THE
ABC CRICKET BOOK
THE FIRST
60 YEARS

THE
ABC CRICKET BOOK
THE FIRST
60 YEARS

Compiled by
JIM MAXWELL

an
ABC
BOOK

Published by ABC Books for the
AUSTRALIAN BROADCASTING CORPORATION
GPO Box 9994 Sydney NSW 2001

Copyright © Australian Broadcasting Corporation
and Jim Maxwell, 1994

First published October, 1994

National Library of Australia
Cataloguing-in-Publication entry
The ABC cricket book.

    ISBN 0 7333 0406 0.

    1. Cricket–Tournaments. 2. Cricket–Tournaments–Australia.
    3. Cricket–Australia–History–20th century.
    I. Maxwell, Jim. II. Australian Broadcasting Corporation.
    III. Title: Australian Broadcasting Corporation cricket book.

796.35865

Edited by Stuart Neal
Designed by Howard Binns-McDonald
Set in 11/14pt Bembo by Midland Typesetters, Maryborough Victoria
Printed and bound in Australia by Alken Press, Smithfield, NSW

8.1–1995

5 4 3 2 1

INTROD

UCTION

The ABC's first general manager, Harold Parkyn Williams, originated many innovative ideas in the early days of Australian radio. Williams devised ball-by-ball descriptions, which were first delivered by Len Watt on 2FC in December 1925 when he described play in the Australia versus the Rest Test trial. His commentary box was a seat at the northern end of the Sydney Cricket Ground, describing the game into a microphone strung from the picket fence.

In 1930 it was Williams who conceived the idea of commentary from England, an illusory broadcast derived from a coded cable service expanded into word pictures. Williams, the director of News and Sport at 2FC before the establishment of the Australian Broadcasting Commission, died in 1933. His concept was developed by Charles Moses (later Sir Charles, and the ABC's general manager until 1966) into the famous synthetic broadcasts of 1934 and 1938. This sparked the genesis of the *ABC Cricket Book*, or guide, as it was first known in 1934.

Cricket must have boosted radio sales in the 1930s, a phenomenon repeated in the 1980s with the B Sky B's satellite dish experience in Britain when they acquired the rights to telecast matches from the West Indies. Families huddled together around the radio to follow the exploits of their folk hero Bradman and the Aussie boys. The influence of those pioneering cricket broadcasts is mirrored by CJ Dennis.

Dad on the Test

I reckon (said Dad) that the country's pests
Is this here wireless an' these here Tests.
Up to the house and around the door,
Stretchin' their ears for to catch the score,
Leavin' the horses down in the crop,
Can you wonder a farmer goes off pop?
I'm yellin' at Jim or I'm cursin' at Joe
All hours of the day, but it ain't no go
Leavin' their work and hangin' around
When they think I'm down by the fallow ground:
Sneakin' away when I start to rouse
An' as soon as me back's turned, back at the house.
'Who got Wyatt? Is Sutcliffe out?'
What do they care if I rave and shout?
Bribin' young Bill for to leave his job
To twiddle the switches an' twist the knob.
'Has he made his century? Who's in now?'
An' I bought that machine for the price of a cow'.
There's a standing crop an' the rain's not far,
An' the price is rotten, but there you are:
As soon as these cricketin' games begin
The farm goes dilly on listenin' in:
Not only boys and the harvester crew,
But Mum and the girls gits dotty too.
An' I reckon (said Dad) that a man's worst pests
Is this here wireless an' these here Tests.

CJ DENNIS

Dilly and Dotty, or Dad and Dave, the power of radio has been sustained, providing immediacy and entertainment. For sixty years and fifty-two editions, the *ABC Cricket Book* has consistently signposted the radio coverage of Australia's national game. The ABC's commitment and continuity is remarkable. This book records the history of the longest running cricket book in Australia.

1 9 3 4

Radio sparked the first ABC cricket publication. The 1934 booklet was designed to help listeners understand the language of the game while they followed the exploits of their heroes in far away England. Only radio could get away with illusory cricket descriptions, and to prove that there was no dishonesty intended, the synthetic broadcast protagonist, Charles Moses, had a film made of a typical broadcast. He demonstrated exactly how the commentators received the cabled information, decoded it and then described the imagined action to the audience. It was a brilliant concept, and in 1934 and 1938 there were few Australians who did not hear a cricket broadcast.

The original book set a style that remained basically unchanged for sixty years. Only the shape and breadth of content altered. In 1934 the guide's size was 6 inches x 5 inches; a one off, because from 1938 the size, like the smokes it advertised, never varied—a standard 5½ inches x 8½ inches (210mm x 135mm) and yes, like those old bottles, it is still maturing.

Many of the technical terms relating to the pitch seem antiquated in the current context. Remember pitches were uncovered and remained so until 1954 in Australia. Many first day pitches looked like concrete and either became hopelessly unplayable—the dreaded 'sticky'—when it rained, or sometimes cracked or crumbled due to wear, tear and the baking sun.

The influence of the weather and decisions about the use of light or heavy rollers had far more influence on the outcome than can be imagined today.

The field placings for Clarrie Grimmett are intriguing. Tactically the contest must have been challenging. The batsmen often 'took on' the deep field, an approach that most contemporary players would consider a 'no percentage' risk. Terry Jenner recalled the wizened Grimmett asking him why he had a long on and long off rather than inviting the batsmen to go over the top. Clarrie would have been fascinated to see Shane Warne in action—and the rare occurrence of 'freebies'. Other curiosities include the field placings 'late square leg' and 'late point'. Hopefully they were more backward than posthumous. The terms 'full tosser' and 'fourer' are outmoded, but occasionally in his later years of silvery commentary Alan McGilvray used these descriptive words.

McGilvray tells a story against himself about a studio call to fill when rain stopped play. He tossed with Vic Richardson about which one would elaborate on the merits of using a light or heavy roller. An hour later, 'What do you think, Arthur?' the customary throw to former England captain Arthur Gilligan, was greeted with, 'I wouldn't use a roller at all'.

FOREWORD

The 1934 English Tour of the Eighteenth Australian Cricket Team already promises contests keenly and evenly fought, champion pitted against champion, skilful team-work met by skilful team-work and, above all, a determined attempt by Woodfull's men to wrest back the "Ashes" which Jardine's team carried home to England in 1933.

The vast majority of Australians will watch closely from day to day the performances of their representatives, studying their "form" under the altered conditions and estimating their chances of ultimate success in their mission.

The Australian Broadcasting Commission will throughout the tour broadcast authentic and detailed descriptions of the play—the observations of experts expertly recounted; and this booklet is offered to listeners in the hope that it will assist them to understand those descriptions fully and to follow the tour with yet greater interest.

M. W. Parsford

L. S. Chipperfield

H. M. Woodfull
(Captain)

Alan Kippax

Stan McCabe

C. V. Grimmett

Harold Bushby
(Manager)

W. C. Bull
(Treasurer)

W. J. O'Reilly

Woodfull

D.G. Bradman
(Vice-Captain)

Len Darling

W.M. Woodfull

W.A. Oldfield

L.O'B. Fleetwood Smith

Ern Bromley

W.A. Brown

B.A. Barnett

THE PLAYERS

WILLIAM M. WOODFULL, Captain: Age, 36; captains the Carlton, Victorian and Australian Elevens; has led Australia since 1930; opening right-handed batsman of excellent defence, scoring mostly from drive and cut; sound out-field; associated with W. H. Ponsford in many notable opening partnerships; has batted with great consistency in both England and Australia and captained the team which won the Ashes in England in 1930, when his batting average for all matches was 58.07.

DON. G. BRADMAN, Vice-Captain: Age, 25; plays for North Sydney, New South Wales, and Australia; outstanding batsman of all time; holder of many records; brilliant stroke-producer all round wicket; magnificent out-field; slow leg-break bowler, occasionally useful as partnership-breaker.

BEN. A. BARNETT: Age 25; keeps wickets for Hawthorn-East Melbourne and Victoria; extremely agile; fast stumper and reliable catch; opening left-hand batsman for his Club; has scored consistently in Shield Games this season, mostly with drives and hooks; once promising slow bowler.

ERNEST G. BROMLEY: Age 21; St. Kilda, Victorian (formerly West Australian) and Australian Elevens; left-hand batsman of extraordinary power; has performed well when team has been in trouble; favours drive, hook and glance; smart runner between wickets; brilliant fieldsman, out-field or cover; change medium-pace left-hand bowler with unusually big "natural" break, but lacks bowling experience; played first-grade in Perth at age of eleven.

WILLIAM A. BROWN: Age 21; opening bat for Marrickville and New South Wales; correct and restrained batsman, favouring forward play; has had an excellent season; good out-field.

ALLAN G. CHIPPERFIELD: Age 27; Newcast (formerly Western Suburbs) and New Sou Wales all-rounder; forcing batsman; at tim hits with great power; slow leg-break bowl with well-concealed "wrong-'un," good pace c the wicket and low trajectory; extremely rel able slip-field.

LEONARD S. DARLING: Age 24; dashing lef handed batsman (first or second wicket dow for Melbourne (formerly South-Melbourne), Vi toria and Australia; greatly improved; excellent field man, out-field, mid-off or cover; useful chang medium-pace, right-hand bowler, with pace c wicket; keeps runs down.

HANS I. EBELING: Age 29; opening fas medium bowler for Melbourne and Victor bowls unusually big in-swinger and smaller ou swing; usually bowls without luck; correct bat man, useful in later batting positions; sou slip fieldsman.

LEO. O'B. FLEETWOOD-SMITH: Age 24; slo left-hand bowler for Melbourne (formerly S Kilda) and Victoria; bowls off-break to rig hander on or about middle stump, breaking leg; extraordinarily well-concealed "wron 'un"; heavy top-spin; dependable slips field man.

CLARENCE B. GRIMMETT: Age 41; Kensingtc South Australian (formerly Victorian) and Au tralian slow right-hand leg-break bowle bowls "wrong-'un" and straight-break, dro sharply, good pace off wicket, immaculate lengt more than 300 wickets in Shield Games; ha taken 81 wickets in Test Matches against En land, and 33 against South Africa; correct bat man, favouring cuts and glances, useful lat in innings; good off-side field.

7

LAN F. KIPPAX: Age 36; captains Waverley d New South Wales; has been Vice-Captain Australia; right-hand batsman of perfect 'le; plays every stroke gracefully; good de- ice; has made welcome return to form; suc- ssful bat on all wickets; Test Match average 'sus England 35.8; sound off-side fieldsman.

AN J. McCABE: Age 23; plays with Mosman, w South Wales and Australia; enterprising, st-scoring batsman, strokes all round wicket. st Match average against England, 39.6; 'ht-hand medium-pace off-break bowler with asional well-flighted "wrong-'un"; good fields- n, usually placed in slips.

A. OLDFIELD: Age 36; Gordon, New South les, and Australian wicket-keeper; Aus- lia's regular "keeper" since 1921; came into minence with A.I.F. team; an artist behind stumps in every way; neat and correct bat, th crisp strokes; Test Match average, 27.32.

WILLIAM J. O'REILLY: Age 28; right-hand slow-medium leg-break bowler for North Syd- ney, New South Wales, and Australia; difficult "wrong-'un" and clever change of pace; re- markable accuracy and endurance; sensational introduction into Test Cricket last season; slip fieldsman with good reach; powerful, but uncer- tain, left-hand batsman.

WILLIAM H. PONSFORD: Age 33; opening right- hand batsman for Melbourne (formerly St. Kilda), Victoria and Australia; free batsman; strongest on on-side; many records to his credit; made enormous scores at opening of first-class cricket career, incuding 437 against Queensland and 429 against Tasmania; still probable cen- tury-maker; safe out-field.

TIM. W. WALL: Age 29; fast bowler for Pros- pect, South Australia and Australia; maintains pace well; gets good height from wicket; swings new ball both ways; performs best in import- ant games; has taken 50 wickets in Test Matches and secured 57 in all games on last English Tour; plays straight bat and has good defence when required; excellent fieldsman at mid-off or mid-on.

THE OFFICIALS

HAROLD BUSHBY (Manager): Mr. Bushby s for many years a well-known cricketer in North of Tasmania and since 1915 has taken active interest in the management of the ne; ever since that date he has been an cutive member of the Tasmanian Cricket ncil and has been a member of the Austra- Board of Cricket Control at intervals since rtly after the War. In 1926 he visited Eng- d as one of the Australian Delegation to the erial Cricket Conference. By profession Mr. shby is a solicitor and practices in Launces- .

Mr. WILLIAM C. BULL (Treasurer): Mr. Bull is well and favourably known in Sydney both as an old player and as an office-bearer. He has been a member of the New South Wales Cricket Association for over twenty-four years, and for the last fifteen has held a seat on the Executive Committee. In 1925 he was elected to the Australian Board of Control and became Treasurer of that body in 1930. He has occu- pied both positions ever since election.

8

AUSTRALIA TOUR
OF ENGLAND **1934**

THE FIXTURES

May

2, 3, 4—Worcestershire.
5, 7, 8—Leicestershire.
9, 10, 11—Cambridge University.
12, 14, 15—M.C.C.
16, 17, 18—Essex.
19, 21, 22—Oxford University.
23, 24, 25—Hampshire.
26, 28, 29—Middlesex.
30, 31, and June 1—Surrey.

June

2, 4, 5—Lancashire.
6, 7—Free.
8, 9, 11, 12—**First Test at Nottingham.**
13, 14, 15—Northamptonshire.
16, 18, 19—Gentlemen of England, at Lords.
20, 21—Free.
22, 23, 25, 26—**Second Test at Lords.**
27, 28, 29—Somerset.
June 30, July 2, 3—Surrey.

July

4, 5—Free.
6, 7, 9, 10—**Third Test at Manchester.**
11, 12, 13—Derbyshire.

July

14, 16, 17—Yorkshire, at Sheffield.
18, 19—Free.
20, 21, 23, 24—**Fourth Test at Leeds.**
25, 26—Durham.
27, 28, 30—Scotland, at Edinburgh.
31—Free.

August

1, 2, 3—Gloucestershire.
4, 6, 7—Glamorganshire.
8, 9, 10—Warwickshire.
11, 13, 14—Nottinghamshire.
15—Army, at Aldershot.
16, 17—Free.
18 to 24—**Fifth Test at The Oval.**
25, 27, 28—Sussex, at Brighton.
29, 30, 31—Kent.

September

1, 3, 4—England XI, at Folkestone.
5, 6—Minor Counties, at The Oval.
7—Free.
8, 10, 11—H.D.G. Leveson-Gower's Scarborough.

There will also be a match at Forres (S land) at the end of the tour, on a c to be arranged.

THE FIELDSMEN

The various positions in which fieldsmen may stand all have special names, as shown in the following diagram (it being remembered that they specify no definite portions of the ground, but positions in relation to batsman facing the bowling at any given time):

Of course, with only eleven fieldsmen, it is not possible to occupy at the one time each of the 28 positions shown; accordingly one places the men in positions best calculated to prevent scoring off bowling of the type which happens to be employed at any given moment. Examples of typical placings follow.

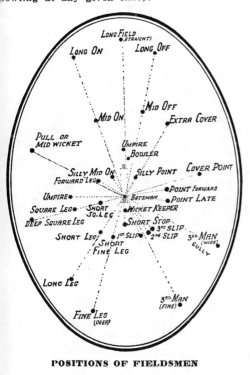

POSITIONS OF FIELDSMEN

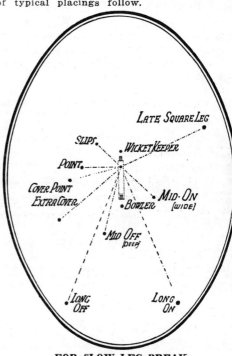

FOR SLOW LEG-BREAK
(modified Off-Theory as bowled by C. V. Grimmett)

Famous Cricket Authorities will Describe the Games

The Australian Broadcasting Commission has been fortunate enough to secure the services of a particularly competent body of former leading players and of authorities on matters concerning cricket to present to the public an authentic and detailed picture of the progress of each of the forthcoming Test Cricket Matches in England. Notable among these are:

M. A. NOBLE: Former Australian Eleven Captain and one of Australia's greatest all-rounders. A sound and powerful batsman, Noble scored in Test Matches 1,905 runs, averaging 30.72, while his medium-pace, well-flighted off-breaks secured him 115 wickets at an average of 24.7. In Sheffield Games his record was even more impressive, for he scored only 4 short of 5,000 and returned the remarkable average of 69.3, while with the ball he accounted for 158 wickets at an average of 22.7. His fielding, too, was outstanding. Noble's voice is already well known to listeners to National Stations, since he has for some time given them the benefit of his acute observations and mature judgment during representative games in Australia in the last few years. His record is as follows:—

Batting

	Inns.	Not Out	H.S.	Runs	Average
In Australia	167	13	281	7,498	48.68
In England	195	19	284	6,217	35.82

	Inns.	Not Out	H.S.	Runs	Average
In S. Africa	5	1	53*	92	23.0
	367	33	284	13,807	41.3

*Not out.

Bowling

	Balls	Maidens	Runs	Wkts.	Average
In Australia	18,439	815	7,806	334	23.3
In England	14,745	716	6,309	264	23.8
In S. Africa	264	8	165	6	27.5
	33,448	1,539	14,280	604	23.6

CLEM. HILL: No less famous than the great Captain, the wonderful South Australian left-handed batsman, Clem. Hill, is acknowledged as the greatest left-hander of his time and still holds many notable records, including the highest Sheffield Shield score (365 not out) ever recorded against New South Wales. His batting average in Test Matches against England is 35.46 for a total of 2,660 runs. Against South Africa he scored 752 runs at an average of 62.6 and in Sheffield Shield Games he has compiled the amazing aggregate of 6,274 runs, with an average of over 5 per innings. His record shows:—

Batting

	Inns.	Not Out	H.S.	Runs	Average
In Australia	235	11	365*	11,384	50.8
In England	170	8	181	5,420	33.4
In America	5	—	42	65	13.0
In S. Africa	5	1	142	327	81.7
	415	20	365*	17,196	43.5

*Not out.

Famous Cricket Authorities will Describe the Games

C. E. PELLEW: Brilliant product of the famous A.I.F. Team, C. E. (''Nip'') Pellew is one of the most picturesque figures of Australian post-War cricket; his small and wiry figure, sleek, fair hair and deeply sun-tanned face will always be associated with crisp, brisk, and enterprising batting, tremendous speed (he was once a champion sprinter) between the wickets and superb cover-point fielding. He was as effective as he was picturesque and his long partnership of 173 against England with J. M. Gregory on the Melbourne Cricket Ground in the 1920-21 series will never be forgotten by those who were fortunate enough to see it. His record is as follows:—

Batting

	Inns.	Not Out	H.S.	Runs	Average
In Australia . .	55	2	271	2,041	38.5
In England . .	39	3	146	924	25.66
	94	5	271	2,965	33.31

E. L. a'BECKETT: By way of contrast, a distinguished member of the younger generation of cricketers has been included, namely, E. L. a'Beckett, LL.B. (Melb.), whom, unfortunately, injuries and illnesses have recently kept out of first-class cricket. After a remarkably successful sporting career at Melbourne Church of England Grammar School and Melbourne University, a'Beckett was hailed as one of the most promising all-rounders in Australia, and his first performance for Victoria in a Sheffield Shield game was to take 6

wickets for 119 runs against a strong N.S.W. team in Sydney in 1928, while early in the next season he scored 113 and 95 in the two innings of another match against N.S.W., played on the Melbourne Ground. a'Beckett is familiar with English conditions in recent years, for he was a member of the 17th Australian Team which went away in 1930 and then secured 397 runs and took 19 wickets. His record already is:—

Batting

	Inns.	Not Out	H.S.	Runs	Average
In Australia . .	43	2	152	1,239	30.21
In England . .	21	5	67*	397	24.81
	64	7	152	1,636	28.70

*Not out.

Bowling

	Balls	Maidens	Runs	Wkts.	Average
In Australia . .	7,173	158	2,434	84	28.97
In England . .	1,992	110	629	19	33.10
	9,165	268	3,063	103	29.73

O. WENDELL BILL: Until this season opening batsman for New South Wales, Wendell Bill will be travelling to England by the same boat as the Team. He will be present at all Matches and at Lunch, Tea and Stumps each day will give, by Radio Telephone, to listeners to National Stations, his impression of the play in the period immediately preceding. Wendell Bill is a sound batsman and a good judge of all aspects of the game and has the advantage of having batted against the bowling of the English Team which toured Australia last year. In representative games his record is as follows:—

Batting

	Inns.	Not Out	H.S.	Runs	Average
In Australia . .	38	3	153	1,295	37.00

Famous Cricket Authorities will Describe the Games

MR. L. G. WATT: Has broadcast descriptions of cricket matches from the Sydney Cricket Ground for eight seasons, including International and Interstate matches. Mr. Watt and the late Mr. H. P. Williams were the first to give what is known as "ball-for-ball" descriptions of a cricket match in New South Wales. Mr. Watt played grade cricket for Central Cumberland from 1907 to 1915. His cricket descriptions are marked by a cool, unhurried and clear speech, keen observation and sound judgment. Mr. Watt knows most of the cricketers of yesterday and to-day, and, what is more important, knows their views on the game. This season he has frequently been heard describing all important representative and grade cricket matches in Sydney.

MR. MEL. MORRIS is one of the best known sporting commentators in Melbourne. He was educated at Wesley College and earned fame in practically every sport. As a schoolboy his name was a household word with the Victorian public, and, ere he left school, senior clubs were clamouring for his services. He attended Wesley College from 1905 to 1911 and excelled at Australian Rules Football, in which he proved a clever and brainy player. He also won laurels for his skill at tennis and cricket, while as a gymnast and runner he won many prizes. After leaving college, he played amateur football with the Old Wesleyans. On the outbreak of war, Morris, a comparative youngster, joined the colours, and he served with the 103rd Howitzer Battery. Returning from overseas, he joined up with the Elsternwick team and did much to get that club going again on a sound basis. After a season or two with Elsternwick, he graduated to the Richmond League team, where as a half-forward, rover, and general utility player he performed magnificently. He was captain and coach in 1926 and later joined the Brunswick Association team as a coach. He has been sporting commentator for 3LO for six years and has broadcast most of the chief sporting events of the Commonwealth from Football Finals and Test Matches to Road Races, Cycling and Swimming Championships.

MR. C. J. A. MOSES: As a sporting announcer in Melbourne from 1930 to 1932 and as Sporting Editor of the Australian Broadcasting Commission's New South Wales Branch since January 1933, Mr. Moses has become widely known for his descriptions of many forms of sport. He first commenced his career as a cricket describer when the West Indies Team played in Melbourne in 1930, and since then has broadcast International and Interstate matches from the Melbourne and Sydney Cricket Grounds, and also Pennant and Grade competition games in both cities. During last season Mr. Moses unwittingly deceived many listeners with his "remote" descriptions from 2FC Sydney of the Third and Fourth Test Matches against England which were played in Adelaide and Brisbane respectively. As a cricketer Mr. Moses captained his school in England and played for the Royal Military College, Sandhurst, and later in regimental matches in the British Army.

22

Famous Cricket Authorities will Describe the Games

MR. R. H. CAMPBELL, "prince of cricket statisticians," will bring to the service of the National Cricket Broadcasts all his amazing lore of the history of Test and first-class Australian cricket. There is not an incident of the matches, however trifling, that has escaped the notice of this remarkable historian, whose records cover the entire period since the inception of Test Cricket. Mr. Campbell saw the first Test Match in London and as he always took a keen interest in the Australians, he began, ile still a lad, the compilation of cricket statistics ich now give him supreme authority to speak whenr a point of cricket history arises. His chronological ords are so complete that they cover not only the res but such details as weather on each day of all matches and amusing and irrelevant incidents of the ne, on which his opinion is continually being sought. example, when a cat walked on to the Melbourne cket Ground during a Test Match he was asked if t was a "record." He replied immediately that it s the third cat to invade the playing arena during a st Game. His records show one unique performance ich may never occur again, when the late "Jack" ons of South Australia, playing against England in

Adelaide, lifted a ball high to the boundary where it landed on the back of a sleeping dog. Mr. Campbell's statistics show that the dog is still running. All this marvellous fund of historical data will be drawn upon by Mr. Campbell to throw interesting sidelights upon the incidents of the forthcoming Tests, so that listeners may have accurate and unique information to enhance their interest in the broadcast.

MR. NORMAN McCANCE, whose wit, personality and accurate knowledge contributed so greatly, some years ago, to the public interest in wrestling. A journalist and a man of wide interests, Norman McCance knows cricket as he knows all other subjects, and this fact, combined with his keen observation and knowledge of the players themselves, will commend his descriptions to listeners. Norman McCance has had extensive experience of broadcasting work of all types and has proved as much at  home and as easy to listen to whether detailing the more fearsome contests at the Stadium or extolling the beauties of the song of the Harz Mountain Roller Canary or giving intimate detail of the lives and habits of goldfish.

UNPARALLELED SERVICE

With the expert assistance of this highly qualified and deservedly popular body of men, d with its own extensive and carefully prepared organisation, The Australian Broadcasting mmission will provide a service to its listeners which for vividness, completeness and, above , accuracy, has never been rivalled. You will see the play as the player sees it, if you listen to the National Stations.

AUSTRALIA TOUR OF ENGLAND 1934

TECHNICAL TERMS

In the describing of any game it is unfortunately necessary to make use of a number of technical terms which have grown up with the sport and are customarily employed by t players; such terms are especially valuable in that they convey briefly and clearly a complica series of actions, events or circumstances otherwise almost incapable of lucid description. I those, however, who are not familiar with their application, they are apt to be bewildering, a it is for the benefit of such listeners that some attempt is made here to explain a few of th most frequently heard.

THE BATSMAN

(Assuming him to bat right-handed, which means that when he takes up his position the crease his left foot will be in front of his right.)

"STRAIGHT BAT": The bat is held perpendicular to the pitch, thus eliminating much of the danger which comes from failure to judge accurately the height of the ball.

"CROSS BAT": The bottom of the bat further to off or to leg than the handle.

"PLAY FORWARD": Step and lean towards the ball in an attempt to intercept it before it has time to break or swing to off or leg, after hitting the pitch, sufficiently to pass the bat.

"PLAY BACK": Step back towards one's wicket and watch the direction of the ball after hitting the pitch and place the bat in its path.

"MIS-HIT": To hit imperfectly, usually from edge of bat, often in the air and often in a direction not intended.

"DRIVE": To step forward with the left foot and swing bat straight through in the direction from which the ball is coming, to send it in front of the wicket.

"ON-DRIVE": To drive (as above) to the on-side, the left foot being placed slightly to the left of where the ball lands.

"OFF-DRIVE": To drive (as above) to the off-side by stepping in that direction.

"COVER-DRIVE": To drive (as above) but towards position known as "cover point," the left foot being placed out in the same direction.

(Drives are "forward" strokes and are almost invariably played from balls which land well up towards the batsman's crease.)

"SQUARE-CUT": To step back and to the off-s with the right foot and bring the bat down w a sharp flick flat on top of the ball so that goes out to the off-side at right angles to wicket.

"LATE-CUT": The same stroke as the square-c played at a later stage of the ball's flight, back foot being taken to the off and back most as far as the stumps and the bat be turned so that the end of it points down towa slips.

(Cuts are usually played from short-pitch bowling on or outside the off-stump.)

"CROSS-BAT COVER-HIT": This stroke is pla from short-pitched bowling outside the stump, by placing the left foot forward and the off and hitting with a horizontal bat, face of which is square-on to the bowler. ball travels towards cover-point.

"PULL": Also played from short bowling direc at any stump. The bat is horizontal and fa towards the bowler. The batsman steps b and to the off with his right foot and hits acr his body, which is more or less directly in with the ball; the ball travels to the on-s in the general direction of mid-wicket.

"Hook": The same as "pull" except that ball is on or outside the leg stump and is when passing, or actually past, the batsman, that it travels between square and fine leg.

26

THE BATSMAN

LANCE": Played from bowling of any length or outside the leg stump, by turning one's bat, which is perpendicular to the pitch, so that the face shows out towards "mid-wicket" and the ball, having glanced it, runs down towards fine leg.

THE BOWLER

LENGTH": "Good length" is not a defined term, since it varies with the pace and type of the bowling and the condition of the pitch. A good length ball is one which lands in the most difficult spot for the batsman to play or score from ball of that particular type. Roughly, it varies from 15 feet to 4 feet in front of the batsman—feet referring to fast bowling and 4 feet to slow bowling. A ball which lands nearer the bowler than good length is described as "short" and the opposite is described as "over-pitched."

HALF-VOLLEY": A "half-volley" is a ball which the batsman hits when it is just rising from the pitch.

FULL TOSSER": A "full tosser" is a ball which reaches the batsman on the full.

YORKER": A "yorker" is a ball which lands on the batsman's crease, though by moving forward can make a slightly shorter ball into a yorker."

FLYER": A short-pitched fast ball which rises head high.

BUMPER": A "bumper" is a ball which rises high and at a sharper angle than it would rise from a normal wicket.

SHOOTER": This is a ball which scarcely rises at all after hitting the pitch.

MAKING PACE": Two types of ball are described as "making pace" after hitting the pitch:—
(a) The only real increase in pace comes from over-spin (i.e. the ball is spinning in the air in such a way that the part of it facing the batsman is continually turning downward and the part toward the bowler turning upward), in which case when the ball hits the pitch the spinning of the ball throws it forward with renewed speed; (b) The other type slips through more quickly than the normal ball would, but does not actually rebound faster than it hit the pitch. In such a case the ball, whether by reason of under-spin (the reverse of over-spin) or of an unusually low angle of contact does not, when it strikes the pitch, lose as much pace as is usual.

"IN-SWINGER": This is a ball bowled entirely without spin, but one which changes direction in the air from off to leg by reason of wind-resistance to the seam. The part of the seam which runs around the front of the ball is turned to point towards the batsman's legs, while the ball is aimed to the off-side of the wicket.

"OUT-SWINGER": An "out-swinger" is simply the reverse of an "in-swinger."

"IN-SWERVE": An "in-swerve" swerves in the air from off to leg before the ball hits the pitch; it results from leg-break spin; i.e., the ball revolves as it travels down the pitch, so that the part of it facing the batsman is revolving continually from the leg-side to the off.

"OUT-SWERVE": This is swerve in the air, from leg to off, before the ball hits the pitch, and results from off-break spin, the opposite to leg break spin.

(In the case of "swing" the change in direction of the ball in the air continues and is accentuated when the ball strikes the pitch; in the case of "swerve," however, the effect of the spin upon the pitch is the reverse of its effect on the air, so that, for example, an off-break swerves out to the off before striking the ground and then breaks in towards the leg.)

"OFF-BREAK": An "off-break" is a change in the direction taken by the ball after hitting the pitch, so that it will travel more towards the leg side than before.

27

"LEG-BREAK": Again the result of spin, and the reverse of off-break.

"STRAIGHT-BREAK": This is a ball bowled apparently in the same manner as either the "off" or "leg-break" (usually the latter) which actually retains its original direction after hitting the pitch, since the spin has, in fact, been purely "over-spin" (described under "Making Pace").

"WRONG-'UN": A "wrong-'un" is a ball bowled apparently in the manner of a leg-break, but actually by turning the hand so much further than usual that the spin is reversed and the ball breaks from off to leg. This is also called a "googly" or "bosie" (the latter after its first successful exponent, Bosanquet).

"FLIGHT": Batsmen become accustomed to telling as soon as a ball leaves the bowler's hand where it may be expected to land. "Flight" is the term applied to any variation, as the result of spin, from the ordinary direct line from hand to pitch, which is likely to upset the batsman's calculation and result in a false stroke.

(a) A **"Dropper"** is a ball with over-spin which the air resistance causes to fall more sharply than the batsman would normally expect, so that it lands shorter than anticipated;

(b) A **"Floater"** is a ball bowled with under-spin which the air-resistance underneath it carries further down the wicket towards the batsman than would otherwise have been the case.

DID YOU KNOW?

The English Selection Committee for the forthcoming Test Matches consists of Sir F. S. Jackson, Mr. T. A. Higson and Mr. P. A. Perrin.

That English summertime ("daylight saving"), which is one hour in advance of Greenwich Mean Time, will be operating in England.

That, according to present arrangements the first day's play in each match will commence at 11 a.m., and the remainder at 11.30 a.m., but that this is to be subject to further discussion.

THE PITCH

(The word "wicket" is, unfortunately, used in two senses; in one it describes the stumps and bails, and in the other it describes the pitch on which the stumps stand; in describing the condition of the pitch, it is customary to speak of it as a "fast, sticky or crumbling (etcetera) wicket").

"Shirt-front" Wicket is the term used to describe a pitch which has been rolled, watered and baked until the surface is practically glazed. The ball rises from it with very little loss of speed and at uniform height; spin has practically no effect on it and the ball breaks little. This type of wicket is scarcely ever seen in England.

"Hard-and-Fast" Wicket: A modification of a "shirt-front" wicket; there is not the same glazed appearance and not quite the same pace, while spin gives slightly better results.

"Easy" Wicket: This is a wicket from which the ball rises more slowly but perfectly truly. Spin has, as a rule, no more effect on it than on a fast wicket and the bounce of the ball is uniform. Generally it is the most favourable of all wickets to batsmen.

(All the above types of wicket are described as "good wickets").

"Slippery (cutting-through)" Wicket describes a pitch upon which enough rain has fallen to moisten the surface to the depth of up to ⅛ in. without softening the hard foundation beneath it. The effect of a wicket of this type on the ball is to allow it to "cut through" the moistened surface and hit the hard foundation from which it bounces evenly and very fast. The moist surface makes it almost impossible to bowl a break-ball and it is essentially in the batsman's favour, especially as the ball will probably be slippery and difficult to control.

"Soft" Wicket: A soft wicket is also one which has been wet, but on which the moisture has soaked down until the foundations also are

soft. In this case the ball, when bowled, penetrates comparatively deeply and in consequence loses much of its pace. It rebounds slowly and high (since it hits the forward edge of the hole which it itself has made); this wicket offers good resistance to spin and results in an abnormally large break, but the slowness gives the batsman every opportunity of watching the ball and, although requiring a special technique, this type of wicket is really more in favour of batsmen than bowlers.

"Sticky (Drying)" Wicket: When the "Slippery Wicket" described above begins to dry it becomes an "Easy Wicket," since only a narrow layer has been affected by the moisture, and since the foundation has remained firm. When, however, a "Soft Wicket" begins to dry it can take one of two courses. In the first case, if it dries fairly quickly under the influence of a hot sun and/or a strong wind, it usually becomes what is known as "Sticky" or "Drying." The ball breaks and rises sharply, for the dry crust over the soft, wet foundation gives an unnatural "bite" to the ball and a general rubber-like resilience to the whole pitch. It is one of the most difficult of all wickets from a batsman's point of view, and is particularly suitable for left-handed bowling.

"Slow" Wicket: The other alternative to the quick-drying "Sticky Wicket" is a slow, dead wicket, which results from a general even drying of the pitch. The surface and the foundations dry at much the same speed and the generally slightly soft nature of the pitch leaves it without any sort of "life"; the ball breaks a good deal but very slowly, and at uniform height and speed.

"Fiery" Wicket: When the "Sticky Wicket" has reached an advanced stage in the quick-drying process it becomes "fiery"—also described as "bumping." It still retains the resilience which it had before, although it has lost some of the "bite"; the result is that any

39

ball rises fast and at an unnaturally sharp angle, making it extremely difficult for batsman to keep his strokes down. A fast ball hesitates momentarily as it hits the wicket and then is thrown upward before its speed carries it onward again. This type of ball is known as a "bumper."

"Two-paced" Wicket. It often happens, when a wicket has been soaked by a shower of rain, and especially when it has dried quickly, that some parts of it become solid again more rapidly than others, so that one has a combination of the "Sticky," "Fiery" and "Soft" wickets. The result is that when a ball hits one part of it, it comes through fast and with little turn, and when it hits another it bounces slowly and high and breaks a good deal. This, again, is extremely difficult for the batsman. The difficulty is accentuated still further by the fact that often the bowling, while the pitch was still soft, made little holes in it which have not been completely rolled out and from which the ball rebounds at unexpected angles, so that the batsman has to contend with a most awkward combination of heights and paces.

(All the above group of wickets generally come under the heading of "Wet Wickets").

"Cracking" Wicket. After long use in hot weather wickets are apt to crack; that is to say, definite cracks open in them. This may have no effect whatever on the manner in which the ball rises from them, provided the cracks are sufficiently small. If, however, they widen, as they sometimes do, until they measure up to even ¼ in. across, then occasionally a ball will bounce unnaturally from the edge of one of them.

"Crumbling" Wicket. Again, in the course of a long match in hot weather, the wicket will sometimes crumble; that is to say, small pieces of turf will be chipped out of it and will leave small holes. After this process has continued for some time definite "patches" will develop where the smooth hard surface has been broken down (either by consistent pitching of

the ball in the same spot or by the batsmen's or bowlers' feet) into a series of small lumps of turf; "patches" or "spots" such as these give great assistance to a bowler, since the height to which the ball will rise from them and the extent to which it will break are far from certain. The tendency is to break more and bounce lower.

"Dusting" Wicket. After a time the crumbling process brings these patches to a condition in which they are filled with dust instead of small hard lumps, and from such "dust-spots" the ball will very often shoot (travel fast along the ground or very little above it; a shooter is one of the most dangerous of balls for any batsman to meet).

(The wickets in this group are known generally as "Wearing Wickets.")

One or two additional types of Pitch may be mentioned. They are not so much conditions as definite types of wicket, depending not on weather conditions but on the actual nature of the soil and the mode of preparation.

"Grassy" Wicket. A grassy wicket is one from which the grass has not been shaved on a level with the ground in the customary manner, but has been rolled down into the surface during the course of preparation. Such wickets usually play very truly, but the general tendency is for them to be slightly slower and more easily gripped by the spin of the ball than is the case with other wickets.

"Spongy" Wicket. A spongy wicket is one in which the roots of the grass have grown thickly and to a considerable depth, so that no amount of rolling makes the pitch really hard. It plays accurately, but there is always a tendency for the ball to rise a little more sharply and to break a little more from it than one would otherwise expect.

"Dead" Wicket. This term is applied to a pitch which by reason of an insufficiently "packed" foundation is never entirely solid. The surface is hard and smooth but the weakness beneath it keeps the ball low.

POSTSCRIPT

In wintry Australia bakelite boxes and crystal sets crackled to the sound of the battle for the Ashes. Bill Woodfull's team took the series 2–1, winning the fifth Test by a massive innings and 562 runs to regain the Ashes. Following a record 388 run stand in the fourth Test, Ponsford and Bradman hammered 451 at the Oval, averaging 90 runs an hour, both scoring double centuries. Relishing an England attack weakened by the absence of

Bodyline heroes, Larwood and Voce, Australia's two champion batsmen averaged over ninety in the series. Bill O'Reilly and Clarrie Grimmett spun out 53 victims between them, Australia's only blip a loss at Lord's where a combination of some desperate batting and a rain affected pitch gave England victory by an innings on the back of Hedley Verity's left arm spin. His 15 wicket haul at Lord's remained a record until Bob Massie swung out 16 Englishmen on debut thirty-eight years later.

In the wake of the controversial Bodyline Tests of 1932–33 there was enormous public interest in the 1934 tour. In fact, the tour only went ahead after a narrow five to four MCC vote in favour of the invitation being issued. They had been stung by the Australian Cricket Board's celebrated 'undiplomatic' cable from Adelaide in 1933, after Woodfull had stated 'there are two sides out there. One is playing cricket, the other is not'.

A gentlemen's agreement effectively outlawed Bodyline, except for a leg theory burst from Voce in the Nottinghamshire fixture. England did not select Voce nor Bodyline's mentor, Jardine, who retired to the press box. Larwood refused to play, claiming that political influence in the England team selection had given the Australians the side that suited them. Woodfull strove to put past acrimonies behind him. He struggled in the early part of the tour and even suggested standing down but went on to average over 50 in the series. Frank Woolley, who was recalled to the England side at the age of 47, made his farewell appearance, conceding a record number of byes when deputising for Ames behind the stumps.

CHAPTER TWO

1938

To the generation conditioned to cricket televiewing, it must be difficult to imagine that its
parents, grandparents and friends surrounded a
huge radio receiver in the 1930s, riveted to the
Test match commentary. The synthetic broadcasts, so popularly acclaimed in 1934, were
improved upon during Bradman's first tour as
captain. When atmospheric conditions were
favourable, short wave reception was relayed live
from England, giving further impetus to the sales
of Philco and His Master's Voice radiograms.

Any inferiority Australians felt due to their
isolation from the Old Country in those lingering
days of Empire was forgotten when Australia met
England in a Test match. No wonder Bradman
was an icon, and his conquests must have lifted
the spirit of an emerging nation.

D. G. BRADMAN

D. G. BRADMAN, South Australian Captain. Played formerly for N.S.W. Age, 29. Born 27th August, 1908. Probably the greatest batsman and run-getter of all time. Brilliant, dashing and consistent performer under varying conditions. Plays every possible shot, has a quick eye and cleverly uses his feet. Magnificent field in all positions, with deadly return. Slow leg-break bowler, useful as partnership breaker. Holds world's record of 452 n.o. and highest Test score against England of 334. Topped the batting averages of the Australian Team in England, 1930 and 1934. Last season he eclipsed Hill's Australian record aggregate in first-class cricket of 17,221, scored 1,822·runs, averaging 91.52 and in scoring 6,771 at 105.7 in 47 matches passed Hill's Sheffield Shield record of 6,274 in 68 maches. A truly prolific record-breaker.

1

McCabe, S. J. (N.S.W. Captain), Australian Vice-Captain. Born 16th July, 1910. Brilliant all-round. Attacking batsman, at his best first or second wicket down. Square cuts, hooks and drives magnificently. Medium pace bowler and good field. Toured England 1930 and 1934, and South Africa 1935-36, topping the Test batting averages against the Springboks with an average of 84. In 35 Test innings has scored 1569 runs at 49.03, highest score 187 n.o. Has taken 19 wickets at 41.47. In Sheffield Shield matches has scored 2464 runs, average 58.6, highest score 229 n.o. and has taken 48 wickets at 23.6 His Shield batting average last season was 46.22.

Badcock, C. L. Formerly of Tasmania, now represents South Australia. Born 10th April, 1914. A stockily built right hand batsman who opens for South Australia, but is better in No. 5 position. He has been greatly assisted by Bradman, whom he resembles in many strokes. Delights in playing fast bowling and viciously hooks and pulls short deliveries. Very strong on both sides of the wicket, and hits the ball with great power and perfect timing. A fast runner between wickets and brilliant fieldsman. Scored three centuries against last English team in Australia. Highest score, 325, against Victoria.

Barnes, S. G. Plays for N.S.W. Born 5th June, 1916. Youngest of the team. Forceful and enterprising right hand batsman, who scores most of his runs on the "off." Places the ball cleverly and hits with terrific power past point. Employs a "sweep" shot but has not obtained perfect command of this shot. Moves continually across the wicket, looking for "offside" plays and does not score very freely to the "on." Fair change right hand slow bowler and brilliant fieldsman. Scored 815 runs during last season at an average of 67.

AUSTRALIAN TEAM, 1938.

Barnett, B. A. (Victoria). Born 23rd March, 1908. First class wicket-keeper and useful left-handed batsman. Toured England in 1934 and South Africa 1935-6, but has not appeared in a Test owing to the presence of Oldfield. Scored 573 runs in England, averaging 33.7 and 155 in South Africa at 14.09. Has made 1394 runs in Sheffield Shield matches, averaging 26.8 with a best performance of 94. His batting has shown improvement and last year his Sheffield Shield average was 33.16. Should play in his first Test match on the present tour.

Brown, W. A. Played for N.S.W. Now captains Queensland. Born 31st July, 1912. Very correct, safe right-hand opening batsman, with good strokes on either side, and sound defence. Scored 1,392 runs, average 37.62 on 1934 tour and performed exceptionally well in the Tests. In South Africa was associated with McCabe in three first-wicket partnerships, each of which yielded over 100 runs. An excellent fieldsman, particularly in the outfield. Played in two Tests during last English visit. In Sheffield Shield Cricket has scored 1,223 runs at an average of 47.03; highest score, 205.

Chipperfield, A. G. Plays for New South Wales. Born 17th November, 1905. All-rounder. Splendid right-hand bat with good performances on "glue-pots". Handy change bowler specialising in slow leg breaks. Brilliant slip field. Went to England 1934 and played in all Tests for 200 runs, average 28.57, with a top score of 99 in his first Test. Recently in South Africa filled third place in the batting averages and fifth in the bowling of the Australian team. In 1936-7 appeared in three Tests for 155 runs at 38.75. Shield batting average 31.8, with a total of 861. Bowling, 19 wickets at 41.63.

AUSTRALIAN TEAM, 1938.

Fingleton, J. H. Plays for Waverley and N.S.W. Born 28th April, 1908. Right hand opening batsman with magnificent defence and possessing a great variety of strokes which are seldom used in important matches. Uses his feet and plays slow bowling most effectively. Brilliant field in any position, but excels in the cover position. Has very fast low and accurate return to the wicket. Test representative, 1932-3, 1936-7, and toured South Africa with the last Australian team, being an outstanding success with an average of 79.46. With Bradman, holds record for sixth wicket Test partnership—346.

Fleetwood-Smith, L. O. B. (Victoria), Born 30th March, 1910. Unorthodox, slow left hand bowler; spins ball both ways; very cleverly conceals his "wrong-un." Applies tremendous top spin. A very difficult bowler for left-hand batsmen. Has greatly improved control of the ball since last touring England. Bats right hand but enjoys little success. Reliable slips fieldsman. During English tour did not play in Tests, but took 119 wickets at 18.06, and in the fourth Test, 1936-7, took 10 for 229. Toured South Africa, 1935-6, taking 9 Test wickets at 42.22.

Hassett, A. L. (Victoria). Born 28th August, 1913. Right hand opening batsman with excellent temperament 'and the possesser of every shot required. Moves correctly into position and places the ball with great judgment on either side of the wicket. Has very sound defence and times the ball perfectly. A brilliant field with a fast return to the wicket. Batting averages for the last two seasons, 71 and 64 respectively.

McCormick, E. L. Plays for Victoria. Born 16th May, 1906. Tall, fast bowler, maintaining his pace and getting good lift from the wicket. Swings the ball both ways and occasionally brings the ball in sharply from the "off". Possesses a very smooth and easy run to the wicket, and follows through, bringing the ball off with great speed. Fair right hand batsman and reliable fieldsman. In South Africa took 49 wickets at 18.59 and in the last series of Tests against England secured 11 wickets at an average of 28.72.

O'Reilly, W. J. (New South Wales). Born 20th December, 1905. Tall, tireless, slow, medium pace right-hand spin bowler. World's best bowler. Has wonderful control also of length, pace, and flight. Prefers bowling to a "suicide squad". First Test appearance was in 1932-3 and he headed the averages on the 1934 tour with 118 wickets at 16.12. In Tests has taken 80 wickets at an average of 24.92; in 1931-2 Sydney first grade season, 54 wickets at 7.88; in Shield games, 139 wickets at 18.

Waite, M. G. (South Australia). Born 7th January, 1911. A good all-rounder: powerful right hand batsman with strong defence, and medium paced right hand bowler. Bowls with quick action and makes the ball come off the wicket with surprising speed. Has a liking for the new ball. Frequently bowls slows for South Australia and has enjoyed considerable success with both types of bowling. Is a brilliant field in any position and has an excellent temperament.

AUSTRALIAN TEAM, 1938.

Walker, C. W. (South Australia). Born February 19, 1909. A brilliant wicketkeeper; has filled this position very successfully for all types of bowling; handles slow bowling very effectively, having "kept" for Grimmett for many seasons. A quick stumper and safe catch. Bats right hand and has a good defence and very nice shots. Frequently opens for South Australia. Toured England with Australian XI. in 1930, but has yet to participate in a Test.

Ward, F. A. (South Australia). Born 23rd February, 1909. Slow right hand bowler and keeps good length, spinning considerably. Conceals a good "wrong-un" and attains success with "top spin", drops quickly and swerves very late in heavy atmosphere. Dependable, defensive right hand batsman without possessing a great variety of shots.. A good field. During the season before last he took 53 wickets at an average of 28.41, and last season, 51 at 21.56.

White, E. S. (N.S.W.) Born 17th May, 1913. Tall, medium slow left hand bowler and right hand batsman. A very accurate bowler, concentrating upon leg stump, and spins an occasional ball from the leg on hard wickets. Also cleverly conceals both a fast and slower delivery. Good defensive batsman and frequently plays really good shots, possessing a powerful off drive. A reliable fieldsman, very safe in the air. Highest score, 108 against South Australia.

10

SOME PROMINENT ENGLISH CRICKETERS

W. R. HAMMOND.   W. J EDRICH.

HAMMOND, W. R. (Gloucestershire): Born 19th June, 1903. Stylish right-hand batsman, powerful on the "off." Very good medium pace right-hand bowler. Brilliant slip field. Visited Australia in 1928-29, 1932-33, and 1936-37. Scored 3,252 runs (highest score 217) at 65.04 during 1937, and took 48 wickets at 22.79. In 25 Tests against Australia has compiled 2,281 runs, average 55.63, and captured 36 wickets at 42.94.

EDRICH, W. J. (Middlesex): Born 26th March, 1916. Right-handed bat. The most successful young player in England to-day. Scored 2,000 runs in the 1936 English season, and 2,154, average 44.87, last season. Has a particular liking for fast bowling. Toured India with Lord Tennyson's team and scored 1,000 runs. An excellent fieldsman.

COMPTON, D. C. S. (Middlesex): Born 23rd May, 1918. A fine batsman. Bats right-handed and bowls sometimes for his County with his left arm. Played first class cricket at 18, and scored 1,004 runs, average 34.62, for the season. Last year compiled 1,980 runs at 47.14, 65 against N.Z.; the second Englishman to get his "Cap" at 19.

BARNETT, C. J. (Gloucestershire): Born 3rd July, 1910. Brilliant batsman, good field and change medium pace bowler. In Australia, 1936-37, was second to Hammond in batting averages, playing in all Tests for 395 runs at 43.88. Scored 2,489 runs at 40.14 in 1937.

D. C. S. COMPTON   C. J. BARNETT.

21

SOME PROMINENT ENGLISH CRICKETERS.

J. HARDSTAFF.

G. O. ALLEN.

HARDSTAFF, J. (Nottinghamshire): Born 3rd July, 1911 First played for Notts at 19. Has erect stance, easy footwork, powerful and fluid stroke play. Brilliant outfield. Played against South Africa and then came to New Zealand and Australia, 1935-6, and to Australia 1936-7, and played 10 innings for 311 runs, averaging 31.10.

ALLEN, G. O. (Captain of Middlesex): Born 31st July, 1902. Toured Australia with 1932-33 and 1936-37 M.C.C. teams, leading the latter. Fast bowler, and reliable right-handed batsman. Brilliant fieldsman, especially at short-leg. In 13 Tests against Australia has taken 43 wickets at 38.44, and scored 479 runs, average 23.95. Born in Australia, but has lived in England from early boyhood. Cambridge University "Blue."

FARNES, K. (Essex): Born 8th July, 1911. Very tall, well built, fast bowler, with an easy run and considerable lift from the wicket. Headed the English bowling averages against Australia in 1934 with 10 wickets at 22.9, and took 11 wickets at 23.36 in Australia, 1936-37. A poor bat, fair field. Cambridge "Blue."

VERITY, H. (Yorkshire): Born 18th May, 1905. Medium slow left-hand spin bowler. Enjoys more success in England than in Australia, but commanded respect whilst here, 1932-33 and 1936-37. In 14 Tests against Australia has taken 45 wickets at 28.95, and scored 292 runs at 19.46. At Lords in 1934 he took 15 wickets for 104 runs. Excellent defending bat who has on occasions opened for England. Good field.

K. FARNES.

H. VERITY.

W VOCE.

W. E BOWES.

VOCE, W. (Nottinghamshire): Born 8th August, 1909. Fast left-hand bowler. A tall, well-built man using his height to obtain quick lift from the wicket. Swings the new ball either way and occasionally brings it across very quickly from the leg. Always dangerous in the opening overs. Not a good batsman, but a very safe field. Has accounted for 41 Australian Test batsmen at 24.24 runs each.

BOWES, W. E. (Yorkshire): Born 25th July, 1908. Fast bowler with kick from the wicket. Wears glasses. Visited Australia with Jardine's team and played against the Australians in Test Matches in England Has taken 20 Australian Test wickets at 27.8, and last year in England took 82 wickets at 19.58. A weak batsman.

AMES, L. E. G. (Kent): Born 3rd December, 1905. A good, reliable wicket-keeper. Represented his County at 21, and probably the best batsman-wicket-keeper in the world. Has always been a menace to Australian bowlers, especially on the slower English wickets. In 15 Tests has scored 540 runs, averaging 24.54, and last season scored 2,437 (highest score 201 n.o.), average 48.89.

LEYLAND, M. (Yorkshire): Born 20th July, 1900. Very dogged and powerful left-hand batsman. Bowls left hand and spins the ball considerable from the leg. Seldom bowls in Test Matches, but frequently for his County. A good outfield. Toured Australia, 1928-29, 1932-33, 1936-37. In 19 Tests against Australia has scored 1,518 runs at 52.34 being the most successful batsman in 1934. Was troubled by Fleetwood-Smith in 1936-37.

L. E. G. AMES.

M. LEYLAND.

SOME PROMINENT ENGLISH CRICKETERS.

L. HUTTON.

E. PAYNTER,

HUTTON, L. (Yorkshire): Born 23rd June, 1916 One of England's brightest Test "hopes." Opening batsman, possessing full repertoire of strokes, a glorious off-drive and stout defence. Has a "big match temperament." Change leg-break bowler and brilliant field. Played for the Minor Counties when 16 and entered first-class cricket at 17. Last season recorded 8 centuries for his County, another in the Test trial, and one for England against New Zealand; made 2,888 runs at 56.62 (highest score 271 n.o.) and was third to Hammond and Hardstaff in the averages.

PAYNTER, E. (Lancashire): Born 5th November, 1901. Nimble-footed left-handed batsman. His plucky innings, when a sick man, during the Brisbane Test in 1932-33 will be remembered by all cricket enthusiasts. On that tour he played in 3 Tests for 184 runs, averaging 61.33. Should be an effective counter to O'Reilly. A very smart fieldsman. Last season scored 2,904 runs (highest score 322), average 53.77. Will probably appear in his first Test on an English ground during this series.

GODDARD, T. W. (Gloucestershire): Born 1st October, 1900. Originally fast but now slow bowler, spinning consistently with long, strong fingers and very supple wrist. Flights well and uses height of 6ft. 3in. Frequently bowls round the wicket, to three or more leg fieldsmen, but latterly depending more upon stumping and l.b.w. Toured South Africa, 1930-31; played in England against Australia, 1930, and N.Z. 1937. Took greatest number of wickets last season, 248 at 16.76.

SMITH, C. I. J. (Middlesex): Born 25th August, 1906. Very robust, 6ft. 5in., and over 15 stone. Bowls fast, good length swingers, with the occasional "flyer." May use packed slip field or "suicide squad." In recent M.C.C. match took 6—139, including Bradman. Captured 149 wickets at 17.47 last season. Has taken 617 first-class wickets at 18.58 runs each. A lusty, erratic bat.

T. W. GODDARD.

C. I. J. SMITH.

FAMOUS CRICKET AUTHORITIES WILL DESCRIBE THE GAMES

The Australian Broadcasting Commission has been fortunate enough to secure the services of a particularly competent body of former leading players and of authorities on matters concerning cricket to present to the public an authentic and detailed picture of the progress of each of the forthcoming Test Cricket Matches in England.

A. E. R. GILLIGAN.

GILLIGAN, A. E. R.: Captain of 1924-25 M.C.C. team in Australia. Fast bowler, brilliant field, and fair bat. One of England's most popular captains. Gilligan had a long and distinguished record with Sussex, playing as an amateur, 1920-31, and captaining the team 1922-29. Gilligan went to South Africa with the English 1922-23 team, then captained England against the South Africans at Home in 1924, and captained England against India, in India, 1926-27. Another of Arthur Gilligan's sporting interests was hockey; he represented Sussex in 1921. Mr Gilligan's cricket resumes during the 1936-37 visit of England's cricketers to Australia were amongst the highlights of Test broadcasts. He has a most unbiased outlook, and his comments on this occasion will be anticipated with interest.

WOODFULL, W.M.: Former captain of Victoria and Australian Test Captain during 1930 and 1934 tours and the 1932-33 Australian season. Also visited England under H. L. Collins, 1926, and played in all Tests against England in 1928-29 series. Was first, second and fourth in the batting averages on his three tours. Carried his bat for Australia at Brisbane in 1928-29 season for 30 runs and at Adelaide four years later for 73 runs; and in Tests was associated in four first-wicket partnerships and five second-wicket partnerships, yielding more than 100 runs each. A shrewd judge and cool leader.

W. M. WOODFULL.

OLDFIELD, W. A. Wicket-keeper for N.S.W. and Australia. His wizardry behind "the sticks" ensured him his place in every Australian team, from 1921, the year he seconded H. Carter in England, until the selection of the present team.

Attained fame as a member of the renowned A.I.F. team, and is the only recognised "keeper" to score more than a thousand runs in Tests between England and Australia—1,116 runs, average 23.25, in 38 games. He also played 43 Sheffield Shield matches for 1,517 runs, averaging 25.71. During the second Test of the last series he exceeded the record held by A. Lilley, of England, of 84 dismissals, in these games.

As a broadcaster, has already made a niche for himself as an interesting and competent talker on cricket topics.

27

M. A. NOBLE.

NOBLE, M. A.: Former Australian Eleven Captain and one of Australia's greatest all-rounders. A sound and powerful batsman, Noble scored in Test Matches, 1,905 runs, averaging 30.72, while his medium-pace, well-flighted off-breaks secured him 115 wickets at an average of 24.7. In Sheffield Games his record was even more impressive, for he scored only 4 short of 5,000 and returned the remarkable average of 69.3, while he accounted for 158 wickets at 22.7. His fielding, too, was outstanding. Mr. Noble's voice is already well known to listeners to National Stations, since he has for some time given them the benefit of his acute observations and mature judgment.

V. Y. RICHARDSON.

RICHARDSON, V. Y.: Has played for South Australia in 78 Sheffield Shield Matches and scored 6,148 runs at an average of 43. Richardson was an outstanding cricket personality, a great leader and inspiration to his team, and was recognised as one of the finest fieldsmen in any position that the game has seen. Very courageous opening batsman, who has been a great asset to Australia. Toured England on two occasions and New Zealand twice. Captained Australia in Africa. Has played Australian Rules for South Australia and was captain for several years; in addition has a reputation as a first-class baseballer. Is now a first-class cricket broadcaster whose descriptions and expert comments are appreciated by all cricket fans.

A. D McGILVRAY.

McGILVRAY, A. D.: Captained New South Wales in all its first class matches in 1935-36, and is regarded as a leader of outstanding ability. Bats left hand and bowls right hand, accurate medium pace. Played in 15 Sheffield Shield games and scored 510 runs, average 24.28, highest score 68, and has taken 18 wickets at 52.72 runs per wicket. Finished at the head of bowling averages in 1935-36, Sydney first grade season, having taken 32 wickets at 9.43. A brilliant close-in field in front of the wicket and a very safe slip-field. Is a very keen student of the game, and his cricket descriptions and resumes during the past year have shown him to be an admirable broadcaster as well.

E. K. SHOLL.

SHOLL, E. K., of the Commission's Head Office staff, is organising the cable service from which the synthetic ball-to-ball descriptions will be constructed. Mr. Sholl accompanied the Australian Team to South Africa in 1935-36, and was responsible for the cricket cables on that occasion. During the last M.C.C. tour he accompanied the team to all States, and was frequently heard in ball-by-ball descriptions from the National Stations. He will be heard in similar commentaries on short wave from the Test grounds during the present series. An LL.B. and cricket and boxing "Blue" of Melbourne University, Mr. Sholl recently had first grade experience in Sydney as a slow bowler with Paddington. His knowledge of cricket is that of a capable player and of a keen student of the game.

HOOKER H.: Played with N.S.W. 1924-32 and in 15 Shield games took 58 wickets at 26.32, and scored 364 runs, averaging 24.26. In 1928-29 season he was associated with Alan Kippax in the world's record 10th wicket partnership of 307 against Victoria at Melbourne. In the return match captured four wickets in four balls—the only occasion by an Australian in first-class cricket in this country. Played against English XI.'s, 1924-25, 1928-29-30, 1932-33, 1936-37, and was a member of an Australian XI against England in 1928. An experienced broadcaster with a flair for describing sporting events such as cricket and football. Has broadcast from 2NC, Newcastle, for many years.

H. HOOKER.

MORRIS, MEL., is one of the best-known sporting commentators in Victoria. He was educated at Wesley College and excelled at Australian Rules Football. He also won laurels for tennis and cricket, while as a gymnast and runner he won many prizes. Returning from military service, he played with the Elsternwick and Richmond League Football Clubs, performing magnificently as half-forward, rover and general utility player. Captain and coach of Richmond in 1926, he later coached the Brunswick Association's team. He has been the Commission's Victorian sporting editor since its inception, and has broadcast most of the chief sporting events of the Commonwealth from Football Finals and Test Matches to Road Races, Cycling and Swimming Championships

MEL. MORRIS.

CHANCE, J.: Entered the Radio world in 1933 via 2FC Children's Session. His first experience of Sporting Broadcasts was with a Brisbane Commercial Station, when he broadcast wrestling, boxing, and. during the Australians' tour of South Africa, synthetic cricket descriptions. Joining the Queensland National Stations in September of last year, he covered various sporting events before being transferred to Sydney in January of this year. when he assisted with commentaries during the Empire Games and Centenary Celebrations. Since then Mr. Chance has described boxing, cricket, football and such features as the Clouston and Ricketts flight.

J CHANCE.

LEGGETT, D. G.: Federal Officer for Outside Broadcasts. Since becoming a member of the Commission's staff in 1935, has had experience in numerous departments and in three States. Recently relinquished the post of School Broadcasts Officer in Queensland to enter upon his present duties. Is a graduate and a "double blue" of Sydney University, and last year won the Queensland Pentathlon and Decathlon titles. Has been heard in a wide variety of sporting broadcasts, notably during the recent Empire Games.

Mr. Leggett is in charge of the organisation of the present Cricket Broadcasts, and will be glad to receive any suggestions for their improvement.

D. G. LEGGETT.

AUSTRALIA TOUR OF ENGLAND 1938

BOWLERS' FIELD PLACEMENTS

THE FIELDSMEN (At right).

The various positions in which fieldsmen may stand all have special names, as shown in the following diagram (it being remembered that they specify no definite portions of the ground, but positions in relation to batsmen facing the bowling at any given time):

Of course, with only eleven fieldsmen, it is not possible to occupy at the one time each of the 28 positions shown; accordingly one places the men in positions best calculated to prevent scoring off bowling of the type which happens to be employed at any given moment.

POSITIONS OF FIELDSMEN.

WAITE AND McCABE (At left).
Field assumes bowlers are swinging in to batsmen. If swinging away, two men only required on leg side.

Waite: This field would be used, particularly as Waite swings ball in from the "off". Second slip may be taken across to a position between mid on and square leg, and square leg would move a little behind wicket; this is only when ball is new and swinging considerably. When ball is old square leg may move to extra cover; If wicket slow second slip takes cover position, thus leaving only one slip with three men on leg.

McCabe: Square leg or second slip takes up extra cover position according to pace of wicket; McCabe chiefly swings away from batsmen, in which case, square leg takes short gully position, i.e. between point and second slip, and fine leg would move to square leg, leaving cover positions fairly open, inviting batsman to drive the ball in the hope that he may snick one.

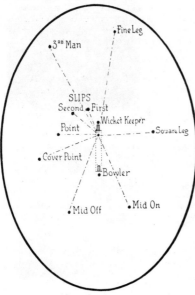

30

THE ORIGIN OF THE ASHES

The famous "Ashes Match" was played on Kennington Oval at the end of August, 1882, and was won by Australia by seven runs. In 1878 the first white team had given England a taste of Australian cricket quality. In less than 12 hours it defeated a powerful M.C.C. team by nine wickets, and established its reputation at a single stroke. In Marylebone's 1st innings Spofforth took 6 wickets for 4 runs, and Boyle 3 for 14. In the 2nd innings Boyle took 6 wickets for 3 runs, and Spofforth 4 for 16, including the champion "W.G." in each innings.

Australia lost the only Test played in 1880 by 5 wickets. W. G. Grace made 152, and Murdoch capped this achievement by scoring 153 not out. Australia was heavily handicapped by the absence of Spofforth, who was on the injured list.

With these facts before them the English selectors took no chances in picking their team for the match at Kennington in 1882. In consequence the contest between the old lion and the young was a true test of strength. Of all the thrilling matches which have been staged between England and Australia there is none that pulsated to the same extent as the "Ashes Match." Space forbids a detailed account, but the finale as described by a great personality in the world of cricket should convey some idea of its immensity. Says he: "It was the most exciting finish I have ever seen, and I should not like to see such another.

"It is impossible to describe the state the people were in just before the end of the game. Men who were noted for their coolness at critical moments were trembling like a leaf. Some were shivering with cold. Some even fainted. At times there was an awful silence. When it was all over, I saw a friend of mine who was sitting over a chair looking unutterably miserable. I slapped him on the back and told him to cheer up; said he: 'Old chap, I feel I should like to cry,' and I think a good many of us felt the same way just then.

"The excitement in England was as nothing to that in Australia. The Australian cricketers were heroes, but modest in victory, for, as Pardon relates, 'The Demon was talking to me in the dressing room a few moments after the game was over when the loving cup was passing round. Horby, Lyttleton, Earl Darnley and others were congratulating Murdoch and his men on their magnificent uphill fight, and Spofforth said that he could not possibly have had a wicket that suited him better. I know this was the case, and I know also that the Australians behaved with modesty and good taste in their hour of triumph, and that the Englishmen took their beating with a good grace, as gentlemen and good sportsmen should.''

Immediately after the match the following notice appeared, not in "Punch" as many imagine, but in the "Sporting Times":—

Many people imagine that the stumps used in this match were burnt and the ashes deposited in the urn which now holds an honoured position in the Long Room at Lords. This is not so. The urn was fashioned in Australia, the ceremony of filling it with ashes was enacted in

70

Melbourne, the residue from a funeral pyre of stumps being placed therein during the progress of a match against Ivo Bligh's team.

The urn bears an inscription which leads one to the speculation that, if the poet's cricket was no better than his verse, its return was not warranted:—

"When Ivo goes back with the urn, the urn.

Studd, Steel, Read and Tylecote return, return.

The welkin will ring loud,

The great crowd will feel proud,

Seeing Barlow and Bates with the urn, the urn.

And the rest coming home with the urn."

THE ASHES URN.

Presented to the Hon. Ivo Bligh, after his team had won the rubber in Australia in 1882. Now the property of the M.C.C.

Ivo Bligh, apart from his cricket success, found his life's happiness in Australia, for he carried away a bride as well as the urn. He injured his finger during the Victorian match and the fair donor of the handkerchief used to bind up the wound, Miss Morphy, of Melbourne, became, at the conclusion of the tour, the Hon. Mrs. Ivo Bligh, and later, the Countess of Darnley.

"In Affectionate Remembrance

of

ENGLISH CRICKET

which died at the Oval

on

29th August, 1882

Deeply lamented by a large circle of sorrowing friends and acquaintances.

R. I. P.

N.B.—The body will be cremated and the Ashes taken to Australia."

By courtesy of the N.S.W.C.A.

71

AUSTRALIA TOUR OF ENGLAND **1938**

POSTSCRIPT

Australia retained the Ashes in 1938, but England levelled the series with an overwhelming triumph at the Oval. Len Hutton forged an incredible world record 364, England remorselessly compiling a record 7 for 903 declared, and Australia was bowled out for 201 and 123. Bradman did not bat in either innings after twisting his ankle while bowling, nor did injured opener Jack Fingleton, and Australia was whipped by an innings and 579 runs. The margin of defeat remains the largest in Test history.

In the previous Test at Headingley Australia had ensured the Ashes' retention, O'Reilly taking ten wickets and Bradman carefully creating a century on a damp pitch.

A feast of scoring in the first two drawn Tests included McCabe's epic 232 at Trent Bridge at a run a minute. The spectacle prompted Bradman to summon his team onto the players' balcony, commenting, 'You may never see an innings like this again'.

Rival captain Walter Hammond peeled off 240 in the Lord's Test, and Bill Brown reciprocated with 206 not out. This match was the first Test to be televised, and to a small audience: only 17 000 sets were licensed in Britain at the time, so the match crowd would have been vaster than the 'box' fans for the only time in television cricket history!

For trivia buffs, the other first at Lord's was Australia's AG Johnnie Moyes' debut as a television commentator. Moyes, a respected cricket writer, became a familiar cricket voice on Australian radio, and was also editor of the *ABC Cricket Book* in the 1950s.

The 1940s

Relieved and rejoicing when peace was restored in 1945, the cricket loving public responded magnificently to the 1946-47 series. More spectators watched the Tests than in any subsequent series. Bradman, throwing off the twinges of fibrositis and a strained leg muscle, made 187 in Brisbane, then 234 in Sydney, re-establishing his authority and ensuring Australia's superiority. England matched Miller's flair and personality with Denis Compton—the Brylcreem boys. Hutton, Edrich and Washbrook scored runs, but Hammond was past his best. Leg spinner Doug Wright led the bowlers on both sides taking 23 wickets in the series, lacking penetrative support save for the talented Alec Bedser.

The 1946–47 pen portraits include seven players who participated in the famous victory Tests in 1945. Coinciding with the end of the war, these matches were played in a tremendous spirit with over 30 000 fans watching one day's play at Lord's and over 360 000 spectators attending the fifteen days' entertainment of the five-match series. The success of these reunifying contests prompted Dr HV Evatt, Australian Minister for External Affairs, to appeal to the MCC to send a side to Australia as soon as possible. England's subsequent tour also fulfilled one of Prime Minister John Curtin's last wishes when he called for an immediate resumption of Test cricket before his death in 1945.

TWO WORLD FAMOUS CRICKETERS

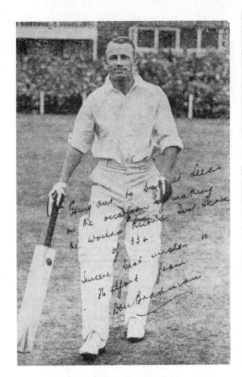

D. G. BRADMAN   **W. R. HAMMOND (English Cap**

BRADMAN, D. G. (S.A., formerly N.S.W.): Born 27/8/1908. Probably the greatest batsman and run-getter of all time. One of cricket's greatest personalities. Brilliant and dashing performer under all conditions. Master of every shot, brilliant foot-work, and from his perfect timing imparts tremendous power into all strokes. Magnificent field in all positions with deadly return. Bowls slow leg breaks, useful as a change bowler. Holds many world's records: highest score of 452 not out; most number of centuries in Tests, 15, including two scores of over 300 and five double centuries; highest aggregate for Tests, 3,840 runs, average 91.42; highest aggregate for any Test series, 974, average 139.14; shares with W. H. Ponsford the two highest Test partnership records of 451 and 388. Greatest run-getter in Sheffield Shield, 8,634 runs, average 112.12. Has scored over 25,000 runs in first class cricket, including 93 centuries. An inspiring leader. Captained Australia in 1936-37 and in England 1938. South Australian Representative on Board of Control and Australian Selector.

HAMMOND, W. R. (Gloucestershire): Born 19/6/1903. One of the greatest cricketers that the world has known. Brilliant right-handed batsman, described by Wisden "As the player with irreproachable style." Has a style of batting in which splendour of manner, grace of execution and muscular power have been combined, rarely equalled in cricket history. Right-handed medium pace bowler and one of England's greatest slip-fielders. Has played in 77 Tests against all countries. In the 29 Tests against Australia has scored 2,684 runs, average 57.10, including 10 centuries with four scores over 200. Has taken 36 wickets, average 44.83. On first tour of Australia, 1928-29, scored over 900 runs in Tests, average 113.22. In the Fourth Test of the series scored 119 not out and 177. Toured Australia also in 1932-33 and 1936-37. Has scored over 160 centuries, highest being 336 not out against New Zealand, 1933. Last season topped the English batting with 1,783 runs, average 84.90. Captained England in the 1938 series against Australia, also against Australian Services and India last season. Truly a grand cricketer.

5

Some Prominent Australian Players

| A. MORRIS | B. A. BARNETT |

MORRIS, A. (N.S.W.): Born 19/1/1922. Forceful yet stylish left-handed opening bat. One of our brightest prospects; likened to Warren Bardsley. An excellent field, especially in slips. Created an Australian record, 1940-41, when aged 18, by scoring a century in each innings at his first interstate appearance, 148 and 111. Enlisted and served in the islands.

BARNETT, B. A. (Victoria): Born 23/3/1908. First class wicket-keeper, useful left-handed batsman. Toured England in 1934, 1938, and South Africa, 1935-36. Has played in four Tests against England. On the 1934 tour of England scored 573 runs, average 33.7, 1938, 809 runs, average 28.89. Has played in 53 Sheffield Shield matches scoring 2,088 runs, average 29.82. Served as Captain in A.I.F. and was P.O.W. for over three years in Malaya. Returned to first class cricket last season and revealed former brilliancy.

| K. R. MILLER | E. TOSHACK |

MILLER, K. R. (Vic.): Born 28/11/1919. Brilliant all-rounder. Forceful stylish right-handed bat, expert on back-foot play. Fast right-hand bowler and good field. Scored 181 against Tas. in first State appearance. Entered Shield cricket, 1939-40, scoring a great 108 v. S.A. Served in England as a pilot, F./O., R.A.A.F. Played with the R.A.A.F. XI and toured with the Aust. Services Team. Headed Aust. and English batting in the five Victory Tests with 443 runs, average 68.28.

TOSHACK, E. R. H. (N.S.W.): Born 15/12/1916. Tall left-handed medium pace bowler noted for accuracy, length and spin. Prefers bowling to on-side field. Has the uncommon ability in left-handers to turn from the off. Bats left-handed. Played for N.S.W. Seconds, 1933-34, then missed seven years owing to illness. Returned to his club last season, gained interstate selection and headed the bowling with 35 wickets, average 15. Performed well with Aust. Team in N.Z.

17

ENGLAND TOUR OF AUSTRALIA **1946-1947**

Some Prominent Australian Players

D. K. CARMODY

D. TALLON

CARMODY, D. K. (N.S.W.): Born 16/2/1919. Right-handed bat, delightful stroke-maker, splendid field. Played Shield cricket, 1938-39-40. Served in Britain as a pilot, Flt.-Lt., R.A.A.F. Captained the R.A.A.F. XI in England and greatly impressed with his fine batting. Following a glorious 137 v. the South of England, Sir Pelham Warner described him as a real stylist and future Test star. Was shot down near Holland and taken p.o.w. After the war toured with Aust. Services Team.

TALLON, D. (Q'ld): Born 17/2/1916. Brilliant wicket keeper. Entertaining right-handed batsman. In Sheffield Shield matches has outstanding performances, both as keeper and batsman. Against N.S.W., 1938-39, caught nine and stumped three. Has also dismissed seven batsmen in one innings. In Shield cricket has scored 2,058 runs, average 33.19, including five centuries. Highest score 193, v. Victoria, 1936. Toured New Zealand as first keeper with Australian XI last season.

J. PETTIFORD

R. S. ELLIS

PETTIFORD, J. (N.S.W.): Born 29/11/1919. Promising all-rounder. Slow right-handed leg-break bowler. Sound batsman and very good field. Served in England as a pilot, F./O., R.A.A.F. Gained prominence for good all round form with the R.A.A.F. and Services XI's overseas. Later suffered ill-health and was not seen to advantage on Aust. Services tour.

ELLIS, R. S. (S. Aust.): Born 25/11/1917. Slow left-handed bowler with natural spin from leg, also bowls the left-hander's "googly." Very safe field. Bats left-handed. Played for S. Aust., 1939-40. Served in England as a pilot, Flt.-Lt., R.A.A.F. Played in the five Victory Tests, dismissed W. R. Hammond four times in seven innings, and took 13 wickets, average 28.6. Toured with the Aust. Services Team.

Some Prominent Australian Players

D. R. CRISTOFANI

C. McCOOL

CRISTOFANI, D. R. (N.S.W.): Born 14/11/1920. Right-handed slow bowler and batsman. Entered interstate cricket, 1941. Served in England as a Flt.-Lt., R.A.A.F. Had outstanding successes with bat and ball in Services cricket. Played in three Victory Tests. Captured five wickets for 55 and made 110 n.o. in the Fifth Test, while in the three Tests he took 14 wickets, average 14, and batted for an average of 54.6.

McCOOL, C. (Qld.): Born 28/12/1918. Good all-rounder. Formerly played in N.S.W. Attractive right-handed batsman, slow right-handed googly bowler. One of Australia's best slip fields. Represented Qld., 1945-46 season, scoring 520 runs, average 43.3, including one century. Captured 29 wickets, average 23.5. Toured N.Z. with Aust. XI this year, averaging 37 with the bat and taking 7 wickets, average 26.2.

S. G. SISMEY

K. STACKPOLE

SISMEY, S. G. (N.S.W.): Born 15/7/1916. Excellent wicket keeper and right-handed batsman. First played Shield cricket, 1938-39. Served in Britain and Gibraltar as pilot, R.A.A.F., rising to Sqdn. Ldr. Played successfully in Services matches in England and later toured with the Aust. Services Team. Showed fine form with the bat in England.

STACKPOLE, K. (Victoria): Born 31/7/1916. Stockily built, forcing right-handed batsman—looks for runs all the time. One of Victoria's most consistent Club performers. Entered Interstate cricket last season and was an outstanding success. Played two grand fighting innings both against N.S.W. at Melbourne and Sydney. Very good fieldsman, moves fast to the ball with smart return. Prominent in Melbourne football as playing-coach to the Prahan Club.

19

Some Prominent Australian Players

K. J. GRIEVES   **G. TRIBE**

GRIEVES, K. J. (N.S.W.): Born 27/8/1925. Stylish right-handed batsman, with shots all round the wicket. Exceptionally smart slip-field and fair change slow bowler. Entered first grade cricket at 16. Began interstate career, 1945-46, and averaged 55 with the bat. Scored 102 n.o. against the Aust. Services Team. At 21, has the unique record of having represented N.S.W. at cricket, baseball and soccer.

TRIBE, G. (Victoria): Born 4/10/1920. Left-handed googly bowler of the Fleetwood-Smith type. Gets considerable break both from leg and the off, and flights the ball well. Reliable batsman and very good field. Played Interstate cricket last season and bowled particularly well. Against Queensland at Brisbane, captured 9 wickets for 45, and at Melbourne took 6 wickets for 101, also showed good form against New South Wales and South Australia.

BROWN, W. A. (Q'ld.): Born 31/7/1912. Champion opening batsman, right-handed, with temperament reminiscent of J. B. Hobbs. Correct yet stylish stroke maker. Brilliant fieldsman. Toured England, 1934 and 1938, Sth. Africa, 1935-36. Carried his bat for 206 n.o. at Lords. Has scored three centuries in Tests against England and one against Sth. Africa. Captained Aust. Team in N.Z. tour last year.

HASSETT, A. L. (Vic.): Born 28/8/1913. Brilliant right-handed batsman, with nimble feet, very sound defence and perfect timing. Brilliant field. Played Shield cricket from 1935, scoring 2,488 runs, average 60.68. Toured England, 1938, for 1,607 runs, average 50.24. Captained Australian Services' Team. Topped the batting in English first-class matches with 867 runs, average 72.25. Golf handicap 4. Was Vic. schoolboy tennis champion in 1931.

SAGGERS, R. (N.S.W.): Born 15/5/1917. Outstanding wicket keeper, neat and smart in his work, reminds one of W. A. Oldfield. Stylish right-handed batsman with good repertoire of strokes. Entered Shield cricket, 1939-40. Shares world's wicket keeping record with W. F. Price of Middlesex, by dismissing seven batsmen, all caught, in one innings. Prolific run-getter in club cricket; scored 1,150, average 80, 1942-43.

BARNES, S. G. (N.S.W.): Born 5/6/1916. Youngest member of Aust. Team to tour England, 1938; toured N.Z. with Aust. side last year. Brilliant all-rounder. Forceful and enterprising right-handed bat. Ranked among world's best. Good change right-handed slow bowler, brilliant field and can keep wickets. Scored six successive centuries in interstate matches, 1940-41. Has scored 4,892 runs in first-class cricket, average 55.

LINDWALL, R. (N.S.W.): Born 3/11/1921. Fast right-handed bowler with long, easy run and smooth action. Has courage and stamina to bowl for long spells. Bats right-handed Played for N.S.W., 1941. Enlisted and served in the islands. Returned to cricket last season, won a place in the team for N.Z. and in first-class matches captured 40 wickets at 26.6 runs a piece. Surprised by scoring 134 n.o. against Queensland. Plays first-grade Rugby League.

Some Prominent Australian Players

A. L. HASSETT

W. A. BROWN

R. SAGGERS

S. G. BARNES

R. LINDWALL

ENGLAND TOUR
OF AUSTRALIA **1946-1947**

Some Prominent Australian Players

F. FREER   **W. JOHNSTON**

FREER, F. (Victoria): Born 4/12/1916. Tall, right-handed medium off spin bowler, nice easy action and is able to swerve the ball both ways. Bats right-hand and is a good field. Holds record for Victorian Pennant cricket when in 1943-44 season secured 88 wickets at an average of 12.5. Last season took 7 wickets for 29 against Queensland and also bowled well against New South Wales. Has also represented Victoria at Interstate baseball.

JOHNSTON, W. (Vic.): Born 6/2/1922. Fast medium left-hand bowler who gets pace and lift with the new ball and effective spin when the wicket wears. Said to resemble the Englishman, Bill Voce, though bowls to orthodox field. Takes comparatively short run. Safe field with excellent returns from outfield. Plays baseball in off season. Bowled splendidly against N.S.W. last year on fast Sydney wicket.

HAMENCE, R. A. (South Australia): Born 25/11/1915. Stylish right-handed batsman. Uses his feet well, particularly against slow bowlers. In Sheffield Shield cricket has scored 1,032 runs at an average of 30. After serving with the forces, returned to the South Australian side last season and showed excellent form. Scored brilliant 74 not out, out of a total of 106 against N.S.W. last year. Good out-fielder with splendid return to the wicket. Toured New Zealand with the Australian XI last season.

DOOLAND, B. (S.A.): Born 1/11/23. Right-handed slow bowler of very promising type. Is faster through the air than most slow bowlers. Last season took 31 wickets, average 28.08, from 187.7 overs, including 12 maidens. Captured 9 Vic. wickets and accomplished the hat-trick. Brilliant fieldsman in slips or infield. Likely successor to C. V. Grimmett. Interstate baseballer.

MEULEMAN, K. (Victoria): Born 5/9/1923. Right-handed opening batsman. Stylish stroke maker, uses his feet well. Entered Interstate cricket last season and performed splendidly. Scored a brilliant 153 against South Australia. Was Victoria's most prolific run-getter last season. Good fieldsman, particularly in the outfield, with splendid return to the wicket. Toured New Zealand last year with the Australian XI and was a success as opening batsman with W. A. Brown.

ROGERS, R. E. (Qld.): Born 24/8/1916. Forceful left-handed opening batsman. Drives powerfully and is a good man in a pinch. In Sheffield Shield has scored 1,514, average 32.2, and has six centuries to his credit in first-class cricket. Fair change medium pace bowler and splendid fieldsman, particularly in the outfield.

ALLEY, W. E. (N.S.W.): Born 3/2/1919. Hard-hitting left-handed bat, fair right-handed medium-pace bowler, brilliant outfield. Gained prominence by scoring over 1,000 runs in two successive grade cricket seasons. Totalled 1,413, average 70.65, in 1943-44, and equalled Victor Trumper's club record of six successive centuries. Scored three centuries and average 69 in interstate games last season. Has big match temperament.

R. A. HAMENCE

Some Prominent Australian Players

B. DOOLAND

K. MEULEMAN

R. E. ROGERS

W. E. ALLEY

23

ENGLAND TOUR
OF AUSTRALIA 1946-1947

Special Commentators for ABC Broadcasts

VICTOR RICHARDSON is a former Australian Test captain and opening batsman. A popular broadcaster whose commentaries have been a feature of A.B.C. cricket broadcasts for many years and who will be heard again in the broadcasts of the major matches of the season with Alan McGilvray.

J. H. FINGLETON will broadcast about the Test matches. As a first-class practising journalist and a former Test cricketer, he is well qualified to analyse the play in the Tests, as was evident in his constructive resumes of last year's international matches.

ALAN McGILVRAY is a former New South Wales captain and all-rounder, a keen student of cricket and an experienced broadcaster. Travelled throughout the Commonwealth with the M.C.C. team last season to broadcast for the A.B.C.

S. P. FOENANDER of the "Ceylon Observer" is a journalist and broadcaster of long standing. He has reported international cricket in India and some 25 Anglo-Australian Test matches in England and Australia. Mr. Foenander is the author of the several articles on Indian cricket and cricketers which appear in this book.

3

THE STORY OF INDIAN CRICKET
By S. P. FOENANDER

The history of cricket in India dates back nearly 200 years. The game was played in Calcutta as long ago as 1751, according to records still preserved. The Calcutta Cricket Club, composed mainly of English military and civilian players, was responsible for introducing the game into Eastern Inda, while to the Parsis belongs the honour of having started cricket in Bombay exactly a century ago. Dr. M. E. Pavri, one of the greatest cricketers produced by India prior to the coming of Ranjitsinhji, in his comprehensive history of Indian cricket, entitled "Parsi Cricket," tells the story of the progress made by Indian cricket in the province of Bombay and later all over India.

The first cricket club founded in Bombay in 1848, was called The Oriental Cricket Club. In the 1870's the Parsis established a better known club, called the Elphinstone Cricket Club, which exists to-day. These two clubs were responsible for the development of the game among the Parsis, who were the first cricketers of India to send a touring team to England.

The records of Indian cricket published to-day only tell us of the visits to England of All India teams from 1911, but, in 1887 the first Parsi team visited England, played 28 matches, won one, lost 19, and drew 8. A year later a second Parsi team toured England and did better than the previous one. It was led by P. D. Kanga, and matches were played all over England. A feature of the Parsi cricket was the fine bowling of Dr. Pavri, who captured 170 wickets at 11 runs each.

Indian cricket took a definite step forward after the appointment of Lord Harris, famous old Oxford University and All England captain, and later President of the M.C.C., as Governor of Bombay. Lord Harris did much to encourage cricket among all communities, including the Hindus and Muslims, who now gradually began to challenge the supremacy of the Parsis. The offer of a Harris Shield for competition among the clubs of Bombay helped to raise the standard of the game, and when Lord Hawke's team, G. F. Vernon's team, and later, Sir K. J. Key's team visited India, the standard of cricket among the Indians was definitely higher than it had been before the advent of Lord Harris.

The big annual match in Bombay used to be the one between the Europeans and the Parsis, and later the Hindus came into the competition to make it a triangular one. Indian cricket received much encouragement by the visits paid by G. F. Vernon's team in 1889-1890, and by Lord Hawke's team in 1892. The inclusion in Lord Hawke's team of the famous All England captain of later years, Sir. F. Stanley Jackson, lent additional interest to the tour of that strong side all over India. A sensation was created at Bombay when the Parsis beat the English tourists by 109 runs in their first meeting. In the return game the Parsis were beaten by only 7 runs. The English team included several well known county cricketers, so that the achievement of the Parsis was remarkably good.

One of the strongest English sides to tour India was the Oxford Authentics team in 1902-1903, captained by Sir K. Key, and including A. H. Hornby, afterwards Captain of Lancashire. Then there was a long lapse of years before an English team visited India.

In the meantime the Indians developed their Quadrangular tournament in Bombay, in which the Muslims now competed with the Europeans, the Parsis and the Hindus. Up to the year 1936 the Quadrangular Tournament, held in Bombay, was the most important of all the cricket contests in India, and it did much to develop the standard of Indian cricket that was gradually approaching international standard from about the year 1912.

In the Quadrangular Tournament over a period of 25 years, between

4

1912 and 1936, the Hindus won the Championship 6 times, the Europeans 4 times, and the Parsis and Muslims 3 times each.

In 1937, "The Rest" were included in this Tournament, which now became known as the Pentangular. The Rest were made up of cricketers who did not belong to the four communities engaged in the Quadrangular Tourney.

Between the years 1937-1947, the Muslims and the Hindus each won the Championship four times. They were definitely the two most powerful cricket communities in India, having taken the place of the Parsis and Europeans, who were predominant in Indian cricket before 1912.

The first representative Indian team to tour England was the one led by the Maharajah of Patiala in 1911, and included Dr. H. D. Kanga, who had played for Middlesex, Colonel K. M. Mistry, a truly great left hand batsman, and J. S. Warden an excellent allrounder. But Indian cricket was still far short of international class, as the results of the tour proved without a doubt, for of the 14 first-class games played, the tourists won only 2 and lost 10. They had still not been given the honour of playing Test cricket.

A country that can produce a Ranji, a Duleep, a C. K. Nayuda, a Pataudi, and a V. M. Merchant, with its vast population, many of them as crazy about the game as the most enthusiastic in England and Australia, is bound sooner or later to challenge the supremacy of the older cricket nations. The foundation of the fame that the Jam Sahib of Nawanagar won on the cricket fields of England and Australia, was laid in his native state of Jamnagar, where he first learnt the game from Englishmen. But it was in England that the unequalled talent and genius of Ranji was developed to its full. Ranji, and later, Duleepsinhji and Pataudi, emphasised the natural skill that Indians possessed for cricket.

These three outstanding Indians, each in his time performed the remarkable feat of scoring a century in his first Test appearance for England against Australia. This is a fact that adds more glamour to the story of India's rise to cricket eminence. But great and outstanding though Ranjitsinhji, Duleepsinhji and Pataudi—all three mainly products of English coaching and experience in big cricket—have been, there are scores of other cricketers produced by India in the past quarter century who challenge comparison with the first-class cricketers of other countries.

In the last ten years Indian cricket has advanced by leaps and bounds, as is shown by the results of the Annual Inter-Provincial tournaments for the Ranji Trophy started in 1934. Some of the biggest totals and highest individual scores of over 150 have been compiled in these annual competitions, that have spread more interest throughout India than the Pentangulars have done in Bombay. Inter-zonal contests, begun in 1946, have also played their part in developing cricket tremendously, while the visits to India of Jack Ryder's team in 1935,-36, and of the Australian Services team in 1945, not to mention the M.C.C. tours of India in 1926-27, in 1933-34 and 1937-38, have all contributed very materially to the advancement of Indian cricket.

The last tour in England of the Indian cricket team led by the Nawab of Pataudi, proved more clearly than any previous tour had done that, in spite of the adverse climatic conditions under which the Indian cricketers had to perform, India can now worthily hold its own in Test cricket with England and Australia.

PRONUNCIATIONS: Indian names are continually, more or less Anglicised, and it is often difficult to tell which is the most suitable of various pronunciations to use. E.g., the short "a" is something like the "u" in "but" or the "a" in "about." Anglicised it becomes the "a" in "bat." Occasionally the "a" is like "ah." "i," at the end of a word, is "ee." "i" is never "eye." "u" is sometimes long "oo," sometimes short "oo." All syllables have about the same stress on them.

AUSTRALIAN TEAMS IN INDIA

J. RYDER'S TEAM

During the summer of 1935-36 an unofficial Australian team toured India under the auspices of the Maharajah of Patiala. The team consisted of a blend of former internationals and young players, and had been gathered together by Frank Tarrant, one-time Victorian and Middlesex cricketer, who acted as manager and played in some matches.

The players were: J. Ryder (Victoria and Australia), C. G. Macartney (N.S. Wales and Australia), H. Ironmonger (Victoria and Australia), H. S. Love (N.S.W. and Australia), L. E. Nagel (Victoria and Australia), R. K. Oxenham (Queensland and Australia), A. H. Allsopp (Victoria). F. J. Bryant (Western Australia), J. L. Ellis (Victoria), Tom W. Leather (Victoria), F. Mair (N.S. Wales) and R. O. Morrisby (Tasmania).

The Australians opened their tour at Colombo against Ceylon, and were unbeaten until the seventeenth match, when All India won the third representative game by 68 runs.

Probably, the heat and the constant travelling were telling on the visitors by this time. Anyway, shortly afterwards, Moin-ud-Dowlah, 5 for 413 declared, trounced them by an innings and 115 runs, in the worst defeat sustained by a visiting team at the hands of an Indian eleven. Amarnath scored 144. and the former All India bowler, Amar Singh, captured 11 wickets for 87.

India won the fourth and final representative fixture by 33 runs. The Australians had won the first game against All India by 9 wickets, and the second by 8 wickets.

Altogether, the Australians played 23 matches, won 11, lost 3, and drew 9. Ryder scored over 1000 runs, and R. K. Oxenham took more than 100 wickets.

AUSTRALIAN SERVICES TEAM

On the way home from England at the end of 1945, the Services team played a series of 10 matches in India, including one at Colombo. Two matches were won, two were lost and the remainder were drawn. Of the three representative games played at Bombay, Calcutta and Madras, two were drawn and the third resulted in a victory for India by 6 wickets.

The Australians did not extend their opponents in India as they had done during their tour of Britain, but this was no doubt due in some degree to the absence of their opening bowlers, R. G. Williams and A. G. Cheetham, and to the after effects of their strenuous British programme of nearly 50 matches.

Lindsay Hassett, captain of the side, hit up 4 centuries, 2 of them in the match against the Princes' XI, and he also topped the batting averages with 87.40. D. K. Carmody proved a steady opening batsman with an average of 45.50, and a century against All India. J. Pettiford scored 2 centuries against All India and R. S. Whittington scored one. K. R. Miller was outstanding as an allrounder, scoring 2 centuries and sharing the bowling honours of the visit with C. F. T. Price.

J. Pettiford scored most runs in the representative matches, and also had the best average, 67.25. C. G. Pepper took most wickets, 16, at 33.75. while C. F. T. Price with 7 at 20.28, headed the averages.

While the Australians scored 11 single centuries in 10 matches, their opponents made 9 single and 2 double centuries. Of the present tourists, R. S. Modi scored 203 for India and 168 for the Indian Universities, L. Amarnath made 113 for India and 163 for Princes' XI, and Mushtaq Ali, 108 for the Princes' XI.

COMPTON IN INDIA.—Denis Compton, while on service in India, played for Holkar in the 1944-5 National Championship series. He batted 4 times for 372 runs, incl. 249 n.o.

56

INDIA TOUR OF AUSTRALIA **1947-1948**

PATAUDI

The Nawab of Pataudi, Iftikhan Ali, born on March 19, 1910, is ranked with K. S. Ranjitsinhji and K. S. Duleepsinhji as India's three outstanding batsmen in international cricket. There is much similarity in their careers, for all three practically learnt their cricket in England, had the honour of playing for England against Australia, and each scored a century in his first Test. Pataudi did so in 1932 at Sydney, as a member of D. R. Jardine's team. Each of them also had the distinction of scoring a century for the Gentlemen versus the Players.

Pataudi in style was less brilliant than "Ranji" and "Duleep," but he combined solid defence with powerful driving and other facile strokes all round the wicket. Like the other two famous Indians, Pataudi gained his Blue for cricket, and went further and gained his Hockey and Billiards Blue, too. In fact, Pataudi was not only a cricket International, but also a Hockey International, for he represented India in the 1928 All India Olympic team.

There are other rare records that Pataudi has created in 'Varsity cricket. On his first appearance against Cambridge he scored a century, 106, and in the second innings he just missed getting another hundred, scoring 84. It was in 1929 that he attained cricket immortality by scoring 238 in the Inter-Varsity match, this being the highest score ever made by an Oxford or Cambridge batsman in the Battle of the Blues. He is one of the very few 'Varsity batsmen who has scored two centuries in Inter-Varsity matches. In 1931 Pataudi performed another amazing feat, when he equalled Tom Hayward's record of scoring 4 centuries in one week. This he did for Oxford University. In his last year at Oxford he reached the record total of 1,307, averaging 93.35, and hitting up six centuries.

After he left Oxford Pataudi turned out for Worcestershire and scored heavily in County cricket. He gained his distinction of being the first Worcestershire batsman to score three double centuries in a season —two of them in successive innings.

On his visit to Australia with the M.C.C. team in 1932-1933, Pataudi started the tour brilliantly, scoring two centuries in succession. He then capped this feat with a century in his first Test with Australia. Subsequently he fractured a finger bone in his right hand and was out of the game for a while. As an out fieldsman, too, he was splendid and proved himself a great favourite with the Hillites, especially after the following incident. Some of the crowd used to call him Gandhi, and he took it good-naturedly. One day one of the crowd on the Hill cried out to Pataudi, "Say, Gandhi, where's your goat?" Pataudi's reply—"Oh! He is now on the other side of the fence," not only silenced the would-be wit, but created a tremendous roar of laughter. After that no one ever called Pataudi, "Gandhi."

Talking of Pataudi's skill in billiards, it might be mentioned that on the 1932-33 tour, while in Sydney, "Pat" often visited Horace Lindrum's saloon and engaged in many a game with Australia's snooker champion and Eddie Paynter.

Owing to ill-health, Pataudi dropped out of big cricket for several years, but he made a welcome return to the game in 1946, when he led the All India team in England.

DOPED WICKETS MENACE INDIAN CRICKET

Doped wickets were the subject of some interesting comments by an Indian cricket writer, Berry Sarbadhikary, which appeared in "The Cricket Annual," after the Indian tour of England in 1946. They are of particular interest to Australian cricket enthusiasts, in view of the Australian visit to England next year.

"In general, our batting strength on bone-dry wickets (although often

PATAUDI   RANJI TROPHY

THE RANJI TROPHY

The trophy perpetuates the memory of the late Kumar Shri Ranjit-sinhji. It is a gold cup, two feet high, valued at £500 and is competed for annually by the Provincial Cricket Associations of India.

The Associations are divided into four zones, eastern, western, northern and southern. Each Zone conducts a knockout competition and the winners play off for the Ranji Trophy and the National Championship.

---

marred by an unnecessarily negative attitude) against the counties was never in doubt, nor was our pronounced weakness on wickets that turned.

"It was on soft wickets that we failed—a vital failure, because most of our younger hopes, except Modi, were involved in it. The holes in their batting technique—the result of years of playing on nothing but doped wickets—were too big not to give them away with a vengeance. The greater is the pity because India offers a wide scope for the preparation of varied wickets ranging from the hard-and-fast to the green-top and the turning. Fortunately, Duleepsinhji, I know, has taken up the cudgels against the 'doped' wicket in India, and perhaps President de Mello will now lend him a hand, with an eye to the future."

SOME LONG INNINGS

When scoring 234 v. England, at Sydney, during the recent Test series, S. Barnes batted for ten hours and forty-two minutes, an innings which for duration of time is second only to Hutton's 364 in thirteen hours and seventeen minutes, v. Australia, in 1938. The only other innings lasting over ten hours have been:—

V. M. Merchant	359 n.o.	v.	Maharashtra	1943-4
H. Moses	297 n.o.	v.	Victoria	1887-8
F. C. Thompson	275 n.o.	v.	New South Wales	1930-1
W. H. Ponsford	437	v.	Queensland	1927-8
A. Shrewsbury	267	v.	Middlesex	1887
A. Sandham	325	v.	West Indies	1929-30

In the second Test match v. Australia, in 1924-5, H. Sutcliffe made scores of 176 and 127, for which he batted in all for 13½ hours—the longest time for two innings in a match. S. Barnes' 234 is the slowest score of over 200 ever made, but though he batted over six hours before reaching his first hundred, there have been a few hundreds even slower, the slowest of which was probably W. H. Denton's score of 102 v. Derbyshire in 1914, for which he was at the wicket for no less than seven hours.

—by George Brodribb, in a recent issue of "The Cricketer."

63

ENGLISH CRICKET COMMENTATORS

ARTHUR GILLIGAN   REX ALSTON   JOHN ARLOTT

GILLIGAN, ARTHUR: Came into prominence in the cricket world when he succeeded H. L. Wilson as captain of the Sussex XI. At the end of that season played for England against Yorkshire. Subsequently enjoyed a notable career in first-class cricket. Captained the M.C.C. team to Australia, 1924-25, and to India in 1926-27. Gave his first broadcast for the B.B.C. when he gave an eye-witness account of a County Game in 1937, and continued throughout the season. Served during last war as a Squadron Leader in the R.A.F. Came to Australia for the visit of the 1936-37 M.C.C. team to broadcast for the A.B.C. His outstanding commentaries were a wonderful success, and the response by listeners throughout the Commonwealth was amazing.

ALSTON, REX: Educated at Clare College, Cambridge, and was Master at Bedford School for seventeen years. Member of the Bedfordshire and Hertfordshire National Fitness Council from its inauguration to the outbreak of war. Captain of College cricket—played Rugby for College, and got running Blue. For five or six years played cricket for Bedfordshire, and was County captain for two years. Played Rugby for Bedford, East Midlands and Rosslyn Park. Joined the B.B.C. in January, 1942, as Billeting Officer; transferred to Overseas Presentation in June, 1942, as announcer; joined North Region Home Presentation in September, 1942. Went to Birmingham as Midlands Talks Producer in May, 1944. In 1945 transferred to London to broadcast commentaries—Assistant, Outside Broadcasting Department. His hobbies are all forms of sport and gardening.

ARLOTT, JOHN: Joined B.B.C. on 3/9/45 as Talks Producer in the Eastern Service, giving weekly poetry programmes for all Overseas Services—gave cricket talks in Home Service, in October, '44, and May, '45. Has taken part in three "Transatlantic Call" and three "Country Magazine" programmes, and appeared in "Britain's Our Doorstep" feature in 1945—a most versatile broadcaster. Has also gained prominence as a poet, as a number of his own poems have been published. Film commentaries for M.O.I. include, "Make Rich the Land," "English Village," "The Royal Show," and "National Parks," in which he acted as a farmer. Recreations include cricket and other sports. Has been 12th man for Hants, and played in charity matches with Worcestershire. Married, with one son. Family has been on the land for generations.

A.B.C. COMMENTATORS
IN ENGLAND

ALAN McGILVRAY   DUDLEY LEGGETT

McGILVRAY, ALAN: Former N.S.W. captain, and very keen student of the game. Represented N.S.W. in Sheffield Shield matches and against overseas teams. As a pupil of Sydney Grammar, represented All Schools against N.S.W.C.A. twice, and later captained N.S.W. Colts and Seconds. Played for Paddington and Waverley Clubs. Headed Sydney grade bowling in 1935-36 and batting in the next season—a very rare distinction. His deep knowledge of cricket is recognised by all players and officials. Has broadcast cricket for the A.B.C. since 1934, including all first-class matches during M.C.C. tour, 1946-47, and the Indian tour. A really excellent commentator—one of the best in the history of broadcasting. Flying to England in May as a member of the B.B.C. team, to broadcast the Tests direct on short-wave.

LEGGETT, DUDLEY: The A.B.C.'s Federal Sporting Supervisor. Is travelling with the team, and as well as being responsible for the despatch of any cables necessary, is liaison officer between the B.B.C. and A.B.C. in the arrangement of all broadcasts covering the many outstanding sporting events, including the Olympic Games, Davis Cup and Wimbledon, and the tour by the Australian Rugby League team. Has been employed by the A.B.C. since 1935, and has organised all the Test Cricket broadcasts since then. Did some excellent broadcasts as a war correspondent for the A.B.C. During his career has described many sporting events.

26

A.B.C. COMMENTATORS
IN AUSTRALIA

BERNARD KERR   HALFORD HOOKER

KERR, BERNARD: Began broadcasting career in 1932. After assisting in Sporting Department was appointed Sporting Editor for New South Wales in 1938. Has held position ever since, and is now Acting Federal Sporting Supervisor. Described many sporting events, the most important being Sheffield Shield and Test cricket, Rugby League Tests against England and New Zealand, Soccer Tests against Palestine, India, China and South Africa, Interstate and Australian Lawn and Hardcourt Tennis Championships, and Davis Cup Challenge Round, 1946. Member of the A.I.F., and in 1945 appointed Sporting Editor, Australian Army Amenities Broadcasting Section, broadcasting special sporting bulletins on shortwave to thousands of troops in the Islands.

HOOKER, HALFORD: Before broadcasting was very well known as a cricketer. Represented N.S.W. in Shield and International matches from 1924-32. Is always remembered as the holder of the world's record tenth wicket partnership, with Alan Kippax, of 307, against Victoria at Melbourne, in the 1928-29 season. In return match took 4 wickets in 4 balls—a record by an Australian in this country that still stands. Has a splendid club record with Mosman, both with bat and ball, heading both averages on one occasion. Is widely known for his excellent work on the air, the most important broadcasts being Cricket, Rugby League and Soccer Tests. Since 1934 has been attached to the Newcastle Studios of the A.B.C. Is naturally very much appreciated by listeners interested in sport in the area.

Editor's Note: The comentators shown on this page, and the next, are members of the A.B.C. team who will present any synthetic descriptions necessary. The A.B.C. Sporting Service is desirous of relaying descriptions of the Tests on short-wave. However, it is realised that if reception is not favourable, listeners will expect a coverage by cables. This form of presentation in the past has been extremely popular. Thousands have appreciated the illusion and atmosphere created, and it is fully expected that these commentators, after a little experience, will maintain the high standard of similar presentations during previous tours by an Australian team.

DON BRADMAN SCORING HIS 100th CENTURY

On 15th November, 1947, playing for an Australian XI against India on the Sydney Cricket Ground, Don Bradman played a superb innings of 172 in compiling 100 centuries in first-class cricket. He received a hearty and breath-taking ovation from a thrilled crowd of 32,000. His score of 172, made just three minutes short of three hours, included 18 boundaries and one six. Scoring was made at a very fast rate after the century in 132 minutes —150 in 161 minutes, and 172 in 177 minutes. Keith Miller, his partner, also played a great knock, and the partnership of 252 lasted 154 minutes—the last 50 in 16 minutes.

SYDNEY CRICKET GROUND 15th NOVEMBER, 1947.

35

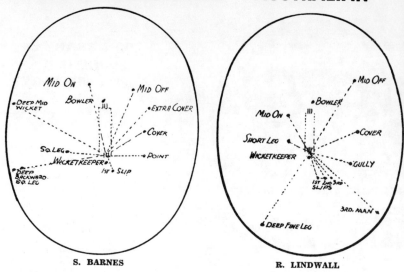

S. BARNES   R. LINDWALL

BARNES, S.: Slow bowler. Faster through air than McCool and Ring—thus needing fieldsmen backward of square leg. Deep mid-wicket's position could vary from there towards straight hit. Employs good over-spinner, which whips off wicket and often gains l.b.w. decisions.

LINDWALL, R.: Fast bowler. Field would change according to his pace and a square-leg and mid-off may be required. Fieldsmen used for either or both these positions would come from firstly, 3rd slip—secondly, gully.

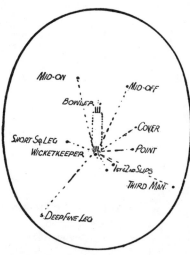

K. MILLER AND S. LOXTON

MILLER, K.: Fast bowler. Field would change according to his pace and a square-leg and mid-off may be required. Fieldsmen used for either or both these positions would come from, firstly, 3rd slip—secondly, gully.

LOXTON, S.: Medium fast. Field is often varied, according to movement of ball in the air and of wicket. Movement of square-leg and gully fieldsmen to extra cover and mid-off, give a defensive field, whilst square-leg to 3rd slip would be an attacking field if ball was swinging away.

40

JOHNSTON, W.: This field placed for fast medium deliveries. Sometimes square leg would be replaced by putting him at short gully. When bowling medium paced leg spinners field would alter thus—2nd slip to extra cover—3rd man to gully—deep fine to short fine leg. Mid-on would field fairly wide as left-hand over wicket bowler would cover a fair area in fielding his own bowling.

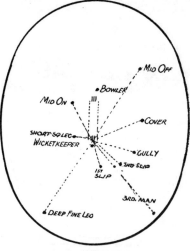

W. JOHNSTON

ENGLISH BOWLERS

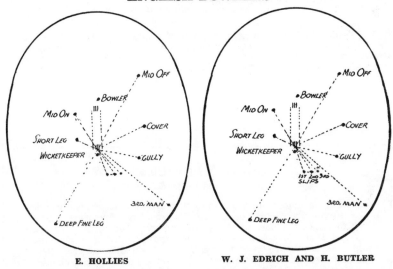

E. HOLLIES

W. J. EDRICH AND H. BUTLER

HOLLIES, E.: Right-hand googly and spin bowler. Has shown a great deal of promise and probably next best to Wright. Most hostile on rain-affected wicket.

EDRICH, W. J., and BUTLER, H.: Edrich well known as most energetic attacking bowler, throwing everything into his action. Butler possesses more speed and hostility, but inclined to break down with back complaint.

41

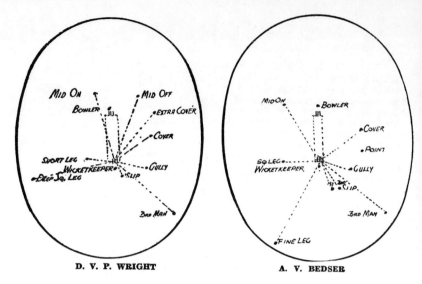

D. V. P. WRIGHT   A. V. BEDSER

WRIGHT, D. V. P.: Bowls leg spinners faster than usual leg-break bowler. Has unusual and pronounced "hop" in his approach. His accuracy allows him to do without long-on. Against an attacking batsman fields mid-off much deeper and straighter. England's best bowler.

BEDSER, A. V.: Stout-hearted bowler. Attacks all the time. Employs short on-side field to his fast medium deliveries. On easy-paced wicket strengthens off-side field by bringing short leg to point, with gully fielding wider and deeper. With Wright, England's bowling hope.

ENGLISH CRICKET
By Neville Cardus

It is far more than a game, this cricket. It somehow holds the mirror up to English nature. We are not hypocrites, but we try to make the best of things of contrary appeal. It was once alleged that W. G. Grace now and again cheated. I asked an old Gloucestershire "pro" to speak frankly on this subject. "Nay!" he protested with loud emphasis, "never. The 'Old Man' cheat?— 'e were too clever for that."

42

POSTSCRIPT

Bradman's final playing years coincided with the emergence of some great Australian cricketers. Fast bowlers Ray Lindwall and Keith Miller were match winners, their deeds overshadowing the equally impressive Bill Johnston, who was the leading wicket taker alongside Lindwall in 1948 (27 wickets). Arthur Morris and Neil Harvey began their illustrious left-handed careers, and Brown, Hassett and Barnes resumed after the six year war tumult. Don Tallon, overlooked in 1938, became a superb custodian; sharp stumper and swift catcher. And Bradman's powers were not dimmed by the years. He averaged over a hundred in the twilight time of his late thirties, captaining the side shrewdly, maintaining his unbeaten series record.

In 1948 Australia were undefeated on tour, scoring 721 in a day against Essex and capping their Ashes victory at Leeds, scoring 404 to win by 7 wickets on the final day. At The Oval Arthur Morris completed a brilliant 196, England were dismissed for 52 and 188, but the match is probably best remembered because a player was bowled for a duck. Of course, it was Bradman's last Test innings and an anticlimactic conclusion to an amazing, prolific career.

Alan McGilvray covered his first tour for the ABC, joining Rex Alston and the former Hampshire policeman, John Arlott, in the commentary box. McGilvray had seen India in its first Australian tour the previous summer. Weakened by four withdrawals, the Indians struggled to compete against a powerful home side. They probably got the worst of the conditions, caught out on a Brisbane sticky, and were beaten by an innings in the first Test. Bradman struck four centuries in six innings and nineteen-year-old

Neil Harvey made 153 on debut. Vijay Hazare, the only Christian in the Indian side, scored a century in each innings at the Adelaide Oval, but the tour lives in the memory of many for the birth of the expression 'doing a Mankad'. In the second Test in Sydney, left-arm spinner Vinoo Mankad ran out Bill Brown at the bowlers' end when he backed up too far—another Test first. Letters to the newspaper editors called Mankad's behaviour unsportsmanlike and, hearing of this, Brown rang Mankad saying that he (Brown) was to blame. In the fifth Test Brown was run out for 99, not at the bowlers' end, but with twist of irony by a direct hit from Mankad fielding at point.

The 1950s

The post-Bradman era, and the Don's continued presence as a selector and then Chairman of the Board of Control, had a significant influence on the shape of the game and its leadership. The search for 'another Bradman' consumed the press, with Ian Craig and then Norm O'Neill prematurely earmarked for immortality.

Lindwall and Miller battered the West Indies in 1950–51 and South Africa performed outstandingly to draw the 1952–53 series 2–2.

Australia lost the Ashes in 1953 and after defeats in 1954–55 and 1956 they were rejuvenated by Richie Benaud's inspired leadership, regaining the Ashes 4-0 in 1958–59.

One of the topics reviewed in this collection of material for the seven publications of the 'fifties is 'broadcasting cricket'. Written by Bernard Kerr, who became a committed head of ABC Sport in later years, it is a fascinating insight into the technique of cricket broadcasting—in fact, all sports commentary on radio. Readers may have noticed that one of the major differences today is that the atmosphere in the box is more relaxed and the style more conversational than in 1951.

Sir Donald Bradman analyses the varying conditions batsmen would encounter in 1953. Pitches were still uncovered and the new ball was available after 65 overs. Cricket balls were hand-stitched too, so the balance was far more in favour of bowlers than today, when in a dry English summer it is easier to get past the gatemen at Lord's than to hit the outside edge.

Clarrie Grimmett recalls his England experience and the adjustment required on slower pitches: 'The ball must be kept up to all batsmen to preclude any possibility of back play. They must be forced to play forward and feel for the ball'. It is a theory improved upon by Shane Warne, whose flipper has imperilled batsmen who 'play back'.

Radios were an expensive household 'necessity'. The Phillips Challenger cost eighteen guineas ($37.80) in 1950 when the average weekly wage was about seven pounds ($14). And that was half the price of a huge Philco or His Master's Voice radiogram in 1938, when thirty-five guineas ($73.50) was a starting point for family entertainment. New technology is never cheap but, as television buyers discovered, eventually such 'necessities' became affordable. This cheapening story has been repeated with every technological marvel we take for granted today.

The comparative cost of ABC Cricket Books is harder to follow. As the quality of paper improved and colour was introduced to the cover, the price rose from ninepence (8 cents) to a shilling (10 cents) in 1950 and then massively doubled to two shillings in 1951. Amazingly, the price did not go up for another seventeen years. The word inflation was not yet in economic vogue and probably had more relevance to the pressure of pneumatic tyres on a new Holden.

The 1958–59 series was the first to be televised in Australia. It was the start of a long association between the ABC and the Australian Board of Control, which officially ended on television in 1990.

F. R. BROWN

BROWN, F. R.: (Northants). Born 16/12/1910. Forcing right hand batsman, dangerous leg break bowler, fine field. Can also bowl off breaks and seamers. Toured Australia and New Zealand 1932-33. Has gained six England caps between 1931 and 1937. Captain England v. New Zealand in 1949, scored doubles in 1932 and 1949. Popular and exceptionally talented cricket. Excellent captain — attacks all the time. Strict disciplinarian. His captaincy could be one of the successes of the tour.

HASSETT, A. L.: (Victoria). Born 28/8/1913. Vice-captain of 1948 tour of England. Has played 14 Tests against England, scoring 832 runs in 32 innings, including 2 centuries — average 37.82. Captained Australian team in South Africa, 1949-50. Second in Test batting averages, scoring 402 runs from 6 innings, highest score 167 — average 67.00. In all first class matches scored 889 runs—average 68.39. Brilliant, nimble footed right hand batsman with amazing power of concentration and strong defence. Grand fieldsman and excellent leader. Former schoolboy tennis champion and sound golfer.

L. HASSETT

6

IN SEARCH OF THE "ASHES"

The M.C.C. touring team for Australia arrived at Fremantle on October 9. John Arlott, well-known B.B.C. cricket commentator, who has followed the fortunes of English cricket since the war — against India, South Africa, Australia, New Zealand and the West Indies — introduces the team and makes a critical appreciation of its chances on Australian wickets.

(By Courtesy of "London Calling")

Since England lost the rubber of 1950 to a better side in Goddard's West Indians, hope runs higher than expectation as to the M.C.C. regaining the Ashes in Australia. Nevertheless, there is very little informed dissatisfaction with the work of the selectors. There is no surprise felt in their having returned to the idea of Brown as captain — only in the fact that they should ever have discarded him after his leadership against the 1949 New Zealanders.

Brown still bowls, though at a reduced pace, the leg-breaks and googlies which first won him an England cap, but he can also turn his hand to medium-pace swingers or to good-length off-spinners. A bold bat, with a solid basic technique and a fieldsman still safe and nippy for all his bulk, he will rank as at least a useful player. As captain, he toured Australia before any other member of the side, which must help him to establish an authority over the entire side as no younger player could do.

While Brown has the graces of an easy manner and a pretty wit, he is a mature thinker and a firm captain. He will discipline this touring side as he did the Northants side which he has led to a striking revival since his return to first-class cricket last year. He knows the game and will sacrifice no cricketing advantage to court popularity. I expect Brown's captaincy to be one of the successes of the tour.

The Test eleven will obviously be built round the batting of Hutton and Compton, the wicket-keeping of Evans, and the bowling of Wright and Bedser. All the remaining players, except perhaps the efficient Surrey wicket-keeper, McIntyre, a reliable reserve to the more-accomplished Evans, stand a chance of playing in the Tests. If the side is to come near success, Compton and Hutton must regularly make high scores, Evans must produce his most brilliant form, and Wright and Bedser must take good wickets cheaply.

Washbrook's late acceptance of the invitation to make the tour gives additional confidence in the batting. While the fast bowlers always "fancy themselves" against him, he, with a characteristic jaunty confidence, fancies himself against them. If his hooking and square cutting sometimes bring about his downfall, they have also chalked him up many quick and early runs on his way to Test hundreds, and, on his last appearance against Australia, in Leeds in 1948, he looked the master of the situation. If there are other batsmen who may have been considered, Washbrook's superb fielding at cover makes him an automatic choice.

In the shadow of the skill of Hutton — surely the most accomplished batting technician in the game to-day — and the immense psychological fillip which a fit Compton gives to any batting side, the commanding back-foot aggression which Simpson has held in abeyance through the Tests of 1950 may flower again on fast wickets. With such a start, the fast scoring of Parkhouse will be a major asset, for he is perhaps the most uninhibited stroke-player in England to-day.

Sheppard, of Sussex and Cambridge University, has a good brain and temperament, and the concentration and basic technique to make a great, solid batsman. Dewes may find his methods seriously exposed by Australian bowling strategy, but I am certain that he will never be faulted for courage or concentration.

Wright, still the only bowler in England capable of utterly beating great batsmen on good wickets, had the steadiest of all his Test bowling spells in the last Test against the West Indies. This gives encouragement for his peak form is, with Compton's fitness, the major condition of the English team's success.

38

Bailey, whose batting in the lower half of the order can be an immense asset is, one fears, for all his efforts, not fast enough to be an economic proposition as a shock bowler in short spells, and he lacks the stamina to make a stock bowler in Australia. Both these tasks are therefore likely to devolve upon the monstrously overworked Alec. Bedser.

John Warr is still increasing a pace already considerable by current English standards. He has the height to make the ball lift, an immense willing confidence, and may easily displace Bailey if he "comes on" as much as the selectors no doubt expect.

I fancy Hollies' flight, steadiness and strategy will worry all but the best Australian batsmen, and in his best form he will be destructive on bad wickets and command respect on good ones.

Berry, of Lancashire, and Close, of Yorkshire, make the trip, like Sheppard in the hope that their distinct promise may develop during the tour into cricketing greatness. Berry belongs, as a slow left-arm bowler, in the school of Wilfred Rhodes; he has flight, slight spin, immaculate control of a skilfully varied length, an imperviousness to punishment, and a sense of strategy remarkable in one so young.

Close, after a first season in 1949 in which he became the youngest player ever to complete the double of 1,000 runs and 100 wickets and the youngest who ever won an England cap, then went into the services.

PREVIEW OF TOUR
by ARTHUR GILLIGAN

The very greatest interest was taken in England about the selection of the English team to tour Australia, though many considered the M.C.C. Cricket Committee were slow in announcing the names of the players. After Norman Yardley and George Mann had declined the captaincy, Freddy Brown, on the eve of the M.C.C. Cricket Committee choosing the captain and team for Australia, scored a brilliant century in the Gentlemen v. Players match, then took the first three of the Players wickets with some fine bowling and was immediately asked to captain the present team. This was an extremely popular choice. Denis Compton, who had a knee operation during the 1950 season, made a fine recovery and was elected vice-captain. He is the first professional cricketer to receive this honour, and the news was well received both in Australia and England. Freddy Brown has a very useful team with a few veterans and a generous sprinkling of the young brigade. There are seven under the age of 27, the youngest being Brian Close, who made his debut for England v. New Zealand at Manchester in 1949, at the age of 18. Close is the youngest player to appear for England in Test cricket. David Sheppard (21) has already played some fine innings both for Cambridge and Sussex, and a useful future lies ahead with added experience. Amongst the old hands Hutton and Washbrook opened in the 1946-47 Australian tour, and did very well during the South African 1948-49 tour. Denis Compton, a most lovable figure on any cricket ground, should do well again, whilst of the newcomers Reggie Simpson, Gilbert Parkhouse, John Dewes and Trevor Bailey can be relied upon to get useful scores. The bowling may prove to be our weak link in the chain, but England will pin her faith in Bedser, Bailey and Warr as the fast attack, with Brown, Hollies, Wright, Berry and Close to provide the spinners. Doug. Wright still remains England's greatest bowler, and much will be expected of him during the Test matches. Everybody in England realises that Australia has a formidable team, but I think that Freddy Brown will make an ideal captain and will have his team with him to a man. His leadership is inspiring and he will certainly make Australia fight each Test match to the bitter end. I am making no forecast as to the ultimate result — so much depends on the luck of the toss and the luck of the weather — but one thing is certain, that we shall witness some really good Test matches during the 1950-51 tour, though we shall all miss that wonder batsman, Sir Donald Bradman, who has always been a thorn in any English team for the past 18 years. Anyway, here's good luck to Brown and his team, and some grand cricket is certain.

39

ENGLAND TOUR
OF AUSTRALIA **1950-1951**

WITH THE AUSTRALIANS IN ENGLAND

by ALAN McGILVRAY

To play for Australia in England is surely a goal sought by all cricketers, and in so doing one is entrusted with definite responsibilities. I was incapable of attaining that objective, but was fortunate to find myself in England in 1948 with the responsibility of describing the activities of our fellows and their opponents and to bring the stories they provided into the homes of thousands of listeners.

In many years of cricket I never felt the emptiness and fear that was my experience as I winged my way to England to fulfil my purpose. My first meeting with my old friend Arthur Gilligan reassured me and, as I sat before the microphone at Hove in the match against Sussex, I felt more confident in that Arthur was there was the occasional "What do you think, Alan," etc.

However, a County match is not a Test match, and within a week we were at Nottingham for the First Test. Arthur joined me in the opening commentary, and we spoke to Australia — what a thrill it was. I was really nervous. As I left the microphone after my first twenty minutes' spell that empty feeling returned and I thought of all I had not done. Surely I spoke too quickly forgot this and that, omitted to mention so-and-so. I anxiously awaited the cables I knew my wife, family and friends would send me, giving their opinions on the reception. Strangely they were pleasing, so I gradually regained my confidence and felt a whole lot better after the first day, and really settled down to my task.

The B.B.C. invited me to talk about the Australian listener. I spoke of the nightly interest we people take in Test matches — of the homes and parties, and generally how people lived whilst a Test match is being played in England. I generally found it difficult to convince the people of England that such things could really happen. Given the same opportunity of night broadcasts, I am sure English people would do as we do, for it is my opinion that although we are a cricket loving country, there is more interest taken in the game there than here.

Cricket accommodation is poor in comparison, for few grounds would hold more than 30,000, but the endless and daily queues outside the full ground convinced me of the sincerity of English followers. During the Second Test at Lords, I noticed and spoke to several people who slept outside the ground every night of the complete five days. To ensure their positions in the queue that numbered hundreds, they would leave the ground no later than fifteen minutes before play ended for the day and take up their positions, make bed and prepare meals on the footpaths outside the walls of the ground. First in one of these queues every day was a woman who told me the only time she left her position was to prepare her husband's Sunday mid-day dinner.

Of the five Test match grounds, Nottingham, Lords, Manchester, Headingley and The Oval, none compare either in accommodation or surface with Melbourne and Sydney. Wickets contained more grass, and appeared more lively but were not overprepared as are some in this country, and naturally did not wear as well. I inspected all wickets at the conclusion of each Test and found them very well worn, the worst being Headingley, where both bowler and batsmen had worn holes sime six inches deep. From my position directly behind the wicket and about forty feet high in the stand, I could not see the batsman's foot as he took up his position at the crease to face the bowler. This particular hole was very deep and wide, and as I stood on the wicket I could not understand how any side could score over 400 runs on the last day on such a mess of turf — a truly great performance.

Clearly England needed some fortune to beat this very great Australian side. Its efficiency started with its leader, Sir Donald Bradman, who, apart from being the greatest captain I have ever seen, had with him a well balanced batting and bowling combination, together with brilliant fielders who just did not drop catches.

4

England, on the other hand, were inconsistent, both in selection and performance. Compton revealed his greatness, but he lacked support. Despite the many fine performances of several younger players, they failed to gain recognition. The selection of players, namely Crapp, Emmett, Dollery, Cranston and Laker, played right into Australia's hands. Finally the selectors placed Yardley in charge of the Fourth Test without a slow bowler, and upon a wicket already mentioned. This was a travesty to any captain, for he must have longed for Wright and Hollies. Any average slow bowler could have bowled Australia out that day upon such a wicket. In desperation he called Hutton into the attack. Hutton tries to spin the ball, but could not be classed as even average. However, realising the possibilities on such a wicket, Bradman danced right out and took the bat out on him to the extent of 32 runs off three six-ball overs, and put him out of the attack. Yardley looked for a spinner, tried Hutton, failed in a good purpose, and then came in for most unwarranted criticism. With over 400 runs on the board, what captain would not try any kind of spinner.

Compton spun the ball viciously and was difficult to handle. He trapped Hassett, had Morris missed twice and Bradman once, and thus England threw away a Test match. Never will I forget the dejection of the spectators after that match. Here they had this great Australian team at bay — their first possible victory in years — a Test victory that would have thrilled England, but it didn't happen. As play commenced on the last day at Headingley I felt and admit without reservation, hoped for an English victory, for England two Tests drawn, put up a great fighting display, and a win would have done much to revive their confidence.

On the contrary the Fifth Test match debacle wherein England were all out for 52 in their first innings after winning the toss, revealed the opposite effect. From the defeat came a constructive selection for the final Test, chiefly in Dewes and Hollies. They had little chance to show their best for Dewes, the solidly built and good looking Middlesex player was very nervous and completely overawed in facing Lindwall and Miller, whilst Hollies more than fulfilled expectations by bowling Bradman second ball, but with insufficient runs on the board in England's first innings the match was a foregone conclusion and resulted in an innings victory.

We saw Hollies at Egbaston when playing for Warwickshire, and he took eight Australian wickets in one innings. This stocky fair haired slow bowler has a lot of ability, especially in flight, and should perform well on the coming tour. He is approaching forty years and faces a strenuous tour. As he suffers from a sustained knee injury it can be assumed that if Brown finds he can spin the ball on Australian wickets, he will be "reserved" for Tests and used sparingly in other games.

In the same match 28-year-old R. T. Simpson was again made twelfth man. Simpson played a good innings for Notts against Australia, was twelfth man in the first Test, and although six or seven other batsmen were chosen in the Second, Third and Fourth Tests, he was not considered until the Fifth Test. Inquiring about this very active and attractive player, a selector replied "he is a little young for this stuff and is essentially a good wicket player." Simpson will score a lot of runs in Australia, and, in doing so, will be a treat to watch.

I wonder what this selector must have thought as he watched 19-year-old Neil Harvey score a century at Headingley in his first Test. I well remember the crowd's sympathetic applause given Harvey as he walked on a Test wicket for the first time with Australia 3 for 60 odd, and I also vividly recall the enthusiastic reception he received as he reached his century. Although the crowd would have liked his wicket I felt, as by brilliant batting he approached his hundred, there was not one person amongst the great sporting following who was not "riding him home."

In their selection of the 1950-51 M.C.C. team the selectors have done what should have been done in 1946-47, and that is, build a team, blending youth with experience. Some will fail undoubtedly, and it would be foolish to attempt

(Continued on Page 37)

ENGLAND TOUR
OF AUSTRALIA **1950-1951**

"AUSTRALIA"—94 SUCCESSIVE GAMES WITHOUT A DEFEAT

"Australia," as distinct from Australian XI.'s, has not suffered a defeat since September 13, 1938. Since then they have played 94 games — they have won 66 and drawn 28, as under:—

2 remaining games of 1938 English tour.
5 games on 1946 New Zealand tour.
5 Test matches against England, 1946-47.
5 Test matches against India, 1947-48.
4 games on the way to England in 1948 — Tasmania 2, Western Ausralia and Ceylon.
34 games on the 1948 English tour.
25 games on the 1949-50 South African tour.
14 games on the 1950 New Zealand tour.

Because of Australia's great superiority many critics have under-rated many sensational and really magnificent victories.

The Australians showed their great all round strength in the 1947 Melbourne Test, when the slow bowler, McCool, made 104 not out; the fast bowler, Ray Lindwall 100; and the wicketkeeper, Don Tallon, 92.

They set a world's record for a first class game when they scored 721 in one day against Essex, which included two Test match bowlers, Trevor Bailey and Peter Smith.

Australia's 1948 Leeds Test win came after England, batting first were 2 for 423 at 3.10 p.m. on the second day.

Although England won the toss and batted in the Oval Test, Australia had a first innings lead at the tea interval — 0 for 54 to 52.

On the South African tour they were dismissed for 84 against Transvaal on a bowler's wicket. However they dismissed Transvaal for 53 to win by 15 runs.

In the Third Test they scored a remarkable win after making only 75 on a wet wicket, and South Africa, at one stage, led by 311 and 2 for 85 to 75.

They also beat Natal Country after making 74 on a wet wicket.

During this unbeaten period Australia played 21 official Test matches. Only Keith Miller played in all 21 games, and he made 1,029 runs, took 57 wickets and 20 catches.

BATTING AVERAGES (first ten)

Neil Harvey	959 runs at	106.55	and 6 centuries
Don. Bradman	1,903 runs at	105.72	and 8 centuries
Arthur Morris	1,830 runs at	67.77	and 9 centuries
Sid. Barnes	998 runs at	66.53	and 3 centuries
Lindsay Hassett	1,395 runs at	58.12	and 5 centuries
Jack Moroney	352 runs at	50.28	and 2 centuries
Sam Loxton	479 runs at	47.90	and 1 century
Keith Miller	1,029 runs at	42.87	and 1 century
Bill Brown	268 runs at	38.28	and 0 centuries
Colin McCool	459 runs at	35.30	and 1 century

BOWLING (10 or more wickets)
Wides and No Balls not included.

Bill Johnston	66 wickets at	18.24
Ray. Lindwall	77 wickets at	19.19
Ern. Toshack	47 wickets at	21.04
Keith Miller	57 wickets at	22.00
Colin McCool	36 wickets at	26.72
Ian Johnson	51 wickets at	27.96

All six bowlers played in the First Test against India in 1947.

FIELDING (10 or more catches)

Don. Tallon	40 and stumped 8
Ron. Saggers	15 and stumped 8
Lindsay Hassett	22
Keith Miller	20
Colin McCool	14
Sid. Barnes	13
Don. Bradman	11
Ian Johnson	10

Many of Tallon's catches were astonishing. In the 1946 Sydney Cricket Ground Test he dived back yards to take a right hand catch after Ian Johnson had dropped Compton's snick off McCool.

In the Manchester Test he caught Emmett off Lindwall so low that his right glove was on the turf.

In the Oval Test he dived out three yards to pick up Hutton's glance off Lindwall.

(Continued from Page 5)

to pick those who will succeed, but from it all will come a basis for future years. It is my opinion that the M.C.C. could beat Australia. I repeat could beat, but much depends on Captain F. R. Brown. He is a venturesome skipper with a tremendous task in front of him. That will not worry him unduly, for he is a man of principle and purpose, and with ordinary luck and solid support he could build this side quickly into a worthwhile combination. His attack is varied, and providing he gets support from his fielders, will test our batsmen, whilst the batting combination commencing with Hutton, Washbrook, Simpson and Compton, is convincing.

Much depends upon the performances of the new players, Dewes, Bailey, Berry, Close, Parkhouse, Sheppard and Warr. They have great prospects and we can be sure that they are going to fight it out the hard way. In addition I expect Wright to be much more effective under Brown. In his previous tour, badly placed fields, and tiring outfield work, together with ill luck that went with him whenever he bowled, prevented him turning in good figures. He was an unlucky bowler, and one who consistently beat all batsmen. Brown will correct his field placing and save him over-exertion in the field, whilst Lady Luck might smile upon him now and again.

Let us not forget we have lost Sir Donald Bradman. Just how much he meant to the side for whom he played, or what effect he had on those against him can never be assessed, although it could, this season, be revealed. I know Alec Bedser will be a lot happier, and most certainly will approach his bowling with considerably more confidence.

Lindwall — a tremendous bowler in England — has suffered by his omission from the last Test in South Africa. No doubt he will be a force to contend with, but I am sure he will not hold the terrors he did in England. He has played a big part in cricket for many years, and has, on occasions, been used as a stock bowler by some inexperienced captains instead of a shock bowler, and over the years this must have its effect. If he can reproduce his form then England will have a hard task; on the other hand, if he does not, I feel sorry for Keith Miller, who would then have a heavy burden to carry.

With the season facing us, containing such uncertainties it should be interesting, and no matter what result, it is with great pleasure we welcome our M.C.C. friends and wish them all "good cricket."

ENGLAND TOUR
OF AUSTRALIA **1950-1951**

C. L. WALCOTT

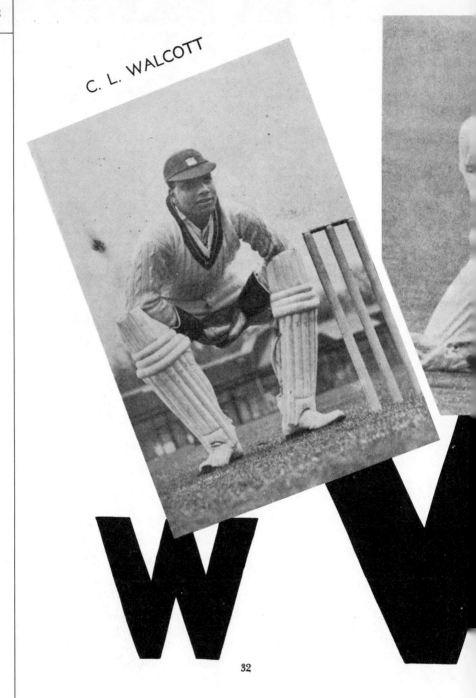

32

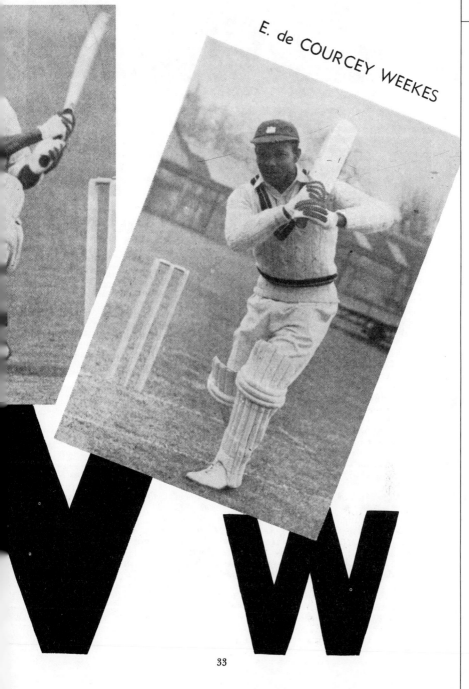

E. de COURCEY WEEKES

33

BROADCASTING CRICKET
By BERNARD KERR

Describing cricket, particularly Test cricket is a most enjoyable task. There are so many dramatic changes in a Test that every happening is vitally important and has a distinct bearing on the ultimate result. Listening to cricket has become firmly established as one of the favourite pastimes of the sport-minded Australian. When Tests are played overseas, sleepy-looking, red-eyed citizens are a common sight as they hurry to their place of business each morning and with the matches in Australia sets are tuned in everywhere, attempts are made to witness at least some portion of play each day and studio telephones run hot with enquiries for scores.

Let me take you behind the scenes! You will find the broadcasting position situated in the grandstand with the technical gear placed in such a manner to completely capture the general atmosphere. You will see on the commentators' table two microphones, one for the describer and the other for the "special" comments man — the job that Arthur Gilligan has done in such a splendid manner.

Commentators have to treat broadcasting rather seriously because so much nervous tension is involved in bringing an accurate report of happenings on the field. You will find that commentators like Alan McGilvray, Victor Richardson, Arthur Gilligan and Johnnie Moyes concentrate to such an extent that the pressure really only eases when an adjournment is taken or stumps have been drawn.

The aim of every man is to provide a sincere and factual description because, in this way, he automatically reacts to every phase of play whether it be sensational, exciting, dull or humorous. The job is not all glamour. Apart from the nervous tension, describing causes great strain on the eyes because the play is not being watched in a relaxed manner. To bring those important details which are appreciated so much by the cricket lover, binoculars are used quite a good deal but not all the time as conditions have to be considered. For instance, at Adelaide where the broadcasting position is side on to the pitch, binoculars are more of a hindrance than a help as they have to be constantly moved from the bowler to the batsman which is most disconcerting. The ideal broadcasting position is one which enables the commentator to look up the pitch. Additional strain is caused by the fact that things happen so quickly, and with the commentator always aiming to be in front of the crowd reaction, he finds himself endeavouring to anticipate, which is a very exacting business. Then again, the weather produces problems because it may be very hot or very cloudy and windy. Behind it all too is the constant thought that once the mike is alive he has the sole responsibility of providing the best service possible to listeners who cannot attend the ground. If the broadcast goes well he has a warm feeling of pleasant satisfaction and if it doesn't he feels exactly the opposite, very much down in the dumps. Although each describer is conscious of carrying out his work along certain set principles you'll find that he has an individual style and you either like him for it or you don't. Arthur Gilligan and Victor Richardson have become famous as a "team" and listeners find themselves intensely interested one moment and highly amused another—Alan McGilvray has become one of the best known commentators wherever cricket is played because of his knowledge of the game, accuracy and brisk style, while a comparative newcomer "Johnnie" Moyes is noted for his logic and sincere manner which at all times carries a tone of authority. Please don't gain the impression that cricket commentators are rather a grim lot and that they find the job rather heavy as they are indeed a very cheerful lot of fellows particularly after stumps.

The photo at the top of this article is the ABC team which broadcast the 4th Test in Adelaide against England from February 2nd-8th, 1951. Top, left to right—Johnnie Moyes, Victor Richardson, Arnold Ewens; Bottom, left to right—Bernard Kerr, Arthur Gilligan, Alan McGilvray.

Although cricket writers and broadcasters have the same intense interest in the game there is a difference in the technique of reporting. I have seen press representatives in action during Test matches and have admired their ability to dash off their copy in the middle of a constant click of typewriters and crowd reaction. The cricket writer on a daily newspaper works under tremendous pressure with one eye on the field and the other on the typewriter and his mind and fingers working at a very lively pace. The cricket describer goes through the same ordeal although there is not as much physical exertion. He has to concentrate even more than the writer and the nervous tension is greater but he has the satisfaction of knowing that when he has spoken about an incident his job has been done. I thought you would like to know how "Johnnie" Moyes feels about it. He had written cricket for years before becoming a member of the ABC team which covered the MCC tour in 1950-51. To complete this article then, here are his comments:—

Newspaper training gives one a sense of news value which is a distinct asset when it comes to broadcasting. Indeed, reviewing a match for a morning paper and doing a broadcast summary have much in common but there are also vital differences.

For example, the writer can sit back and think over the whole day's play, sort out the important incidents, write his copy and pass it over to a sub-editor. If it is a bit long, a few judicious cuts will soon fix that. Sometimes of course, the sub-editor doesn't help and the writer isn't happy when he reads his story in print. On the other hand, a good "sub" can be of real assistance. The commentator, on the other hand, knows that he must be on the air at a fixed time and that his story must be ready. It must be condensed into space allotted — four or five minutes — and that he must not go one word over that time. He must tell, in that short period, the complete story of the day — what happened and why. He must be both writer and sub-editor. If the broadcast falls flat, it is his own work, and he can't blame the "sub."

Therefore, during the day, he never relaxes. He notes down every incident, every changing phase of the game, continually revising his ideas, re-assessing values, cutting here and adding there, so that he has fixed in his mind a coherent story which will flow. It may be that the events of the last twenty minutes may alter the whole complexion of the game. He then must scrap earlier thoughts and conclusions, re-make his broadcast, and work against time in doing it.

He must know exactly what he is going to say when he goes on the air and be enthusiastic about it. If he isn't, then he will bore the listeners. He must be factual and yet not dull. He must give the highlights and yet condense. He cuts his story in advance — not later.

And there is always the knowledge that the broadcast is heard by so many people, not only within Australia, but far beyond its confines. You get a real kick out of that thought.

WEST INDIES TOUR
OF AUSTRALIA **1951-1952**

ARE THEY SUPERMEN ?

By DUDLEY NOURSE, Former South African Captain

I have come to regard the Australian cricketers as something of a race of supermen on the cricket field, fiercely jealous of their cricketing prestige, but wonderfully good companions, shrewd judges, clever plotters, who leave nothing to chance, and superb fielders, which always makes their task so much easier.

PERHAPS, significantly, Arthur David Nourse was scoring a double century in Australia during a summer when another Arthur Nourse was ushered into the world.

It was a compliment to me that I was named Dudley after the then Governor General of Australia, at his request. I say significantly, because while football was my greatest joy as a young lad, it was cricket that absorbed most of my interest in later life, as I followed the footsteps of my father.

Young, with a tour of England to fortify me, I was full of hope that I would be able to combat Grimmett, O'Reilly, Fleetwood-Smith and McCormick. Watching the diabolical accuracy of O'Reilly at nets, and failing to be able to detect Grimmett's "bosey," I was consumed with a fear that I might fail, and was even more determined that I would not let the pair of them cause me sleepless nights. **In my concern over mastering the mysteries of Grimmett and O'Reilly I almost forgot about the ability of McCormick, who captured my wicket five times to Grimmett's three times and O'Reilly twice.**

Yet it was a happy, prosperous season for me (two centuries, my first Test double century, 635 runs in 14 innings). I had climbed another step in the cricketing ladder, even if our optimism did receive a rude shock as the Australians waltzed triumphantly through the land.

I found myself constantly fascinated by the artistry of Stan McCabe; by the glorious fielding of the Australians; by the shrewdness of Vic Richardson's captaincy; by the technique of the opening batsmen, Brown and Fingleton, and their fine understanding of each others play; by the matchless combination of O'Reilly and Grimmett.

Grimmett's subtleties luring one to destruction; O'Reilly's determination always immediately to overthrow a batsman.

These impressions remain almost indelibly in my mind. They were only partly erased when 15 years later we were to be bombarded by the pace of Miller, Lindwall, Walker and Bill Johnston.

Like the rest of the cricketing world, we were out of practice against fast bowling, and could find no effective counter a stratagem. Like many others It was humiliating, to say the least, for a batsman not to be able effectively to counter a strategem. Like many others in this country I admired the confidence of Neil Harvey, the self assurance and ease of Lindsay Hassett's batting, the fielding of Archer, Harvey, Loxton and Miller more particularly, and the general attitude of determination about the lower order batsmen if the upper half had not done so well.

In 1935/36 it was Grimmett and O'Reilly, the spinners, who caused me most worry. In 1949/50 it was the pace of Miller and the change of pace of Bill Johnston that caused me most concern.

My greatest regret is that I was not able to watch Don Bradman at close quarters. I had hoped to profit by his technique. My greatest joy is having had the opportunity of meeting and playing against such fine cricketers.

Here is an Afrikaan's request. The first youngster who tries it on the Springbok captain, Jack Cheetham, is on a well-nigh certain winner.

"HULLO MENEER. SAL U U HANDTEKENING IN MY HANDTE-KENINGBOEK SKRYF?"

What does it mean? Literally, "Hullo, Sir, will you your signature in my autograph book write?

"THE SMOKE THAT THUNDERS"

By LOUIS DUFFUS, Leading South African Critic

When Lindsay Hassett's team sang their way through South Africa three years ago they surpassed all vocal competition until they met the volume of the Victoria Falls. Here the waters of the Zambesi cascade over a 300 foot precipice, smash against the wall of a narrow chasm and rise rumbling high over the land in a spray which the natives call "the smoke that thunders."

SOUTH African cricket has similarly plunged into an abyss, the deepest in its history, through the disappearance from the Test scene in one fell swoop of Dudley Nourse, Eric and Athol Rowan, "Tufty" Mann, Geoff. Chubb, George Fullerton, Clive van Ryneveld and Cuan McCarthy. The attempt to make it rise again is being undertaken not by gradual elevation, but by forcing it against the solid krantz of Australian supremacy.

The qualities which Jack Cheetham's team will pour into the pit, in ample proportions, are youth, courage, ambition and budding talent. They lack experience and stability.

All of them possess the common, encouraging characteristic that their cricket is developing, and most South Africans expect handsome development from such players as John Waite, a tall, lean orthodox batsman and wicket-keeper; from Roy McLean, whose gifts of force and footwork could make him the most colourful member of the side; from 20 year-old Gerald Innes, a stylish stroke-maker; from two well-equipped all-rounders, Hedley Keith, a left-hander, who jumped into prominence by taking 5 for 24 and 5 for 91 for a country side against Hassett's eleven; and Percy Mansell, leg-spin bowler, slip fielder and scorer of 90 in his first Test, who plays in spectacles.

And if the bowlers have no striking record to commend them—except Hugh Tayfield's 7 for 23 when Australia was dismissed for 75 at Durban — they should command outstanding support in the field.

No one is going to beat tom-toms across the veldt to acclaim this team, but their countrymen feel a sober confidence in their potential prowess.

CURRIE CUP AVERAGES: 1951/52

Currie Cup: "A" Section — Batting

	I.	N.O.	H.S.	Runs	Avge.
Norton	11	3	111	535	66.87
Endean	7	2	140	290	58.00
McGlew	9	1	186	438	54.78
Waite	11	1	177	537	53.70
Innes	10	1	139	419	46.55
Keith	10	0	193	458	45.80
McLean	10	1	124	380	42.22
Murray	11	1	97	378	37.80
Cheetham	7	0	58	233	33.28

Currie Cup: "B" Section — Batting

	I.	N.O.	H.S.	Runs	Avge.
Funston	11	0	111	564	51.27
Mansell	12	2	94	485	48.50

Currie Cup: "A" Section — Bowling

	O.	M.	R.	W.	Avge.
Tayfield	316.6	94	756	39	19.38
Keith	272.2	109	456	21	21.71
Watkins	149.2	39	304	12	25.33
Fuller	252	58	669	26	25.73
Murray	250	68	542	19	28.52
Melle	116	27	290	10	29.00

Currie Cup: "B" Section — Bowling

	O.	M.	R.	W.	Avge.
Mansell	243	36	809	49	16.51

SOUTH AFRICA TOUR OF AUSTRALIA **1952-1953**

RUN–GETTING IS MORE DIFFICULT IN ENGLAND

• IS BATTING HARDER IN ENGLAND THAN IN AUSTRALIA, AND IF SO, WHY? IN THIS ARTICLE SIR DONALD BRADMAN DISCUSSES THE QUESTION WHICH IS OF SUCH VITAL INTEREST THIS YEAR WHEN THE AUSTRALIAN TEAM IS TOURING.

WITH the visit of an Australian team to England during 1953, attention will be focussed on all our players, but more particularly on those who have not previously played in the Mother Country.

Enthusiasts will undoubtedly be saying to one another, "Oh, yes, Smith will certainly do well because he has been there before and proved that he can bat on English wickets, b u t Jones will be a failure because the conditions will not suit him."

Why should anyone say that a cricketer who has performed creditably in Australia is unlikely to succeed in England? Why shouldn't a good batsman make runs with the same ease in both countries? The answer is that a fully - equipped player may be expected to do well under any circumstances.

It is of course true that some players have achieved great success in Australia only to fail miserably when sent overseas, and undoubtedly this is because conditions in the two countries vary so greatly.

As a general principle, it is not very wide of the mark to say that strong back players usually do well in Eng-

land, because they have more time in which to follow the ball off the pitch. Those who constantly play forward do not find things quite so easy.

The method of stroke production whilst basically the same, must be adapted to the slower type of pitch. This applies not only from country to country, but often from week to week so far as England is concerned.

Before I first went there in 1930 I had a favourite shot in which I played back to a ball short of a l e n g t h on the stumps and drove it b e t w e e n the bowler and mid-on.

I visualised that this would be a simpler stroke in England and one which I could use m o r e frequently because I imagined I would have more time to see the ball. In a c t u a l fact, I could not play it at all over there, because the ball came along too slowly to get the necessary p o w e r into the stroke, and instead of hitting it past the bowler, I found I had to hit that ball wide of mid-on with a type of pull shot.

Pitches in Australia are made of a heavy black soil, whereas those in England are sometimes rolled out on the natural earth, or are prepared from a chocolate coloured marl. They are not nearly as hard as Australian pitches, whilst the grasses are mostly fine-leafed and not of the couch variety. No scythe is used, and the time of preparation is much shorter.

Whereas we often play virtually on the bare soil in Australia because the grass is cut right down to the earth, most English wickets have a nice coating of green leafy grass, from which the behaviour of the ball is quite different.

When matches are played on what we call a "green top," it is common to see a little ball mark where each delivery has pitched, and when these dry out, it is interesting to note the pattern on the ground where the ball has been landing. For a bowler of the Bedser calibre, that area is a very small one.

Usually it is possible to turn the ball on an English wicket. "Tich" Freeman, a slow bowler who was really good in England, turned the ball a lot and was difficult to play, yet in Australia he did not meet with the same success. Here the explanation seemed to be that in order to obtain spin from our harder ground he had to throw the ball slightly higher.

Consequently he was slower through the air and this enabled the batsman to jump out and get to the pitch of the ball for a drive.

Mostly the English light is dull. Personally I loved it and enjoyed batting without a cap when there was no glare, but sometimes it becomes very gloomy, and with the ball also dark and retaining its sheen because of a grassy pitch and soft outfield, it is difficult to detect the spin through the air.

The atmosphere is frequently heavy and this, coupled with these other features, enables the swing bowlers to keep moving the ball about all day.

Don't forget also that playing six days a week for 5 months on end with playing hours sometimes from 11 a.m. until 6.30 p.m. is a very tiring business. Some players thrive on it; others cannot stand up to the work.

Another interesting feature is that they have daylight saving in England so that although play commences at say 11 a.m. by the clock, it may only be 9.30 a.m. by the sun. This often means dew on the grass, and a somewhat strange light, to which Australians are unaccustomed.

The frequency of rain is the cause of many wickets being damp, and although an English wet wicket is not as bad as an Australian "sticky" dog, it still calls for tremendous skill and concentration.

English professional bowlers are experts at handling their local conditions. County bowlers of no particular fame bowl a good length to a well-placed field, and runs are hard to obtain even in the less important games. Where two country matches are played each week, it means playing against a completely different set of bowlers on grounds that have perhaps not been seen before. Some of these have sight-boards at one end only—notably Lord's. With a dull light this is a great handicap, for spectators moving behind the bowler can interrupt a batsman's vision and concentration.

Moreover, a sightboard at one end and no board at the other doesn't help the player to settle down with any degree of certainty. He must virtually be adaptable to change from over to over.

The difference in food, water and climate all have to be considered. Experience has shown that most Australian players, even in tip-top condition, average several pounds heavier in England. I have known big men to be almost a stone heavier and this additional weight can be a handicap.

Then, too, I should mention the cold.

I have actually been on the field at Worcester with light snow flakes falling, and believe me, this doesn't assist your certainty of touch whether it be batting or bowling. The fingers lose their sensitivity, and the delicate control vanishes.

In one match against Derbyshire, I sat huddled before a roaring fire wearing my cricket clothes including a sweater, blazer and overcoat, while waiting to bat. When I reached the wicket I was hit on the leg above the pad by each of the first two balls. Such happenings don't exactly give you confidence at the start of an innings.

4

I often laugh about the day at Scarborough when I was barracked for bowling in a sweater. In due course I gave way and took it off, but continued bowling in the other one which I was wearing underneath.

There you have very briefly some of the fundamental difficulties and I have yet to find anyone who can give me a cast-iron formula which will show in advance whether a player will succeed in both countries or not. Only experience gives the answer.

I am convinced however, that commonsense plays a vital part in the matter. A great player chould be able to make modifications to his play even daily if necessary. One who sticks rigidly to a style and refuses to learn must pay the penalty.

Finally, a word on statistics. I have stated earlier that I loved English conditions and, if it came to a choice, I would rather bat on a nice English pitch than its Australian counterpart, but I think, taken over a full season's play, the vast majority of batsmen find English conditions more difficult to master.

This appears to be borne out by the averages and as a matter of interest I have compiled the tables set out below in support of the theory :

BATTING

Season	Highest average by English batsman on Australian tour	Highest average by Australian batsman on English tour
1896	....	31.8
1897/8	54.8	....
1901/2	58	....
1902	....	48.4
1907/8	51.9	....
1909	....	46.3
1911/12	55	....
1912	....	51.9
1920/21	62	....
1921	....	58.3
1924/5	73	....
1926	....	57.9

It is rather interesting to point out that whereas an Englishman had a batting average in Australia of over 50 as long ago as 1897/8, and the feat had been accomplished no less than 9 times

by Englishmen up to 1911/12, it was not until 1912 that an Australian (Bardsley) succeeded in doing so in England.

The legendary Trumper could not go beyond 48 in his four tours of England, his other figures being 34, 35, and 33 respectively.

Another interesting batting comparison is that prior to 1948 only two Australians (excluding myself) had succeeded in having a batting average beyond 60 on an English tour.

At that stage it had been accomplished 9 times by Englishmen in Australia.

To complete the story, bowling figures shown below reverse the picture :

BOWLING

Season	Lowest average by Englishman in Australia	Lowest average by Australian in England
1902	....	14.2
1903/4	15.5	....
1907/8	20.1	....
1909	....	14.9
1911/12	19.2	....
1912	....	16.3
1920/21	26.6	....
1921	....	14.5
1924/5	17.6	....
1926	....	16.2
1936/7	20.6	....
1938	....	14.0

In compiling these figures I have omitted cases where the amount of bowling by a player was so restricted that his average was not a fair comparison.

I think readers will agree that I have made out a reasonable case to support my contention that if you take a full season's play into account, batsmen find it a little harder to defeat the bowler in England than they do in Australia, though in isolated instances this may not be so.

But whether batsmen find it more difficult or not, you may rest assured that the great ambition of Australian players will always be to tour England and to play at Lords.

BOWLING IN AUSTRALIA AND ENGLAND

Clarrie Grimmett took more wickets in Test cricket than any other bowler, and was tremendously successful in England. In this article he discusses the conditions our bowlers will meet during the 1953 tour, and he writes from a wide experience.

CONDITIONS in England are different in many ways from those in Australia and the climate tends to give a varied assortment. Pitches are slower, the atmosphere is heavier, and bleak days are likely, especially during the early part of the tour.

Let me give you my own experience when I first arrived in England. Like the other newcomers I was anxious to get to Lord's to practice, but I soon found that my old flight and pace were useless, the ball being too slow off the pitch.

Increasing my pace through the air and off the pitch allowed me to bowl a shorter length than I otherwise could have done, and thus I was able to restrict the batsman's freedom of movement.

This is one of the first lessons to learn and you find out the vital importance of it as soon as you meet these slower pitches.

In a normal season there are many damp days and pitches that suit bowlers. This tends to encourage right and left-handers who have the pace and accuracy to make use of these conditions. They cultivate swing and swerve and cause quite a lot of trouble when conditions are favourable.

The success of left hand bowlers in England makes it a wise move to select this type in a touring side, but they must be able to fit into the new order of things. It is unusual for them to bowl round the wicket in Australia, but with the more turnable pitches in England they are able to do this. So our left-handers must be able to use the other side of the crease, as must any right hand off-spinners.

One axiom that applies to all bowling is that the ball must be kept up to all batsmen to preclude any possibility of back play. They must be forced to play forward and feel for the ball.

Most pacy bowlers in England can move the ball off the pitch quite a lot. They are assisted by the greater bite the ball gets from it and from the heavier atmosphere which causes it to swing disconcertingly. Under Australian conditions this is not so easy.

One of the most heartbreaking pitches found in England is the "greasy top" which usually occurs when there is fine weather with foggy nights. The surface of the pitch is made greasy by the moisture in the air, but there is not enough to penetrate. Consequently the pitch is firm, the ball just skids off it, and hardly leaves a mark. On these pitches a spin bowler has no hope of turning the ball and must concentrate on variations of flight and pace.

A touring team has advantages as well as problems. Playing together day after day must improve their teamwork, and the captain should be able to sort out the "bits and pieces" and mould the side into the best possible combination. On the other hand they play six days a week, and every third and fourth day players pack and move on somewhere else. This continual cricket could cause staleness.

Key players are groomed for the big matches ahead and need match play, while the "also-rans" are left to cool their heels and gradually become more discontented. This is one of the worst things that can happen, so that unless something unforeseen occurs, seventeen players could be a disadvantage. This would give the skipper a lot of worry because a happy team will pull its weight. On the other hand if accident or sickness claims any victims, the "spare-parts" get a game and are much more contented.

Then again a lot depends on how many key players are in form because if there are only a few of these, the brunt of the work falls on them and they become stale. From a morale point of view the team must not be beaten, so for each game a suitable side has to be chosen. If the touring band is evenly balanced the problem solves itself, for efficient teams can be selected, thus assuring regular spells for the key players.

6

AUSTRALIA'S BIG FOUR

By A. G. MOYES

IN the great array of Australian batsmen from Charles Bannerman, maker of the first Test century, down to Neil Harvey, the youngest of the present-day stars, who are the men who stand out above their fellows in everything that goes to make the complete batsman? I'll nominate Clem Hill, Victor Trumper, Charlie Macartney and Don Bradman as the four greatest Australians I've seen. They were masters of their craft.

The order in which I named them doesn't indicate any preference in ranking. They came into Test cricket that way, the first a left-hander, and the others right-handers.

Clem Hill was a schoolboy prodigy, and an innings of 360 for Prince Alfred College gave notice of what was to follow. He had not long celebrated his eighteenth birthday when he made 150 not out for South Australia against the Englishmen, and a year or two later scored 206 not out against New South Wales to clinch a last-minute place in the 1896 side for England.

The rest of his career is part of the history of Australian cricket: a highest score of 365 not out against New South Wales; four centuries in Tests against England, including a glorious effort of 188 when Australia had lost six wickets for 58; five other innings which finished in the nineties, three of them in succession; 17,208 runs in first-class cricket, and 45 centuries.

Of about average height, thick-set, with powerful forearms, Hill was light and dainty on his feet, and a magnificent hitter of fast bowling. He was a picture of aggression as he stood at the crease, and he believed that it was the bats-man's duty to attack. It's a characteristic possessed by all great players.

Vic. Trumper was the originating genius of a new outlook on batting. Graceful always, with the iron fist inside the velvet glove, he could play all the strokes his contemporaries used, and many more as well.

Tall, and rather slight in build, his gift of timing was superb, and he seemed always in position well ahead of schedule to play his stroke. He was a breaker of bowlers' hearts, although he always gave them a chance because of the risks he took, but there was a transcending perfection about his art, and he lives in memory as one stamped with the ineffaceable mark of genius.

On bad pitches he was masterly, without doubt the greatest of all Australians under those conditions, and even the mighty Wilfred Rhodes was forced to bowl outside the off-stump on a Melbourne "sticky" one day as Trumper smote his bowling hip and thigh.

Trumper was the first batsman to score a Test century before lunch. He made six centuries against England; in 1902 had 2,570 runs and 11 centuries in one of the wettest seasons ever known; 17,150 runs and 43 centuries in first class cricket, and 300 not out his highest score.

Charlie Macartney walked for a time in the humble paths of orthodoxy, but later donned the purple of majesty. Short, compact, audacious, a believer in fours rather than in singles, he also hit a century in a Test before lunch, reached the three figures five times against England, three of them in successive innings.

Macartney was the cheekiest of all, determined always to be the master, attacking from the start of his innings, but having the defence to fall back on when once the attack had been temporarily halted.

4

Victor Trumper shows how to drive

Like Trumper and Hill, he would set out to kill the bowler who was troubling his colleagues, and he had the equipment for the purpose, for his footwork was fast and sure, his wrist was like steel, his eye keen and true, and his ambition unchallengeable.

Macartney's highest was 345 against Notts in about four hours' batting. In all, he made 14,217 runs with 48 centuries. A glorious player who had undoubtedly touched the skirts of that capricious lady, Dame Genius.

And then came Don Bradman to dazzle everyone and to re-write the record books and to dominate Test cricket as no one had ever done before. Short but wiry, remarkably quick on his feet, with the same fundamental determination to attack, a killer of bowlers, calm and thoughtful, he built up a record which may never be beaten. Bradman was an idealist, and a merciless cross-examiner of his own acts which had caused him to lose his wicket, thus introducing a touch of realism which also included the knowledge that it is runs scored which win a cricket match. The public demanded runs, and he supplied them as no one had ever done before, full measure and running over.

In all first-class cricket he scored 28,067 runs at 95.14 an innings. He made 117 centuries, 19 of them in Tests against England; had a highest score of 452 not out; passed the 300 mark six times, twice in Tests against England, and in one of them, the first, 100 before lunch. He made a century once in less than every three innings. In all Tests, he had an average of 99.94 runs an innings. The immensity of it all is staggering! How can we place anyone before him?

So there they are, my "Big Four," one of them, Trumper, an opening batsman, and the others all batting at the fall of the first wicket. Superb players, and they studied the art, practised hard to perfect themselves. Natural skill? Of course, but they worked for their success, and there is a lesson in this for all who would follow them on the path leading to cricket glory.

5

1956 AUSTRALIAN TOUR OF ENGLAND

By BRUCE DOOLAND

THE outcome of the 1956 Test series in England could well depend largely on the ability of the Australian batsmen to cope with the battery of pace bowlers which is at the call of the English selectors.

The combination of Tyson and Statham, that proved so destructive during the last M.C.C. tour of Australia in 1954-5, will not, to my mind, be as effective in England as in this country. The slower nature of the majority of English wickets will not prove as helpful as the faster pitches on which the Tests were played in Australia.

This will apply particularly to Frank Tyson, who depends wholly on speed and will not have the added nip from the wicket. Also, there was a doubt during the last English County season as to the fitness of Tyson. He missed nearly half of the County season with his county, Northamptonshire, and was unable to participate in a couple of Tests against South Africa, owing to a recurrent injury to his heel.

The long County season, playing six days a week, may well cause this injury to be troublesome again.

Statham is a particularly fine bowler and, unlike Tyson, does not necessarily depend on sheer pace, but is able to maintain his accuracy and speed, at the same time making the ball move off the wicket with the seam. He should be a constant menace to the Australians and the conditions over the other side will suit him more than in this country.

Should this combination not prove successful, the English selectors can call on two other speed merchants in Trueman and Loader. Trueman is a very good bowler, particularly under English conditions, which allow him to move the ball in the air and to maintain that movement much longer than he would in Australia. Loader also depends on swing, mainly away from the batsman.

I think that Statham will be equally as effective and, perhaps, more so than he was here, but rather fancy that both Trueman and Loader will be more dangerous to the Australian tourists than Tyson.

The value of bowlers of the type and calibre of Lock and Laker, particularly on the Oval wicket, cannot be over-emphasised. This pitch, which is recognised as a spinner's paradise even as early as the second day, is ideal for finger spinners who are able to bowl for long periods economically. Lock and Laker make full use of the pitch which is on their home ground, both being Surrey players. Lock pushes the ball through at nearly medium pace, still maintaining his spin and accuracy, thus cutting out any possibility of the batsmen using their feet in an endeavour to kill the spin.

Lock, in my opinion, is a certainty for the Tests, and I rate him as the best attacking spinner in England.

His only serious rival as a left-arm spinner is Johnny Wardle. This Yorkshireman is more of a defensive bowler, but has the advantage, on a good wicket, of being able to revert to left-arm leg-spin and googly, which may finally influence the selectors.

During the last County season Bob Appleyard was unable to play in the Tests against South Africa, owing to a strained groin, but with a winter's rest I see no reason why he should not be fit again.

Should he regain his past form, it is hard to see him being passed over. Effective as Laker is on the Oval wicket, Appleyard will probably be preferred, owing to his ability to bowl with the seam on green tops and to revert to his natural off-spinners when the occasion demands.

4

BRUCE DOOLAND

The man who carried the English bowling attack since the war, Alec Bedser, is by no means finished and is still a great force to be reckoned with.

Australians who watched him last summer saw an unfit Bedser, not fully recovered from an illness early in the tour. Added to this, his only Test appearance was on the easy-paced Brisbane wicket, when none of the M.C.C. bowlers showed to any advantage.

I feel sure that had he been given another Test chance during that tour he would have been as successful as he was in the past.

Apart from those already known to Australians, there were no outstanding bowlers last English season, with the possible exception of Middlesex's Fred Titmus. He was tried in Tests with not a great

deal of success. He is an off spinner of the same type as Jim Laker but is lacking at the moment in experience. However, he could prove to be a serious rival for a place in the English attack.

From the batting point of view, England is not in such a happy position. The choice of opening batsmen presents a problem that is very acute indeed, and it will be even worse should Len Hutton not be fit enough to make a comeback into Test cricket.

The only exception, perhaps, is Worcestershire's left hander, Peter Richardson, who has just completed his two years National Service and, as yet, has not had an international trial.

Although he played a limited number of first class matches last season during his training, he was not as successful as predicted, but with his National Service behind him and full-time concentration on cricket possible, this amateur could well play himself back into his previous form and into the England side.

One of the openers tried last season against the South African tourists was Yorkshire's Brian Close. Although he carried out his job in the final Test, I don't fancy him as a Test class opening bat, and would be much more suited lower down where he could play his natural attacking game. He is also a useful off spinner, but as England is well placed in this department it would not necessarily influence the selectors to prefer him to a steadier batsman.

It looks absolutely certain that Peter May will lead the side. This young batsman since he first met the Australian tourists in England in 1953 has improved considerably, and the added responsibility of captaincy has not affected his batting. May will prove the major stumbling block to the Australians.

After his successful tour of Australia, Colin Cowdrey had a very mediocre season in County cricket.

5

He did not play for the first half, owing to his National Service, but played for his County, Kent, during the latter half, and was unable to get going in the majority of his innings.

However, he is a good enough player to overcome this and should regain his form at the start of next season. If so, he would then be assured of a Test place.

Denis Compton's knee injury, and subsequent operation, places him as a very doubtful starter and only time can prove whether he will be able to undertake a strenuous season. Should he be fit, there are few better players in England at the moment.

I rather doubt whether Gloucestershire's Tom Graveney will be given many more chances. He has been tried at nearly every position in the batting order and, whilst he is a glorious stroke maker, he does not seem to have the concentration so vitally needed for Tests, and rather rules himself out by his inconsistency.

A young batsman who could easily oppose the Australians is Ken Barrington of Surrey. At the end of the last County season he was awarded a prize for the "most promising young cricketer of the year."

He has been playing regularly only for the past two seasons and, although he played in a couple of Tests against South Africa without much success, he could come into the reckoning next year. He is a forceful right hander with a wide variety of strokes, but whether he has the experience necessary in England remains to be seen.

New members of the Australian touring team will find a great difference in the playing conditions in England to those experienced here. To start with, the hours of play are at least an hour longer daily, and this, coupled with cricket for six days a week, makes a very tiring combination, particularly towards the end of the tour.

Nearly every wicket in England has different characteristics, and the batting and bowling must be modified to suit the varying conditions.

The "Green Top", with its hard surface and plenty of green grass, is ideally suited to the fast and medium-paced bowlers, as it has plenty of pace, and enables the seam bowlers to make the ball move both ways off the pitch for long periods.

The English rain-affected pitches are not in any way as dangerous as their counterparts in Australia, and they rarely behave in such a nasty manner as a "sticky dog" does here. A finger-spinner of the off, or left-arm leg spin variety, is a "must" to take the full advantage of the condition of the pitch.

On the majority of wickets in England it is much easier to turn the ball and, consequently, the spinners find it more effective to push the ball through a little faster than would be the case here. This also tends to give the added "zip" needed on the slower turf.

On the whole, I rather fancy the chances of the Australians in their quest to regain the "Ashes" this year, and with the young talent available I see no need to fear for the future.

The writer of this article, BRUCE DOOLAND of South Australia, played Test cricket for Australia, and then went to the Lancashire League. He qualified by residence for Notts County and for the past few seasons has had a great record, being probably the finest slow bowler in England. As Dooland knows English conditions and players so well, his views have added interest.

TEST CRICKET CAPTAIN AND OLYMPIC STAR

By A. G. MOYES

IN a year when we have both cricket Test Matches and the Olympic Games, it is well to remember John William Henry Tyler Douglas, known to countless thousands as "Johnny won't hit today", the man who won fame in both.

Douglas is best remembered as a cricketer who led England in Tests against both Australia and South Africa, but there isn't much doubt that he was a better amateur boxer than he was a cricketer. Many excelled him in the summer sport, but in boxing he was undisputed champion of England and in 1908 the outstanding amateur middleweight in the world, as he proved by his win over Australia's R. L. "Snowy" Baker in the Olympic Games in England in that year.

This was an historic fight and the pair were so even that neither the judges nor the referee cared to give a decision after the usual three rounds, and ordered another before declaring Douglas the winner. One great English boxing writer of those days has left it on record that in his opinion Douglas was good enough to win a professional title and he added this:—

"Another magnificent amateur was the Australian middleweight, Reginald Baker. I shall never forget his scrap with J. W. H. T. Douglas in the final Olympic Games Competition at the Northampton Institute. Among the thousands of contests I have watched, this three-rounder stands out as a classic. Douglas received the decision, but there were many sound judges who considered that the fair-headed Australian was not a loser. In my opinion Baker should have received the verdict."

It must have been a grand old scrap if it produced opinions like that, but those who knew the two men could understand just how tough it could be.

Johnny Douglas was that way as a cricketer. For a champion boxer he was amazingly slow on his feet when batting and there was neither grace nor charm about him . . . just plain courage, a capacity to fight, and a will to conquer. Against slow bowlers of quality his leaden feet made him look dreadful, and those who watched him playing, or trying to play Arthur Mailey, will recall how funny it was to everyone but the batsman.

However, Douglas fought back. He used to sit for hours behind the bowler's arm and watch him through powerful binoculars, trying to discover the secret of the spinner's art, and it may have helped him because he gained some success and certainly more assurance before the tour was over. He never managed a century against Australia, his highest in 28 innings being 75 and he averaged 26.76 runs an innings. Against South Africa he averaged 38, and he played an innings of 119.

If Douglas was dull as a batsman, he was lively enough as a bowler. Fast-medium, he would make the ball curl appreciably in the air and his in-swinger was particularly vicious. Taking a short run, he threw his whole bodyweight into each delivery and on the way back to his mark would rub the ball vigorously on his shirt sleeves.

For Essex against Leicester in 1906 he took five wickets in eight balls for 0 runs at one stage, doing the hat trick. He took 13 wickets for 155 against Kent; 13 for 172 for the Gentlemen against the Players; 14 for 156 for Essex against Worcester; 14 for 91 for Essex against Hampshire; and

10

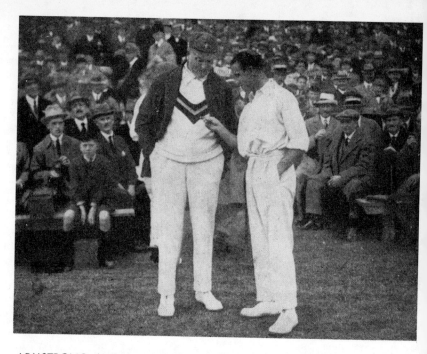

ARMSTRONG (left) and DOUGLAS tossing for innings at Trent Bridge before the start of the First Test in 1921.

four wickets in six balls in a match against Sussex.

At Sydney in 1920-21, Douglas did the hat trick for the M.C.C. against New South Wales.

This great athlete took over the captaincy of the 1911-12 M.C.C. team when P. F. Warner (later Sir Pelham) took ill after playing a century innings at Adelaide, and he came back as captain of the 1920-21 side. In 1924-25 he was a member of the team led by Arthur Gilligan but did little of note during that tour. He also led England a few times against Australia in England.

Douglas, whose highest score in first-class cricket was 210 for Essex, was also a fine soccer player. In the first world war he reached the rank of Lieutenant-Colonel.

There was always a feeling that Douglas lacked a sense of humour but that definitely wasn't the case. He took his sport seriously, played it with all his heart, but he could laugh and, what is more, he could laugh at himself. On one occasion he described an optimst as a "batsman, batting with Johnny Douglas, who backs up for a run."

On 19th December, 1930, he and his father were returning to England from a business trip and while in the Cattegat, the steamer Oberon, on which they were travelling, collided with the Arcturus. Douglas could have saved himself but he rushed downstairs to save his father. Both were drowned, and so the man we all knew as a great fighter went down fighting trying to save the life of another.

11

SOUND AND TELEVISION COVERAGE

OVER the years the A.B.C. Sporting Service has established a fine reputation for the broadcasting of International Sport, particularly cricket. In the coming season the interest in cricket should be particularly high, following Australia's successful tour of South Africa last season. There is certain to be intense enthusiasm — with Australia fighting to regain the "Ashes" on her home grounds.

The Interstate and National programmes will be carefull examined, with the idea of arranging broadcasts to allow listeners in the city and country areas to hear a complete description of the Test Matches. It is realised that country listeners in particular appreciate this service, but at the same time, other important programme features will have to receive consideration.

The broadcasting of Parliament will bring about certain changes in the times of descriptions, but these will be fully publicised in the press and appropriate A.B.C. sessions.

Summaries of each day's play throughout the tour will be given by one of the panel of expert commentators.

The playing times of the TEST matches in **NEW SOUTH WALES and QUEENSLAND are:**

11.30 — 1.00	LUNCH
1.40 — 3.30	TEA
3.50 — 5.30	STUMPS

IN VICTORIA

12.00 — 1.30	LUNCH
2.10 — 4.00	TEA
4.20 — 6.00	STUMPS

IN ADELAIDE
(Quoted in Australian Eastern Time)

12.30 — 2.00	LUNCH
2.40 — 4.30	TEA
4.50 — 6.30	STUMPS

The Tests will be described in full while the periods directly before LUNCH, TEA and STUMPS, during the other M.C.C. and Sheffield Shield matches will be broadcast.

TELEVISION COVERAGE

The last two hours of play in the TEST matches and the M.C.C. matches against the States in Sydney and Melbourne will be telecast. In Sydney, Sheffield Shield matches will be telecast from 1.30 p.m. and in Melbourne the telecast of the Shield matches will begin at 3.00 p.m. Films and telerecordings of the highlights of TEST matches played in other States will be shown in a 30-minutes bulletin at night. Highlights of play will also be seen in the News Bulletins.

3

PLAYERS AUSTRALIANS DO NOT KNOW
By ALEC BEDSER

AUSTRALIANS have seen and know Peter May, Colin Cowdrey and Tom Graveney among the batsmen who are members of the 1958-59 M.C.C. team and they will also remember bowlers Frank Tyson, Brian Statham and Peter Loader, while Godfrey Evans and Trevor Bailey are old friends. Now let us turn our attention to the men who have never been to Australia.

The batsmen who will be new to Australian cricket watchers are Peter Richardson, Subba Row, Willie Watson and Arthur Milton. All of these players have had considerable experience in county cricket and most of them in Test cricket also.

Peter Richardson is a left-hander who has been most successful as an opener for England since he first played a few years ago. Curiously enough his record in county cricket is not so impressive as his Test record. He is a stubborn type of player, scoring most of his runs by deflections on both sides of the wicket, and he very rarely drives the ball. He is gifted with an ideal temperament, nothing seems to ruffle him, and his concentration is a great asset. It remains to be seen how he will fare on the faster Australian wickets, as he is dismissed a lot by being caught at the wicket, even on rather slow English pitches, and he may find the faster pitches more difficult to cope with. He is a good field.

Willie Watson is also a left-handed player and moved from Yorkshire to captain Leicestershire this last season. He has done a fine job for that county and has been opening the innings successfully. Watson, it will be remembered, took part in the match-saving stand with Trevor Bailey at Lord's during the 1953 season in England. He is a fine all-round type of batsman with a pleasing style and any innings by him will be worth watching. His scoring is not restricted to any part of the field, and he has had experience of tours abroad. As befits an international soccer player, he is a fine mover in the field and will prove a very popular tourist.

The other left-hander, Raman Subba Row, was born at Croydon, Surrey, and played first of all for Cambridge University and then for Surrey before throwing in his lot with Northamptonshire. He has had considerable first class experience and visited India with the Commonwealth team, but so far has not toured with an M.C.C. side.

He will, I am sure, get a lot of runs in Australia. His method is more on the lines of the Australian, Ken Mackay, in that he has a very short back-left, but he is able to generate a lot of power in his strokes in spite of this. He is a safe field.

Arthur Milton is the right-hand opening bat for Gloucester. He, too, will be on his first M.C.C. Tour and is also a fine fielder. He played some ten years for his County before gaining Test recognition. Arthur is principally a back-foot player, scoring the majority of his runs by leg side deflections and forcing the ball square to the off side. Although all these players are new to Australia, I feel sure they will soon adapt themselves to the conditions, having all had a considerable amount of experience.

The England attack is composed chiefly of pace bowlers and the one not yet seen in Australia is Fred Trueman, of Yorkshire. Fred Trueman has been the subject of a considerable amount of controversy over the past few years and I am certain some of this is somewhat exaggerated. He is now a fine cricketer and a first class bowler. He has developed enormously over the last few years and in England is able to move the ball considerably.

Obviously, he will not be able to do so much in Australia, but he is a strong fellow and able to bowl for a long time. In addition, he has good control and he will not be easy to score off. Like most fast bowlers today, he has a long drag when delivering the ball. He is a fine close-to-the-wicket fielder and has a powerful throw,

d will turn out, I am sure, to be one
[the personalities of the tour. He
owls very close to the stumps when
elivering the ball and the mark he
aakes could easily be used by an in-
lligent bowler at the other end.

Tony Lock and Jim Laker, of course,
ave not yet been to Australia and all
ustralians will be interested to see
em.

Tony Lock bowls at quite a fast pace
r a left-hander without using much
ght. I feel he will find it most diffi-
llt to turn the ball on Australian
ickets, and therefore his wicket taking
otential will be limited. His principal
ole will no doubt be that of a stock
owler. He is probably the finest short
g in the world to-day in addition to
eing a useful lower end batsman.

Lock's gesticulations will no doubt
muse "The Hill" at Sydney. There is
o more wholehearted cricketer playing
-day.

Jim Laker is the exact opposite to
is county colleague in that he goes
bout his job without the exuberance
nown by Lock. However, he is a fine
owler with immense power of spin
nd flight and is most intelligent.

He has had a lot of experience bowl-
ng on good wickets and I am sure he
ill bowl effectively in Australia if he
ets the slightest assistance from the
itch.

The reserve wicket-keeper to Godfrey
vans is Roy Swetman, who so far
lays for my own County Second XI
ith only an occasional game in the
irst XI. Roy, although only 24 years
f age, looks much younger, an Aus-
alian crowd will think from his ap-
earance that he is still a schoolboy.
lowever, he shows great promise and
he object of course of bringing him
n this tour is to try to find someone
ho will eventually fill Godfrey Evans'
oots and gloves.

Roy is very quick in his movements
nd in some ways not unlike Godfrey
vans in method. This Tour should
reatly improve his keeping an ensure
im a place in the England side for
me years.

There is not any doubt that the
eries will be a close one, and also
he cricket will be slow, made so by
he employment of practically an all
ace attack.

On paper the Australian side will

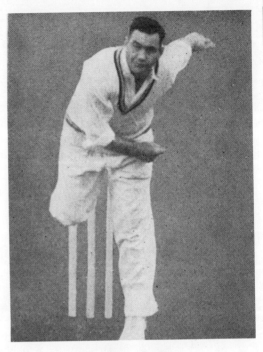

Alec Bedser

be stronger in batting, as it would appear that whatever combination of
players England uses the side will have
a much longer tail.

Alec Bedser, the writer of
this article, was one of the finest,
lively, medium-paced bowlers in
the history of Test Match
cricket. Bedser played in 51
Tests against various countries
and he took 236 wickets at 24.89
runs each. He holds the record
for the number of wickets taken.
He is also one of the four England bowlers to take 100 wickets
against Australia. In the 1953
series in England, Bedser took
39 wickets at 17.48 runs each.
This was a record until beaten
in 1956 by Jim Laker, Bedser's
colleague in the Surrey County
side. The great bowler will be
working with the A.B.C. team of
commentators during the 1958-9
tour.

5

CHAPTER FIVE

The 1960.

The West Indies 1960–61 Australian tour was one of the most fulfilling in the game's history. Rival captains Benaud and Worrell inspired their teams and the attacking, exhilarating cricket won over the public, who had put up with some dull Tests in preceding years.

The series produced a remarkable tied result in Brisbane, a nail-biting last-wicket partnership draw in Adelaide and almost another tie in the decider, when Australia won by two wickets in Melbourne. Richie Benaud recalls this momentous series in the 1968–69 publication, which includes the transcripts of Bradman's, Worrell's and Benaud's valedictory speeches after the fifth Test. Worrell's speech, reproduced by the ABC on an audio cassette *A History of Australia v West Indies Cricket*, is compelling and the spontaneous response from the crowd, heartwarming. Learie Constantine's hope that his countrymen would revert to brilliant methods was realised.

Australia's narrow victory, 2–1, over the West Indies preceded a stirring Ashes battle in 1961. The match at Old Trafford was a classic, Davidson and McKenzie reviving the innings with 98 for the last wicket. Dexter pillaged 76 in England's chase for 256, but when he was dismissed Benaud ran amok. Bowling around the wicket, he took 6 for 70 and Australia retained the Ashes with a 54-run victory.

The return series in 1962–63 did not produce the climax expected, despite some attractive performances from O'Neill, Booth, Davidson, McKenzie and Dexter, Barrington, Cowdrey and Trueman. Harvey and Davidson retired, and during the next season Benaud handed over the captaincy to Simpson.

Australian audiences in 1963–64 saw a great South African side in the making: the Pollock brothers, the effervescent Eddie Barlow, Colin Bland's spectacular fielding, Joe Partridge's late swing and Trevor Goddard's all-round leadership. They possessed the ingredients for success but somehow Australia managed to draw 1–1. Over 500 000 fans watched the Tests, which were Richie Benaud's last in a distinguished 63-match career, scoring over 2000 runs and taking what was then an Australian record 248 Test wickets.

Rain plagued the 1964 Ashes battle, with Burge playing the innings of his life at Leeds, hooking and cutting 160 in an Australian seven-wicket victory. Simpson made 311 at Old Trafford, Barrington replying with 256 in a high scoring draw.

A year later in the Caribbean, Simpson and the rest of his team were ducking and weaving against Hall and Griffith. They became obsessed about the legality of Griffith's action but he wasn't called and, contrarily, the series was decided in Georgetown, where off spinner Lance Gibbs took 9 for 80 in an innings victory. The West Indies' magnificent era under Worrell and then Sobers was winding down, and Australia won the final Test by ten wickets inside three days.

England's 1965–66 mission gave promise of 'bright' cricket from both sides but the batting was far too good overall, only two matches being decided and the series drawn 1–1. Doug Walters launched his match-winning career with hundreds in his first two Tests, and Bob Barber slammed a brilliant 185 in Sydney. In the drawn fifth Test, Bob Cowper ground Australia's only triple hundred in a home Test (307) and veteran wicket-keeper Wally Grout retired with a swag of 187 Test dismissals. His name lives on in the Aussie vernacular, celebrated in the beer drinkers' rhyming slang, 'who's Wally?'.

South Africa emphasised its quality in 1966–67. Australia's batting was in decline and its bowling was too reliant on Graham McKenzie. The story was repeated in 1969–70 when Ali Bacher's team won 4–0. By then Bill Lawry had taken over the captaincy, retaining the Ashes in 1968 in an uninspiring series.

Lawry, Ian Chappell, and Walters who was emerging from National Service duty, carved up an aged and undisciplined West Indies team in 1968–69, Walters attracting the crowds with a record 242 and 103 in the deciding fifth Test, compiling 699 in the series.

In the decade Australia won 33 per cent of the 67 Tests played. Between 1946 and 1960 they were successful in 56 per cent of 77 contests. Significantly, 39 per cent of the 1960s matches were drawn while only 30 per cent stalemated in the previous dominant period. Clearly, some of the opposition was improving while Australia's performance fluctuated. Chappell, anointed by Lawry as a superstar in 1969–70, endured a depressing string of failures on the ill-fated South African tour. His emergence as an inspirational leader in the next decade recaptured public enthusiasm and coincided with an era of fast bowling supremacy.

Hopes for revival of W.I. aggression

WHAT can Australia expect from the West Indies team? In this article, LEARIE CONSTANTINE, the great West Indies all-rounder and one of the most dynamic cricketers in history, tells why his countrymen went down to England, and expresses the hope that in Australia they will revert again to the brilliant methods which are in the real West Indies tradition.

West Indies cricket will again be on trial in Australia as it was in England in 1950. Before that year West Indies had not lost a Test match or a Test series at home, but alas! they have bowed in defeat to Australia in the West Indies; to Pakistan away on the matting; to England in England; and more recently very convincingly to England in the West Indies. It was not, that England had a better team, but England played superior cricket.

For this and other reasons the tour of Australia will be crucial, not only for my country's cricket, but for its capacity to revive and play typical West Indies cricket — blazing the scores, scorching the bowling, and with fieldsmen scurring here and there to save runs, recalling Francis Thompson's beautiful and enchanting lines typifying action and enjoyment —
"As the run stealers flicker to and fro
Oh! my Hornby and my Barlow long
    ago."

Those of you who remember the character of West Indies cricket; its will and capacity to improvise; its tremendous technique in hitting the ball; will mourn the passing of that era. We are optimistic enough to hope that Australia will inspire a revival and make the game worthy of two great antagonists in aggressive mood.

L. N. Constantine

4

It is necessary to go into a few details in order to assess properly the reasons for the recent defeat of the West Indies by England and to indicate at the same time the nature of the job to be done in Australia.

Man for man, the English team could not be compared with the West Indies. The genius of Cowdrey and Peter May and, as well, the potentialities of Subba Row, Ted Dexter, Barrington and Mike Smith, here one had almost the whole story of English batting on the canvas.

The bowling, too, was mainly experimental except for the length and persistence of Statham, the aggressiveness of Freddie Truman of Yorkshire, and the hope expressed in Illingworth and Allen and Barrington's spin. In the old days it used to be said that the bowler had to be very fast or very slow — there was "nowt" for the fellow in between; and this still holds good.

England's fielding was pretty certain to be adequate for Cowdrey specialised in the slips and so did Barrington, while there were young men in Allen, Dexter, Illingworth and company, who, with a good measure of practice, brought things up to the necessary standard.

On the other hand, the West Indies had Worrell, Kanhai and the imperturbable Sobers of whom more will be said as well as Conrad Hunte, Walcott — revived, and Alexander; one of the finest wicket-keepers in the world, although as a captain he left most of us puzzled and perplexed.

In the bowling line there were Hall, faster than Gilchrist, Watson quick and as steady as a rock, and the unconquerable Ramadhin, with left handers Worrell and Sobers thrown in for good measure.

Fielding was the weak spot in West Indies cricket. In fact, it was the poorest that I have seen in International cricket with the possible exception of the 1954 Indians; and there the advantage was thrown away. As for batting — whatever influence Sir Leonard Hutton may have had on players generally, he has certainly planted his approach well and truly into the heads of contemporary West Indies cricketers, changed their entire outlook and attitude to the game, and for the time being destroyed its essential West Indies character.

The English team in the West Indies consistently scored at a faster rate than the West Indies side and that is saying a lot. It will some day be proved to the modernists that attack is the best method of defence, unless one wants to hold up a game and take it into eight and nine days.

If this is the idea, then one must agree that Bailey of Essex and England was a greater player than Sir Donald Bradman of Australia.

But what will Australia have to meet this time? This is the all important question. I wish to comment only on such aspects as I believe will be important to the series.

We have for the first time in the history of the West Indies selected a coloured man as the captain of our team. Usually, it is alleged by my detractors that I have "chips" on my shoulders; that in fact, I am prejudiced, and see everything in terms of colour.

I do not need to deny that, because my friends in Europe, Asia, Africa, America and Australia can bear testimony to the defamatory nature of that statement.

May I say that if this is the first West Indies captain of colour who has ever been appointed to lead a team abroad, then it is not for me to deny a basic prejudice!

Worrell will be a first class captain. He is a student and a good judge of the game. He may play harder than

West Indies captains were wont to do in the past; but his schooling in Lancashire League and International cricket has left him no alternative.

He will be backed up by players, many of whom have graduated in the hard school of competitive cricket in **England.**

A nationalist concept of the recently achieved Federated West Indies with all that it implies will have a greater psychological effect on the players than any single factor operating in the West Indies at the present time. "Boys, we are soon to be a nation." That is important.

Hall is graduating in Lancashire League and a good thing, too, for the gain in direction even at the sacrifice of a little speed must be all to the good.

Watson will be steady and will bowl a dangerous ball which "leaves" the batsman. Worrell will have to decide whether he will be a batsman or an all-rounder, and the same consideration will have to be given to Sobers.

I shall single out one batsman, outstanding in his stroke-play, magnificent in his technique, and a top world class player. That man is Garfield Sobers. He is nicer to watch than was the uninhibited Harvey. He hits the ball harder than O'Neill, and as a fieldsman close to the wicket he takes some beating. He bowls a good length — left hand — and operates the "googley." In short, Gar is a glorious cricketer. Australia will love him and hate him. You'll see.

There is another batsman who hits the ball harder than anyone else in present-day cricket — Cammie Smith. Tall and thin, he moves like an athlete. No side will be able to say it is "safe" after declaring unless Cammie Smith is out.

There is also Kanhai — a glorious stroke-player — who in my opinion pays too great a respect to medium pace bowlers attacking his leg-stump. Nevertheless, he is in the top bracket.

Alas! Gilchrist is out — and Australia misses the opportunity of seeing an unusual cricket character.

In the field West Indies in my opinion, will be deficient. Bowling that ties a batsman down until the decision to gamble becomes an inevitable consequence needs wide thinking and quick movement. West Indies fielding is, and will be, poor, unless Worrel spends a lot of time in the field at practice. There are no specialists in any position on this.

Never in the history of West Indies cricket have I seen such poor anticipation, a reluctance to move off with the bowler, and I have felt that the best and most enjoyable part of the game is not appreciated by those who now play.

But Ramadhin is in the team and if the Australians practice the same immobility as the English batsmen, then he is going to be a tremendous asset to the West Indies side. Valentine is there again and Australia must beware, if only on the principle that at his age there can be a "come-back."

All in all, the result will depend on how many catches the West Indies team take. The story as I see it does not leave me very optimistic. I am hoping that, whatever the results, the matches will be keenly fought.

There will be no incidents — "chucking" or otherwise — and the West Indies will leave friends behind them as both earlier teams have done.

WEST INDIES TOUR
OF AUSTRALIA **1960-1961**

Back Row (from left): A. James (Masseur), B. Boc
Middle Row: P. Burge, R. Gaunt, I. Quic
Front Row: A. W. Grout, A. K. Davidson, R. Benaud (Ca

32

...son, N. O'Neill, L. Kline, B. Jarman, J. Cameron (Scorer).
...e (Treasurer), F. Misson, W. Lawry, G. McKenzie.
...Vebb, Q.C. (Manager), R. N. Harvey, C. C. McDonald, K. Mackay.

33

AUSTRALIA TOUR
OF ENGLAND 1961

One Hundred Years Ago

ON October 18th, 1861, the first English cricket team ever to visit Australia sailed from London on the S.S. "Great Britain", so that we are nearing the centenary of cricket between Australians and Englishmen. The team comprised only 12 men and was assembled through the initiative of a catering firm, Spiers and Pond, of Melbourne.

Those in the team were: H. H. Stephenson (capt.), W. Caffyn, C. Lawrence, W. Mortlock, W. Mudie, G. Griffith, and T. Sewell, of Surrey, T. Hearne from Middlesex, G. Wells from Sussex, R. Iddison and E. Stephenson from Yorkshire, and G. Bennett of Kent.

The team was received with tremendous enthusiasm, so much so that in Melbourne it had to steal away quietly in order to practise. The first game started on January 1, 1862, and it lasted for four days, the tourists scoring 305, and the eighteen Victorians 118 and 92. Top scorer was Caffyn, who made 79, while Griffith made 61.

The players wore hat bands and sashes of different colours so that the spectators who bought score cards could distinguish them. The attendance on the first day was 15,000, and some 45,000 paid the admission charge of 2/6 during the game, so that the sponsors paid all expenses of the tour from this opening match and subsequently made a profit of £11,000. The Englishmen had been guaranteed first-class expenses and £150 a man.

Travelling facilities in those days were rather primitive and when the team left Melbourne to play their second match at Beechworth, in the Ovens district of Victoria, they travelled some 200 miles in a coach drawn by five horses, a wearying journey. However, they won the match comfortably enough.

The journey to Sydney was made by sea and a crowd of some 15,000 people gave them a royal welcome. The players were entertained to a public breakfast and at dinner in the evening. The match lasted for four days, the Englishmen scoring 175 and 66, and the home side, consisting of 22 players, managed 127 in the first

William Caffyn.
Courtesy Surrey County Cricket Club.

3

One hundred years ago — continued

innings, but only 65 in the second.

Then to Bathurst by coach, but a thunderstorm prevented the match being finished; and then back to Sydney, where a combined New South Wales and Victorian side—22 of them —scored a handsome 12-wicket victory, the Englishmen scoring 60 and 75, and the combined side 101 and 35 for eight wickets.

In Hobart a band of the Rifle Corps played the team to its hotel, and Tasmania was beaten by four wickets. This was followed by another match in Melbourne, "Surrey v. The World", the latter winning by five wickets. Bennett made 72 and Caffyn 75 not out and each was presented with £10 by the Melbourne Cricket Club.

Matches at Ballarat and Sandhurst followed, and then Charles Lawrence played a single wicket match against one of the Bendigo men, allowing him eleven fielders. Neither scored a run in two innings, but Lawrence won because his opponent bowled a wide. At Castlemaine a team of 22 beat the visitors by three wickets, and then Griffith, Lawrence and Iddison played, and beat, 11 of the locals.

The last match of the tour was against 22 players of Victoria, and it was left drawn. At the end of four days the Englishmen needed 12 runs to win and had three wickets in hand, but the local captain stuck rigidly to the original agreement that the game was to be limited to four days and he would not concede extra time.

The Englishmen were offered £1,200 to remain in Australia for another month, which shows just what an attraction they were, but they could not fit it in. As a parting gesture, Spiers and Pond divided half the receipts of the last match between the players so that they went home happy.

This tour, which took place before the days of Test cricket, undoubtedly did much to develop the game in Australia. H. H. Stephenson was a wise counsellor who passed on all he could to the aspiring champions, while Lawrence at once became identified with our cricket. He accepted an offer to remain behind and coach with the Albert Club in Sydney, and one young player whom he handled was Charles Bannerman, later to score the first run and first century in Test match cricket, and also to make the first century for an Australian team in England.

Lawrence also captained the team of Australian Aborigines which toured England in 1868, so that he goes down in history as one of the very first sowers of the seed in this country.

AVERAGES

BATTING

	Matches.	Inns.	N.O.	H.S.	Runs.	Avge.
Caffyn, W.	13	19	1	79	419	23.27
Griffith, G.	13	20	1	61	421	22.15
Mortlock, W.	10	14	1	76	255	19.61
Bennett, G.	13	18	1	72	290	17.05
Iddison, R.	13	18	1	36	244	14.35
Stephenson, E.	11	17	2	60	204	13.60
Wells, G.	12	17	3	48	177	12.64
Stephenson, H. H. (Capt.)	13	20	4	47	188	11.75
Hearne, T.	12	16	2	37	138	9.85
Sewell, T.	12	19	5	41	135	9.64
Mudie, W.	10	15	3	27	111	9.25
Lawrence, C.	12	16	1	20	99	6.60

BOWLING

	O.	M.	R.	W.	Avge.
Wells, G.	65	46	33	9	3.66
Sewell, T.	260	140	229	49	4.67
Griffith, G.	336.3	170	364	74	4.91
Lawrence, C.	174.3	72	243	46	5.28
Bennett, G.	344.1	150	426	75	5.68
Caffyn, W.	444.1	213	495	80	6.18
Stephenson, H. H.	71	31	100	16	6.25
Iddison, R.	477.3	183	681	103	6.61

5

AUSTRALIAN PLAYERS

POINTS ABOUT THE

**The Australian team for England looks weake
than the average but it is generally acknowledged ther
is no such thing as a weak Australian side.**

Nine of the 17 players are making their first tour of England with an Australian team. They are Alan Connolly, Grahame Corling, Bob Cowper, Neil Hawke, Johnny Martin, Ian Redpath, Jack Potter, Rex Sellers and Tom Veivers.

The Australian attack will depend to an unprecedented extent, on bowlers on their first tour and not especially distinguished at that.

Corling, one of the pace bowlers, emerged only during last season after replacing Gordon Rorke in the New South Wales team.

Other bowlers new to English crowds will be Hawke, accurate medium pacer

who uses the seam; rugged Victoria speedster Connolly; two wrist spinner Martin and Sellers, and the thick-se Queenslander Veivers, a left-hand b and a bowler of off-breaks, who ra into some withering fire from Dexte when the M.C.C. team toured Austral in 1962-63

Giant W.A speedster Graha McKenzie is the only touring reco nised bowler who has played befo English County and Test crowd though Martin had a season there Lancashire League with Colne in 196

Martin, small, buoyant and kee reveals character in his cricket and a pleasure to watch

By "Observer"

TOURISTS

No one would have thought of Sellers as a tour candidate a year or two ago but he superseded David Sincock and Ian Chappell this season to win selection.

The strength of the Australian tourists will be in the batting of the old school, Simpson, Booth, Burge, Lawry and O'Neill.

The three new batsmen chosen are all Victorians — Bob Cowper, Ian Redpath and Jack Potter. They are not glamour batsmen.

Only five N.S.W. players are in the party, yet it was only two seasons ago N.S.W. whacked the M.C.C. to look a better side than the whole of Australia put together.

Now Richie Benaud, Alan Davidson and Neil Harvey have dropped out and N.S.W. has been on the decline.

This is a pity from the Australian viewpoint as the best cricketers tend to come out of New South Wales.

◄ ROBERT B. SIMPSON ►

Has scored most runs of present-day Australian cricketers with 12,584 in 260 innings (av. 57.72), and taken 192 wickets with his leg-spinners for 7192 runs. Has hit 33 first class centuries with his 359 against Queensland in Brisbane in October last year highest Australian individual score in post-war cricket. Also established N.S.W. first wicket record stand of 308 with Grahame Thomas against W.A. in Sydney in November last year. Leading Australian rungetter this season (1436 at 65.27) when chosen as Australian captain for English tour. Also scored 1337 runs last Australian season at average 60.77. In 46 Test innings has failed to score a century, having made 1534 runs at 36.52.

AUSTRALIA TOUR
OF UNITED KINGDOM **1964**

SIR FRANK WORRELL SENDS

A WELCOME FROM
THE WEST INDIES

The Aussies will be arriving in good condition immediately after a full State cricket season, and this could be an advantage to them. They will also have the benefit of further moulding their Test Team through the preliminary encounters with Colts and Island sides; this is in direct contrast to the situation which usually confronts the West Indies Team at home.

There is never sufficient match practice before our Test Team goes into "battle" with visiting teams, which means that such things as "running between the wickets," "anticipating a run out" become problems of the highest magnitude.

Let me state here and now that I think man for man we are a better side, but teamwork is vital to the success of a side; and this teamwork is much more readily obtained by members of a touring side than by those of a home side.

The West Indians on a home tour play five or six matches in three months, and this is really not enough cricket to get one into the condition or form that Test matches require.

Should a player fail in the first Test match, his next one is another Test match, failure in which more often than not produces a loss of confidence when the next Test starts. These are some of the problems with which the West Indians will be faced.

Many an individual in the Caribbean, and I dare say in Australia, will be regarding this series as a struggle for international supremacy.

I do not think that international cricket teams can be so precisely compared. One has always got to remember that playing conditions and luck play a tremendous part in the resolution of many cricket matches, especially under the climatic conditions of a place like England.

The West Indians in recent years have had a fair measure of success. The Australians have maintained their string of successes, even if it is argued that the exhibition of talent of their current team is not as impressive as that of yester-year, but one should not overlook the ability of the English team, bogged down as it is by a multiplicity of theories. The English team is a good one which should beat any touring team to England, and given a positive approach to the game should be extremely difficult to beat abroad.

Should the Australians beat the West Indies it would be just to regard them as International champions; but should the reverse occur, then the West Indians will have to beat England and Australia again before they can justifiably argue their case for world supremacy.

The 1965 Australian Team is comprised of men who, because of their success in recent years, have become household names in the West Indies.

4

Local enthusiasts look forward to good batting performances from Bobby Simpson, Bill Lawry, Norman O'Neill, Brian Booth. There is disappointment in the news that Peter Burge will not be making the trip, as cricket lovers in these parts still talk of his century against England at Leeds last July; but the men whom sportsmen really want to see in operation are McKenzie and Hawke. These are the hard-working fit pace bowlers who will severely test our batsmen in the months to come.

The West Indies Team will show few changes from that which played in England in 1963. One opening-batsman's position is being contested by McMorris, Carew, Davis, Bynoe and Griffith, all of whom are quite capable of assisting Conrad Hunte in giving the West Indies a good start. This may well be the problem selection, with local insularities creating an unhealthy environment for the individual who catches the selectors' eyes.

We expect to see the old form of Sobers, Kanhai, Nurse, Solomon and Butcher forming the backbone of the batting. The wicket-keeping will be contested by Allan and Hendriks, if the latter is available.

A great deal of interest is being shown in this Tour.

It is an accepted fact that the Australians can boast a "fighting" spirit unknown in any other cricketing country, and the hope in these parts is that the West Indians, by observation of the Australian approach, will have developed a similar capacity to concentrate and apply themselves, whether things are going well or badly.

The West Indies has got a new Captain in Garfield Sobers, a man who has (1) a profound knowledge of the game, (2) the confidence of his players and (3) a near insatiable desire for activity on the cricket field. We look forward to seeing him in his new role, and hope that the rigours of captaincy do not affect his unequalled prowess on the field.

We have seen captains who tended to underbowl themselves, under the

SIR FRANK WORRELL

impression that it was better to give priority to the other bowlers on the side. We have seen captains over-bowl themselves, which gave one the impression that it was a vote of no confidence in their fellow bowlers. It would be tragic if Sobers failed to strike a mean between these extremes; as by the latter his batting may suffer, and by the former his bowling will suffer.

Bobby Simpson will arrive in the West Indies a confident skipper spurred on no doubt by the success of the Australian team in England. Sobers, on the other hand, might have to feel his way in the early stages of the Tour, as he is unused to this new role; but given the support of the established West Indian players, his lot could be much easier than most people think.

Whatever the outcome of the series, we all look forward to the opportunity of having the Australians as our guests, and we shall do all in our power to see that their stay in these parts will be as enjoyable as ours was in Australia.

5

AUSTRALIA FORMIDABLE

Although Australia has won 13 of the 20 Tests so far played against the West Indies, this second Australian Team to visit the West Indies faces a formidable task.

There is a pleasant blending from spin—Cowper is an off-spinner who has shown his ability to contain English batsmen, but whether he will have a similar effect on the aggressive West Indies players he is about to meet remains to be seen. Cowper is a thoughtful bowler and is not easily discouraged by attack. Leg-spinner Phillpott is the type of bowler the West Indies do not often meet; he has good control, and is quickly adaptable to conditions either in his search for spin or flight. Bobby Simpson has indicated that he is pleased with his present bowling form, and is a most helpful addition to the spin attack, which then leads to Sincock. Here is a match winner on his day, or an expensive hobby. As the Sheffield Shield season progressed he revealed better control, and if he can maintain this control and can couple it with his lively and often unpredictable spin he could be Simpson's answer.

These two teams are indeed interest-

ing, and the series itself open and perhaps explosive. I am not deterred by the expressed optimism in the West Indies, for I have great confidence in the ability of this Australian team and especially in Bobby Simpson; and as he said, "We hold the Sir Frank Worrell Trophy and it is up to the West Indies to take it off us, and they can be assured that will not be easy."

Admittedly, some experience has been gained from the visit of the Australian team which toured the West Indies in 1955 under the leadership of Ian Johnson. But it is unlike a tour of Great Britain, where invariably some members of the touring party have gained practical knowledge from previous visits.

In this case no member of the present team has any local experience, and they are thus at an immediate disadvantage.

In addition, the West Indies players have shown remarkable improvement over the past years, and following their Australian tour in 1960-1 and their

10

Sabina Park, Kingston, where Australia will play the first Test.

FACES TASK

Alan McGilvray, one of Australia's leading c r i c k e t commentators assesses our chances in the West Indies.

He says . . .

3—1 defeat of England in 1963, they present a big problem for Bobby Simpson and his team in their defence of the Sir Frank Worrell Trophy.

Following their last tour of Australia, and encouraged by their success in England, the West Indies, under the guidance of their former Captain, Sir Frank Worrell, set out on an intensive and concentrated coaching plan which has been devised to take from Australia the title of "the top cricketing nation of the world" . . . so this series can now be termed as a World's Championship.

During my last visit to England I had many discussions with Sir Frank Worrell, and he left me in no doubt that it was his desire to achieve this objective and that they intended to launch an all-out offensive to gain this title. How this offensive will operate Australia will shortly find out, but having already selected their First Test Team it is apparent that the West Indies will mainly depend in attack upon their fast battery supported by off-spin and the unorthodox Sobers.

Their batting has depth and brilliance, while their fielding is alive and sound.

The playing conditions submitted by the West Indies Board of Control and accepted by the Australian Board include two important changes which could have a considerable effect on the final result.

Although England and Australia have agreed to play under the experimental rule which limits the field placement on the leg side to five fieldsmen, this was not accepted by the West Indies, and of course means that Australian batsmen may face a concentrated leg-stump attack from the fast bowlers. But it is unlikely that short-pitched deliveries will be consistently encountered, for the conditions provide that the persistent bowling of fast short-pitched balls at the batsman is unfair if it constitutes a systematic attempt at intimidation. *Still the thought will be existent in the batsmen's minds . . . not a very pleasant one when Hall and Griffiths come pounding in to bowl.*

The other alteration is that while a new ball can now be taken after 200 runs have been scored off the old one, a new ball can now be taken after 75 overs' use of the old ball. In the West Indies the over consists of 6 balls, which is the equivalent of 56.2 overs under Australian conditions.

11

WEST INDIES HUNDRED UP

The West Indies will be playing in their 100th Test cricket match when they meet Australia at Kingston, Jamaica, from March 3 to 9.

The West Indies won Test match status in 1928. Their first appearance in a Test was against England at Lords, on June 23, 25, 26, 1928.

England was captained by the late Percy Chapman, and included Herb Sutcliffe, Wally Hammond, Douglas Jardine, Harold Larwood (who strained himself and bowled in only West Indies first innings), Maurice Tate, Percy Freeman and Ernest Tyldesley.

In the West Indies first Test side were two players, Sir Learie Constantine and F. R. Martin, who toured with the first West Indies team to visit Australia in 1930-31.

The West Indies did not play up to expectations in England in 1928, and were beaten by an innings in their Test debut at Lords, as they were in all three Tests that year.

"Everybody was compelled to realise the playing of Test matches between the West Indies and England was a mistake," said Wisden's.

What a different story today! West Indies, in 1950 and again in England in 1963, carried off the Test rubber by three victories to one.

After the 1963 West Indies visit to England, Wisden's said: "No more popular side has ever toured the Old Country."

Australia faces Formidable Task
Continued from page 11

This calls for very skilful manipulation of the attack, especially when the attack contains two very fast bowlers, both in the vicinity of 27 years of age . . . not young by West Indies standards, for fast bowlers. Seventy-five overs represents about four hours of play, and the use by Sobers of Hall and Griffiths during these periods will need careful handling.

Sobers has had little experience in captaincy, and before the tour is over he is going to have some worrying moments in the methods he applies here. Simpson is an experienced captain . . . his attack will comprise young and strong bowlers of medium-fast pace, who will provide him, if required, with more sustained efforts at the bowling crease than Hall and Griffiths will be able to supply Sobers.

This is a most interesting factor in planning, and the astute Simpson will not be lacking—but will Sobers have the same ability, and will Sobers find this onerous task of captaincy affecting his own wonderful ability as either bowler or batsman? The answers to these questions will be known only when the tour is over, but I expect these answers to play a prominent part in the result of the series.

The Australian team is a well-balanced combination, containing 10 batsmen, including Neil Hawke, and eight bowlers, with two excellent wicket-keepers and a keen and sound fielding side.

The latter will be most important, for they can ill-afford to provide Kanhai, Sobers, Hunte and others with more than one opportunity to stay at the batting crease.

The batting has depth, and brilliance, and if the pattern of play that has existed over the past Sheffield Shield season is continued, the West Indies attack could receive some harsh treatment. It does appear that all State captains have fully realised the bat is an offensive weapon.

Simpson holds that view and the question here is: Will the West Indies bowlers later have similar views? In England, Simpson vacated the opening position in his desire to add solidity to the middle batting order, and now in the absence of Burge he may revive that intention. This of course will depend upon the approach of his other opening batsmen, but he has little time to reach such a decision, for only two matches will be played prior to the First Test.

McKenzie has had a comfortable Shield season and is now refreshed after the long tour of Great Britain and India, and is in great form. Hawke has shown tremendous improvement after the same tour, and these two bowlers should form the basis of the Australian attack. This basis has support, and good support from Allan and Mayne . . . both the type necessary for West Indies wickets in so far as to use the term . . . "they dig the ball into the pitch" to get lift and life.

HERE'S A LIST OF FUTURE TOURS

1965:   New Zealand to England
(May to July)
South Africa to England
(June to September)
1965-66: M.C.C. to Australia
1966:   West Indies to England
1967:   India to England
Pakistan to England
1967-68: India to Australia and
New Zealand
1967-68: M.C.C. to West Indies
1968:   Australia to England
1968-69: M.C.C. to South Africa
1970-71: M.C.C. to Australia
1971-72: M.C.C. to India and
Pakistan
1973-74: M.C.C. to South Africa
1974-75: M.C.C. to Australia
1976-77: M.C.C. to West Indies
1977-78: M.C.C. to South Africa

WEST INDIES TEST CAREERS

BATTING AND FIELDING.

	Tests.	Inn.	N.O.	H.S.	Runs	Av.	100's	Ct.
. S. Sobers	47	79	9	365*	4098	58.54	14	54
. B. Kanhai	38	66	2	256	3137	49.01	7	21
. F. Butcher	15	25	3	142	1033	46.95	3	1
. C. Hunte	31	55	5	260	2193	43.86	6	16
S. Solomon	23	38	5	100*	1147	34.75	1	14
Nurse	5	10	1	70	309	34.33	—	5
/. V. Rodriguez	3	4	0	50	80	21.50	—	3
'. W. Hall	28	36	8	50*	459	16.39	—	6
. R. Gibbs	21	28	3	22	206	8.24	—	15
. C. Griffith	6	8	3	13*	37	7.40	—	3
D. Allan	2	3	1	40*	43	21.50	—	8

* Denotes not out.   † Allan also made two stumpings.

BOWLING

	Balls	Mdns.	Runs	Wkts.	Av.
. C. Griffith	1487	57	621	33	18.81
. R. Gibbs	6370	323	2072	94	22.04
'. W. Hall	6579	209	3071	132	23.26
. C. Hunte	96	5	30	1	30.00
'. S. Sobers	8906	370	3432	98	35.02
S. Solomon	534	36	172	1	172.00
/. V. Rodriguez	219	3	143	3	47.66
. B. Kanhai	36	3	7	—	—
. F. Butcher	36	1	17	—	—

13

Changes in Wicketkeeping Techniques

THERE has been considerable difference of opinion in regard to methods used by wicketkeepers. Prior to World War II it was generally accepted that wicketkeepers would stand directly behind the stumps to bowlers of medium and often fast-medium paced deliveries.

Since that period the policy of standing deep to take bowlers of these speeds has been mostly adopted.

England's post-war wicketkeeper Godfrey Evans invariably used the pre-war method of standing up to the wicket, as revealed in the Bedser-Evans combination, a position Evans preferred and which gained support from Bedser who felt it assisted him by giving him a better target.

For the purpose of this comparison Evans, as the only exception in post-war cricket as far as these figures are concerned, has been included amongst the pre-war wicketkeepers.

With both teams the post-war method has proved the more successful from a wicket-taking point of view. But what effect the wicketkeeper had on the batsman by standing up behind him, containing him within his crease, and in so doing supporting his bowlers by preventing the batsman standing out of his crease and thus disorganising the bowler's length (and by also presenting a better target for his bowlers) cannot be established by figures.

It is to be expected byes conceded would be reduced by the latter method.

Percentages of wickets taken by wicketkeepers out of total wickets in 193 matches are:

ABC Commentators

BRIAN JOHNSTON, of the BBC (above), will join the ABC's team of commentators for the M.C.C. Tour of Australia.

Brian Johnston joined the BBC in 1945 after a career which included war service with the Grenadier Guards, with whom he won the M.C. Johnston has made many notable sporting broadcasts for the BBC. He is now making his second tour of Australia with an M.C.C. Touring side.

ABC commentators will be Alan McGilvray, Lindsay Hassett and staff of the sporting departments in the various States.

Television commentators will include Frank Tyson, F. R. (Freddie) Brown and ABC staff men in the various States.

	Caught	Stumped	Total
Pre-war. Dismissals by Australian wicket-keepers	8.04%	4.50%	12.54%
Post-war. Dismissals by Australian wicket-keepers	18.17%	1.58%	19.75%
Pre-war. Dismissals by English wicket-keepers	10.88%	2.39%	13.27%
Post-war. Dismissals by English wicket-keepers	14.78%	1.13%	15.91%
Pre-war. Byes conceded by Australian wicket-keepers		2.176 runs in every 100 runs.	
Post-war. Byes conceded by Australian wicket-keepers		1.896 runs in every 100 runs.	
Pre-war. Byes conceded by English wicket-keepers		2.371 runs in every 100 runs.	
Post-war. Byes conceded by English wicket-keepers		1.552 runs in every 100 runs.	

21

What are Australia's chances?

By Ian Craig, Captain of Australian Team in
South Africa 1957/8

The visit of the sixth Australian team to South Africa this summer represents a complete cycle since the previous tour in 1957/8, for on both tours, a group of relatively untried newcomers has been called upon to take over the full burden of responsibility from the experienced veterans of previous years.

The disappearance of O'Neill, Booth and Grout from the scene, in the manner of Miller, Lindwall and Langley previously, prompts the question "can these newcomers match up to the task as successfully as Benaud, Davidson and others in 1957/8?"

An answer can obviously only be given at some future time, after all the prophesies and predictions of the critics have passed into the record book. However, a brief consideration of how cricket is played in South Africa and how the Australians will adapt to the circumstances, may offer some insight into the prospects of the team.

Perhaps the most important feature of South Africa for the visitors is that the conditions both of climate and for playing are not appreciably different from those of their native land. With the country falling in the latitude strip bounded by Rockhampton in the north and Sydney in the south, it is not unexpected that the climate is warm and temperate, presenting perfect conditions for cricket. The hard firm wickets allow the batsman to play with confidence at the pitch of the ball and across the line of flight producing, as a result, stroke play of the same type as is common in Australia.

Therefore, after a brief acclimatisation to the 6000-feet altitude of Johannesburg and the northern areas, there is little doubt that the Australians will readily adapt to the playing conditions. Performance of the individuals should be relatively easy to predict, making the task for Simpson less onerous than in England, where tour selections must frequently be based on an educated guess of how players will adapt.

South Africa, which for cricketing purposes includes Rhodesia, has a European population of a little over 3.5 million. Of these, the 1.5 million English-speaking people are virtually the only source of South African players, as few of the Afrikaans-speaking population take an interest in cricket. It is, therefore, only to be expected that the general standard of play at provincial level is not as strong as for our Sheffield Shield, and, taking the statistical approach a step further, that Australia should be able to put a much stronger side onto the field than their Test opponents.

Historically there is ample evidence to support this statistical approach. It could be argued that the success of the

4

past two South African tours in Australia refute it, but I do not think this to be true.

On these tours the success could be largely attributed to the development of excellent teamwork and confidence resulting from constant hard cricket. In South Africa, however, these advantages have benefitted the tourists, and it is significant that Australia has not lost even a single match on the five previous tours.

Previously South Africa has suspended their Currie Cup Competition, the equivalent of our Sheffield Shield, during the visits of touring sides. This left the South Africans short of hard match play which results only from competitive cricket. This season it has been decided the Currie Cup competition will be held, which means that with one exception, Eastern Province versus Natal, all other Currie Cup matches will be completed before the first test against Australia.

Simpson must be prepared to capitalise on these advantages right from the outset of the tour and concentrate on gaining the maximum psychological benefit possible.

He should develop teamwork by fostering mutual confidence between his players. He should ensure that all players are given adequate opportunity to reach and maintain top form, a task which may not be easy with the depth of the batting talent available.

He should also resist the temptation to make sporting declarations just to keep provincial matches alive, but instead should pursue victory by the greatest possible margin to instill confidence into his own players.

With proven run-getters like Lawry, Simpson and Cowper forming the basis of a formidable batting order which combines strength and depth, the South Africans will not be able to rest until the last man is back in the pavilion. They will then be confronted with a proven opening attack in Mackenzie and Hawke, supported by fielding which should be first class.

All these features seem to portend a crushing Australian victory, but it would only be an optimistic person who would so predict. What, then, are the factors which make such a prediction risky?

Firstly, Test matches are frequently won or lost either by the mental approach of the players to the task, or by the ability to exploit opponents' weaknesses. How these factors affect the game can never be assessed until the moment at which they occur, and consequently predictions on the result of any Test match do not fully take them into account.

5

South Africa's main weaknesses in the past have been a lack of confidence in their own ability and an inability to cope with top quality wrist-spin bowling. Both these weaknesses could be overcome in this series, with the advent of a new aggressive attitude amongst the South African batsmen.

For Graeme Pollock has developed into one of the world's finest players, with the capacity to tear an attack to shreds. With strong support from Barlow and Bland he may wrest the initiative from the Australians and inspire his colleagues to victory, as he did in the series against England last year. Positive action from this trio could well find Australia short in bowling of quality.

In Chapple, Stackpole and Martin rest Australia's main hopes of exploiting the traditional weakness against wrist spin. Whether they can do this as effectively as Grimmett, O'Reilly and Benaud in the past is doubtful but Simpson must be prepared to encourage them with long spells of bowling in the provincial games to develop them, if possible, to Test standard.

However, if Australia has a question mark against its bowling, so too must South Africa. Apart from Peter Pollock there appears to be little penetration in an attack which is based on medium pace and orthodox finger spin, neither of which have ever menaced Australian batsmen on firm wickets.

With this apparent superiority of the bat over the ball on both sides, the series could well develop into a stalemate with a number of drawn games. This is one of the unfortunate features of modern Test cricket, as evidenced in a number of recent series, and could perhaps be attributed in part to the restrictions which have been placed on bowlers by changes in the laws of the game.

Despite all the "ifs" and "buts" which could be added to the above considerations I favour Australia to win, if only by the margin of a single Test in the only result of the series. Irrespective of the outcome, however, the Australians are certain to return home with vivid memories of South African hospitality, of superb scenery and of the thrilling experiences of the Game Reserves. A South African tour is widely regarded by visiting players as the most enjoyable and relaxed of all tours.

Milestones in South African Cricket

By Robin Jackson (S.A. Cricket Correspondent)

The year 1843 saw the formal establishment of the game of cricket in South Africa. It was in this year that the Port Elizabeth Cricket Club was founded — the first in Africa. For many years all cricket was strictly local; then in 1876 inter-town competition began.

In 1876 the Port Elizabeth Town Council presented the "Champion Bat", and the first Cricket Championship of South Africa took place in Port Elizabeth. As it turned out, Port Elizabeth fared poorly and it came as no surprise that Port Elizabeth brought in the first English professional cricketer ever to coach in South Africa.

Local cricket was again to be reminded of its "below par" standard with the arrival at the Cape of the first side from England in 1888, led by C. Aubrey Smith. The two "stars" of the side were Bobby Abel (the idol of Kennington Oval), and that great Lancastrian, Johnny Briggs, who took more than 300 wickets. Needless to say, the visiting side gave the South Africans plenty to think about with their almost effortless Test wins at Port Elizabeth and Cape Town.

The record against the touring side in 1891 skippered by Walter Read made just as dismal reading, and it was not surprising that the first South African team ever to visit Britain (1894) played, in the main, only second class fixtures.

A marked improvement in the standard of local cricket coincided with the visit of the next English side. From this tour there emerged three personalities who go down in South African cricketing annals as cricketers of international renown — J. H. Sinclair, C. B. Llewellyn and wicket-keeper E. A. Halliwell.

South African cricket received a timely shot-in-the-arm by the man responsible for inaugurating tours by Englishmen to South Africa, Sir Donald Currie. It was Sir Donald who launched cricket on an inter-provincial level. His "Currie Cup" is still the most coveted trophy in South African cricket.

A significant milestone in cricket was reached in 1905 with the arrival of the first team ever sent to this country by the M.C.C. But even more memorable from the South African point of view was that South Africa won this Test series by four matches to one.

Two years later (1907) South Africa was given Test status in England. In 1909, back to South Africa came another M.C.C. side skippered by Leveson-Gower with well-known players such as Hobbs, Rhodes, Woolley, Denton and Blythe. Despite such a formidable array of batting talent, it was the bowling of Faulkner and Vogler that tipped the series South Africa's way by three Tests to two. Only a few months separated this home series with our first in Australia. Highlighted by Faulkner's all-round ability, (732 runs at an average of 73.2 and capturing 10 wickets) South Africa won one of the five Tests played.

7

RICHIE BENAUD RECALLS THE LAST WEST INDIES TOUR OF AUSTRALIA

By Richie Benaud
former Australian Captain

A new era of cricket began in 1960/61 when Frank Worrell's West Indian side visited Australia for what was, to me, the most memorable Test series ever played. Sadly, this tour will be without Sir Frank and his tragic loss is something that affects world cricket, not just West Indian cricket—he was the kind of man who belonged to all countries.

Even now, eight years after the events, that series against the West Indies seems almost incredible in its fluctuation and excitement. For me it all began before the First Test Match in Brisbane with Sir Donald Bradman making a rather guarded, and certainly unusual, request to come along to the team meeting that is always held on the eve of each Test. He didn't tell me beforehand the reason for this but, in fact, it was one of the most important visits ever made to a cricket team by a Chairman of Selectors.

His theme was quite simple—without giving away any selection room secrets he and his co-selectors believed that this could be one of the greatest seasons of cricket ever provided for the Australian public. Naturally he wanted Australia to win but, above all, he wanted to see good cricket for the spectators and he urged the players and myself to provide it throughout the series. It is only guesswork how much

RICHIE BENAUD in action

11

influence that had on the Australians' play in the five Test matches that year but I know from a personal point of view that it had an effect on my own captaincy.

The most immediate effect was in the first game in Brisbane where, at one stage in the afternoon, we were very much in danger of defeat but still kept on pressing for victory. The other side, led by Frank Worrell, were in the reverse situation with victory seeming certain at one time early in the afternoon and then defeat looming as the afternoon went on.

In the end the tie was, in itself, a freak result but the important thing was that the pattern of play had been set with both sides trying to win a match rather than avoid losing it. Later on in Adelaide, Australia was in the position of desperately needing the last two men to exist for an hour and 40 minutes and there was no thought there of searching for victory, rather was it a case of keeping one's fingers crossed and being able to scrape out of the match and go to Melbourne still all square.

It would be greedy to hope to play in two series such as this one for there was more excitement packed into those five matches than into 15 or 20 of the others I played for Australia. But everyone's hopes must be high in Australia this year that the West Indies will provide a lift in the numbers of spectators going through the gates for all the matches. I don't subscribe to the thought that there is any loss of public interest in cricket but it is certainly true that fewer people watch the minor matches these days for there are so many other outlets for them to pursue. To woo them back to watching the game is the task of the cricketers and, not least, the selectors who choose those cricketers—administration must play its part as well.

In thinking of the 1960/61 tour, one should never lose sight of the fact that, before that tied Test in Brisbane, the West Indies had a variable record on the field and they were not pulling in the spectators as they should and, later, did. Although anything up to 50,000 civilians profess to have seen the dying minutes of that tied Test in person, the bare fact

The late FRANK WORRELL, Captain of the 1960-61 West Indies team in Australia

is that only 4,000 were present at the game. Hundreds of thousands saw it on television and I suppose millions more heard it on the radio, with cars stopped at the side of the road and even a half called in beer drinking in the pubs and clubs of the nation.

Since then in Australia we have had a series against England in 1962/63, which promised much and then fizzled into nothing, and an excellent series against South Africa where Graeme Pollock proved himself one of the greatest young batsmen of the century. 1965/66 again saw M.C.C. send a side, with England and Australia drawing the series, and, in 1967/68, India lost all four Test matches, though the last two were closer than eventually appeared on paper.

It is not a dissimilar situation to when

RICHIE BENAUD former
Australian captain

their defeat by England in 1968 will be to the benefit of Australia's spectators.

Prior to that historic day when Sobers set Cowdrey a target at Trinidad, the West Indies were playing with the mantle of world champions' resting heavily on their shoulders. I still rate them, despite that defeat, as having the best team in the world but they will play their cricket with an easier mind now they have been once beaten.

I have seen most major Test series played in the past five years and yet the excitement of 1960/61 is still with me. They tell me that Hall is not at his quickest these days and yet I can still see him charging in to bowl that last bumper at McKay in the Adelaide Test. I will be surprised if, as his critics say, he is over the hill on this current tour. There will again be the magic of Gibbs, who turned the Sydney Test in 1961, and the glorious strokeplay of Kanhai who has turned plenty of Tests in his vivid career.

And, of course, there will be a Sobers. I played with Miller and I captained Davidson for many years and have seen most of the great all-rounders since the war. But, to me, Sobers is the most complete cricketer to have picked up a bat or ball in the past 22 years.

He now has the task, and a big one it will be, of equalling the performances of Frank Worrell's side in that memorable tour. Sobers himself was an integral part of that tour, as he will be of this one, and I am certain he too will have some nostalgic memories as he steps on the field at each of the major Test grounds.

He is a lucky man! Not all of us have the chance to play in two such Test series but, on the West Indies side, Sobers, Hall, Kanhai, Gibbs and Hendriks will do so, though Australia will field a side with none of the faces that appeared eight years ago.

The games will be played for the Frank Worrell Trophy, inaugurated at the conclusion of the 1961 series, and I hope the cricket played this time matches that played and advocated by the great man himself. If the pulsating excitement of eight years ago can be produced, even only in part, then spectators will throng to the grounds and depart content.

the West Indies came eight years ago though, fortunately, Australian spectators have not in the meantime watched slow series such as they put up with in 1958/59 and 1954/55. I would dearly love to see a series similar to that in 1960/61 as the West Indian tour unfolds over the next four months. Perhaps that is wishful thinking and, certainly, one could never really expect the freak results of Brisbane and Adelaide to be repeated.

I have seen the West Indies play in three full series in the past eight years and count myself lucky to have done so. There has been a tendency in recent times, as their cricket has slipped a little, for them to go on the defensive rather than continue in all out attack. I hope this doesn't make itself felt during the current tour and I believe, in a way,

13

EXTRACTS FROM SPEECHES MADE AT MELBOURNE AFTER TH FIFTH TEST OF THE 1960-61 WEST INDIES TOUR OF AUSTRALIA

Sir Donald Bradman

"Ladies & Gentlemen, I'm very sad to say that the time has come to ring down the curtain on this series of Test matches. But, I speak to you today as Chairman of the Australian Board of Control for International Cricket and on my own behalf and on behalf of the cricket-loving public of Australia, I want to pay tribute to the captains and the two teams, who have provided us with such magnificent cricket this summer.

Now, as you know, we had a tie in Brisbane—the most fantastic finish in history, and in order to commemorate that wonderful occasion, the Board of Control created a trophy for permanent competition between Australia and the West Indies . . . and it was decided, in honour of a very brilliant cricketer, who, unfortunately has now played his last Test match in Australia, that we should call it the Frank Worrell Trophy.

As you know, ladies and gentlemen, Frank Worrell has been and, in fact, still is, a great cricketer in the artistic mould, and there aren't very many of them about . . . we regret deeply that we won't have the pleasure of seeing him again. But, in addition, I can tell you he's a grand sportsman and a very gallant loser.

This trophy, which we have here, I'm going to hand to Frank and I'm going to ask him to present it to Richie, who is the winning captain . . . and the next time these two teams meet, which will probably be in the West Indies, then they shall play again for this trophy. You'll find that it has, on the top of it one of the cricket balls used in the famous Tie-Match in Brisbane".

Frank Worrell

. . . (Emotionally upset by this gesture and the crowd's reception)

"Mr. Chairman . . ." (For he's a jolly good fellow . . . sung by some 3,000-4,000 people) "Thank you, ladies and gentlemen. This is indeed a very sad and a happy occasion because the drawing of the stumps this afternoon marked the end of the most sensational, interesting and enjoyable series that any West Indies team has ever been engaged in. It also marks the culmination of a very

The Sir Frank Worrell Trophy,

It is known that Sir Frank Worrell's greatest wish was to return to Australia with Lady Worrell in the hope of presenting the Sir Frank Worrell Trophy to the winning team in this Series. Frank died in March 1967 and thus his wish will not be fulfilled, but his memory will never be erased.

Editor.

ijoyable stay in your country. We ould like to thank all those people for eir very kindly letters and those of you or the lavish hospitality.

We've had a very enjoyable tour and, fortune decreed that this trophy should tay in Australia, we have got to congratulate Richie and his men for the onderful fight-back at Adelaide and or dominating the scene in this match, nd we are looking forward to seeing is trophy in the West Indies, where we hall try to wrest it from you, in the same riendly and exciting manner as it has een won during this series.

I've got two duties to perform: I've ot to present this trophy to Richie and ongratulate him and his men for the onderful cricket, and secondly, I've got little token which I should like to resent him also. Firstly, Richie, congratulations to you and the boys . . ."

He presented his cap, tie and blazer to Richie, amid tumultuous applause.) "I've got a symbol here of a scalp; handing Richie his cap) secondly, you an have my neck, (his tie) and you can ave the upper half of my body (his

blazer). I shall refrain from offering him the lower half of my body because the knees would not stand him in any sense. Thank you all".

Richie Benaud

"Sir Donald Bradman, Frank, ladies and gentlemen . . . Frank was kind enough to say that he was offering me his scalp, and his neck, and the upper half of his body, but I am quite certain that you will agree with me that he himself will remain in the hearts of cricket-lovers in this country for many a long day.

It's always a very sad thing to come to the end of a test series; it's always a very happy thing to have won, and in this particular instance, it is a magnificent moment to stand here in front of all you people and to be able to say that, having played in this, my 50th Test match, I haven't played in five more memorable, nor more enjoyable games, nor have I and my team ever played against a finer bunch of cricketers than these West Indians.

I've come to know Frank pretty well in this particular season; you generally get to know your opposing team and your opposing captain pretty well, and, I would like to tell you that it's not only been a pleasure to play against our visitors (and against Frank) but to play in a series as captain against Frank Worrell has been a privilege.

There's little more I can say, except "Thank you" to all the people out here, who have supported the game and supported cricket this year, and a very, very big "Thank you" to my own team, who gave me such wonderful support during the series, and an even bigger "Thank you" to our West Indian friends and Frank, who have done such a wonderful job. Thank you".

15

AUSTRALIAN CAPTAIN

Bill Lawry

W. M. (BILL) LAWRY
Tests 53. Runs 4478. Av 50.88
H.S. 210.
Catches 21.

Has captained Australia in 11 Test Matches. Won 6 (W.I. 3. India 2, Eng. 1). Lost 2 (Eng. 1. W.I. 1) Drawn 3 (Eng. 2, W.I. 1). Has the third highest aggregate of runs in Tests for Australia, headed by Sir Donald Bradman 6996 runs in 80 innings, and Neil Harvey 6149 runs in 137 innings. Needs only 5 innings to become the third Australian and the second left-hand batsman to play 100 Test Innings. N. Harvey 137 and S. E. Gregory 100. During the two series he has enjoyed as Captain he has led 12 of the chosen party of 15 under his command. Last season against the West Indies revealed the development of the inexperienced side he led in England, and his conscientious efforts and guidance began to show their effect.

He will now lead a team against the World Champions, South Africa with the knowledge that he has several experienced players under him and upon whom he can depend. This should relieve him of a great deal of responsibility, which he rightly carried in England.

8

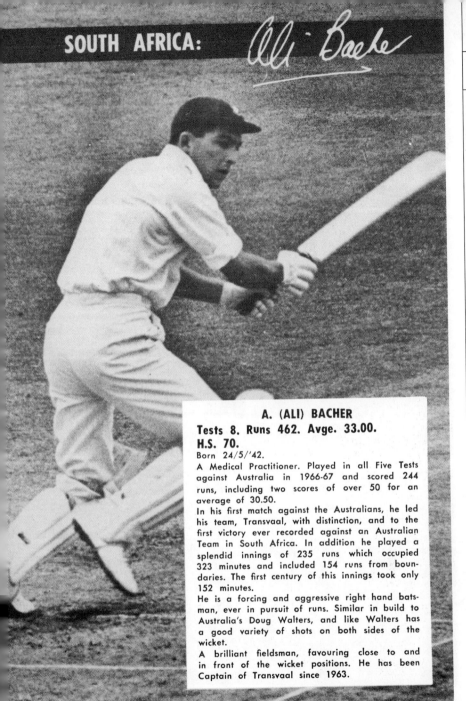

A. (ALI) BACHER

Tests 8. Runs 462. Avge. 33.00.
H.S. 70.

Born 24/5/'42.

A Medical Practitioner. Played in all Five Tests against Australia in 1966-67 and scored 244 runs, including two scores of over 50 for an average of 30.50.

In his first match against the Australians, he led his team, Transvaal, with distinction, and to the first victory ever recorded against an Australian Team in South Africa. In addition he played a splendid innings of 235 runs which occupied 323 minutes and included 154 runs from boundaries. The first century of this innings took only 152 minutes.

He is a forcing and aggressive right hand batsman, ever in pursuit of runs. Similar in build to Australia's Doug Walters, and like Walters has a good variety of shots on both sides of the wicket.

A brilliant fieldsman, favouring close to and in front of the wicket positions. He has been Captain of Transvaal since 1963.

9

CHAPTER SIX

The 1970.

1970–1976

Fast Bowler John Snow rocketed Australia in 1970–71, claiming 31 wickets. Ray Illingworth's team were tough opponents and England's 2–0 victory was deserved.

Greg Chappell made an elegant debut with a hundred in Perth's inaugural Test, but Australia's lack of penetrative bowling saw five different new-ball pairings tried. McKenzie, who had often carried the attack, was dropped after defeat in the fourth Test, his Test career ending with 246 wickets. For the first time in history, Australia dropped its captain and Ian Chappell replaced Bill Lawry for the seventh Test. Dennis Lillee made a promising debut in Adelaide, taking five wickets in England's first innings.

Australia's renaissance under Ian Chappell in 1972 was fired by Lillee's pace. Massie's swing helped Chappell square the series, despite a combination of fuserium disease and Derek Underwood securing an England victory at Headingley.

The push for winning runs on the last day at the Oval was televised live to Australia— Sheahan and Marsh steering Australia home by five wickets. The ABC's huge television audience gave Kerry Packer the initial indication of cricket's commercial potential on the box.

Chappell's inspirational prowess was confirmed in 1973 when he retained the Frank Worrell Trophy in the West Indies. Lillee and Massie broke down, leaving Walker, Hammond, Walters, O'Keeffe and Jenner to share the burden and the spoils. The West Indies missed their great all-rounder Gary Sobers, who, as Tony Cozier sadly surmised, had played his last Test.

No-one anticipated Jeff Thomson's impact on the 1974–75 series. He had taken 0 for 110, bowling with a foot injury, on his debut two seasons earlier. Alongside Lillee he formed one of the most lethal attacks, his javelin-like action making it nearly impossible for batsmen to react effectively. Combined, Lillee and Thomson scythed out 56 victims against England, and then again in 1975–76 on the West Indies visit. They set a standard for aggressive, combative Test cricket which was emulated by the West Indies for the next two decades.

The "synthetic"

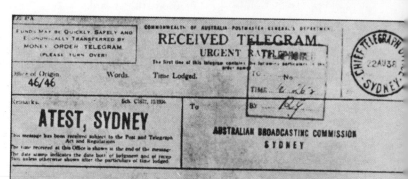

roadcasts of cricket

ALTHOUGH I have taken part in a number of important sporting broadcasts during my career involving such events as Test Cricket, Davis Cup tennis, Commonwealth and Olympic Games, etc., I am sure that nothing has interested me more than synthetic Test descriptions which began in 1934 covering the Australian tour of England.

After so many years I still meet people who want to know how they were done and who tell me, strangely enough, that they were more interested in the synthetic descriptions than the direct broadcasts from England.

In July 1932 the Australian Broadcasting Commission was formed and during the intervening period the Commission has devoted a considerable amount of time to the broadcasting of cricket. Up to this point of time coverage has been provided for 152 Test Matches, including 80 Tests between England and Australia and hundreds of other first class games.

The sensational 1932 "bodyline" series in Australia brought the first full realization of the entertainment value in the broadcasting of cricket. The public reaction, interest and response was so evident that it was decided to extend this type of broadcasting.

Then came a big problem. The next Test series would be played in England and as overseas reception in those years was barely audible, how could this policy be pursued.

A plan was evolved, simple though it now seems, but then surrounded by many fears and doubts. It was to provide a cable service describing every ball bowled in every Test match to the Commission's studios in Market Street, Sydney, from where a ball-by-ball description would be provided. It had been determined that arrangements could be made for a cable sent from any ground in England to reach Sydney in two minutes. This was achieved and in fact, at the start of the series the broadcasts originated in Sydney were only two minutes behind the actual play. As experience was gained this time was reduced to 45 seconds.

There were many presentation problems. Could cricket scenes be described from a message and inside the four bare walls of a studio. They were, and from all over the continent came expressions of appreciation of what was then termed "synthetic" broadcasts.

An A.B.C. representative, and an experienced cricketer, Mr Eric Sholl was sent to England in 1934 to provide the cable information. In Sydney a team of 13 men, consisting of technicians and cricket experts was set up. It was the task of this team to construct and amplify the messages for the commentators to provide ball-by-ball descriptions. (The members of this 1934 team were:—Messrs C. J. A. Moses (now Sir Charles Moses), M. A. Noble, E. L. a'Beckett, Clem Hill, C. E. (Nip) Pellew, Bernard Kerr, P. C. Harrison, Dion Wheeler, Mel Morris, R. H. Campbell, J. L. Hall, J. Duffecy and A. Grey.) That countless people sat up for hours, and many throughout the complete playing period of 8.30 pm to 3.30 am EST on cold winter nights now seems incredible, but they did.

During the early broadcasts mistakes were frequent but quickly corrected. Uncertainty and nervousness existed, for this was a most unusual operation but slowly the team moulded itself into a splendid combination, heartened by the warmth and sincerity of the listeners who were ever in support in expressions of gratitude and appreciation.

Records revealed an amazing increase in radio licences. Sales of radio receiver parts from which people built their own valve but mainly crystal sets broke all records, and it was then reported that

11

electric light plants had to meet unusually heavy demands. The A.B.C. created Test Match fever and it swept the Continent.

In 1938, when a similar operation was performed the uncertain reception conditions, which existed in 1934, had improved. Thus for the first time these thousands of listeners were able to hear eye-witnesses descriptions of the play and resumes that came from the Test grounds in England. This only occurred between 1.30 am and close of play at 3.30 am EST. Frequently this link broke down and then the synthetic broadcasts were continued. Reference is made to these synthetic broadcasts in early A.B.C. Annual Reports and this is a quote from one of these reports:— "Of this type of broadcasts listeners have constantly asked . . . how is it done . . . is it coming from England . . . no attempt had been made to hide the fact that such broadcasts had their origin in the Sydney studios, but the descriptions were so true to life that many people believed them to be coming direct from the ground. Even in the last few months when the scheme of the broadcasts had been revealed more than once by the press and cinema screen,

enquiries have shown that this belief was still held". The accompanying photographs taken during the 1938 series, show some of the stages in the construction of the synthetic commentaries.

Photograph "A" is an example of the type of cable received.

Photograph "B" shows how it was built up and constructed by those in "Photograph "C", which includes Halford Hooker, former NSW player, second from the right who is amplifying cables; John Chance, an A.B.C. sporting commentator and now an announcer, (sitting directly in front of Halford Hooker) is making copies of the amplified message; the late Mel Morris, then Sporting Editor for the Victorian branch, in the bottom left hand corner is checking the fielding charts which are shown in front of him.

Photograph "D" shows a portion of the broadcasting studio. Halford Hooker is here taking his turn at the microphone. The late Victor Richardson, on Hooker's right is awaiting his turn at the microphone and listening to the cable information coming from the G.P.O. and checking the cables as they reached the studio. Sitting in

ont of Hooker is the sound effects operator, ...es Turner, following a carbon copy of the mplified message, and supplying the cor-...ct atmosphere by fading in crowd noises, ...pplause and so on, from two spinning scs on turn tables. The commentator ...ade the sound of the bat meeting the ball, ...d of a ball striking pad, by tapping a ...ooden cup with a pencil held in his ...ght hand, or the heavy rubber band around ..., which produced a dull thud.

Panoramic views of the grounds were of ...reat help in building up the synthetic ...oadcasts, and these were placed in ...ont of the commentator, as shown in ...hotograph "D". When the commentator ...ferred to the ground he did so in relation ... the cabling point, which was clearly ...arked on the large photographs.

Photograph "E" shows the progressive ...coreboard placed in the left hand corner ...f the broadcasting studio. This photograph ...as taken during Sir Leonard Hutton's ...nings where he made his world's record ...core. The operator of the scoreboard is ... Grey, who acted in that capacity during ...e 1934 and 1938 synthetic broadcasts. ...lay started at 8.30 pm EST but the team

assembled an hour before to have discussions, to iron out faults which occurred during the previous evenings' broadcasts and by 8.15 pm all took up their various positions and awaited the arrival of the first three most important cables. The first to tell of the weather, the state of the pitch and ground and any other item of interest.

The next two cables gave detailed information about field placements and the positions of every fieldsman for the two opening overs. The fielding charts were then compiled. One set was kept in the receiving and amplifying room, and another placed in the broadcasting studio for use by the commentator who would occasionally "call" the field placements for the benefit of the listener. This was more than useful for "filling-in" periods when the flow of cables was delayed, as often they were, and thus the commentator had little to talk about. These delays were a constant threat and worry to all concerned, especially to the commentator who had to maintain a constant flow of information. These field placements remained static, and no further reference was made to them, unless a fieldsman was moved from his original position, and then this information would be conveyed immediately by cable. There was however a code evolved here for when a fieldman's name was mentioned in the cable it served to convey he had fielded brilliantly. Then the game would be under way, and invariably the receiving room would come to life with the words "here it comes", meaning of course the arrival of the first cable. The receiving room was ever alive with tension, anxiety and concentration for all were aware of the necessity of keeping the commentator fed with information so that he could keep talking.

Much the same tension and anxiety existed in the broadcasting room, with the commentator ever glancing at the door through which the runner would appear, sometimes with a full message of six balls, often with three balls and occasionally with but one ball on the message, for speed was the essence and the receiving room staff were trying to keep him going. He knew this and then would come the fateful message "no cables" or "keep going old chap" or "sing a song, the listeners won't mind" or some such message, mostly sent in humour, and so very often a sense of humour was needed.

Having received Message 46, the commentator proceeded to describe the over. It was known this was the 34th over, with Fleetwood-Smith bowling to Hammond. The first ball would be described as a full toss, driven through the covers by Hammond for 2 runs but as Hassett's name is mentioned it has conveyed, as previously mentioned, that Hassett has fielded well, by chasing the ball towards the boundary and saving a possible four runs. Second ball, "unchance" is the key word here for it indicated Hammond had hit the ball on the full, past the bowler for four runs, but the bowler did not get a hand to it and thus not a chance and so it would be described.

The third ball is another full toss, no doubt bringing a comment that Fleetwood-Smith was bowling erratically. This was off driven, possibly not well timed for Hammond rarely failed to hit a full toss through the covers for four runs. Here he scored two

runs, but the key to this description surrounds two words in the actual cable "run appeal Hutton". An appeal for a run out has been made against Hutton, it must be at the bowler's end when completing the second run (otherwise the words "keeper's end" would have been mentioned in the cable. The fielding chart showed Hassett at cover so he returned it to the bowler's end. The commentator would colour this description by having Hutton racing down the pitch to make his crease, or even diving at full length, dependent entirely upon the commentator and his enthusiasm about such an incident.

To the fourth delivery Hammond employed one of his favourite shots and swept the ball to the square leg boundary. Again the fielding chart provided the information about who was fielding at deep square-leg and in this case it was Barnes.

The remaining three words, bowler keeper, off pushed conveyed that Hammond had played the first back to the bowler, the second went through to the keeper without a shot being attempted. Had Hammond played at the ball and missed the words "unplayed keeper" would have been used, meaning that he had attempted to hit the ball and missed. Here the commentator would use his imagination by describing the ball beating Hammond off the pitch with leg or off spin. The last ball was played slowly to cover, with McCabe showing on the chart as fielding at close in cover. The word "brightening" on the cable indicated that the weather was brightening and was shown in the remarks column on the message. The commentator could use this either before or during the over, according to the timing he had assessed for Fleetwood-Smith to bowl an over. This would be roughly three minutes and he had to adjust his description to that timing for every over, otherwise he would find himself short of cricket information.

This was a most important factor, to maintain the normal pace of the game so that an even flow of cables sent according to that timing, could be received and described.

14

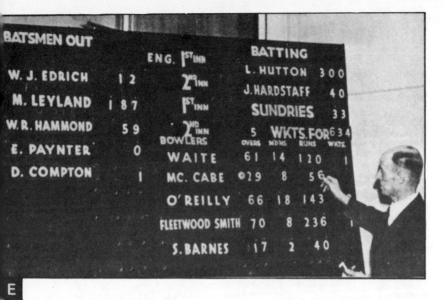

E

Fast bowlers were assessed at about five minutes an over, slow bowlers $2\frac{1}{2}$ to 3 minutes, and some commentators used stop watches so that they would not describe an over too fast. It was remarkable how accurate our broadcasts were when they were checked with the press reports. Although we had to make up our own descriptions of balls that were not scored from we knew the type of bowler and the strength of the batsman and of course we had the exact field placings so with this information our descriptions were close to the mark.

It is quite a long time since 1934 but even though the synthetic descriptions imposed a great strain on all concerned with the presentation they were exciting days and even now I am stirred by my association with them.

BERNARD KERR
DIRECTOR OF SPORTING
BROADCASTS. A.B.C.

ABBREVIATIONS USED IN PEN-PORTRAITS OF PLAYERS

RHB Right hand batsman.
LHB Left hand batsman.
RF Right arm fast bowler.
RFM Right arm fast medium pace bowler.
RM Right arm medium pace bowler.
RS Right arm slow bowler.
ROS Right arm off-spin bowler.
LS Left arm slow bowler.
LSM Left arm slow-medium pace bowler.

15

MCC TOUR
OF AUSTRALIA **1970-1971**

Two captains cricket's mos demanding jol

FORMER ENGLAND Captain E. R. (Ted) Dexter and Australian Captain I. (Ian) Chappell were invited to answer eighteen questions about cricket captaincy.

Ted Dexter played in 62 Tests, and captained England in ten of the 19 Tests he played against Australia. In 1962-63 in Australia his opposing captain was Richie Benaud in 5 Tests. Bobby Simpson also captained Australia in 5 Tests against him in 1964 in England.

As Australia's captain Ian Chappell was asked the questions in the present tense, and as a former captain Ted Dexter's questions were in the past tense. The questions and the answers appear in those terms.

● ● ●

You have played against all Countries who play Test cricket. Who do you regard as your greatest opponents?

CHAPPELL: Your greatest opponents can vary with the respective strengths of the Countries when you actually play against them. I always find, however, that the team which is consistently the toughest to beat is England. This is probably because they play for their living and in playing so much cricket they always have a wealth of experience under all types of conditions.

DEXTER: There is not much doubt from an English point of view that Australian teams have been the hardest to beat. If you actually wind up the winner either in a series or a single Test match against Australia, as an Englishman you really feel you have achieved something.

4

Many captains at the start of a Test match, play with a policy "if I cannot win then I will endeavour not to lose," and so never lose sight of the possibility of a drawn game. As a captain of your Country is/was that your attitude?

CHAPPELL: As a captain of any team I set out with the intention of trying to win from the first ball bowled, and maintain that attitude unless the team gets into a situation where a win is out of the question; and then, of course, it is a backs to the wall job and try and live to fight another day.

DEXTER: I think it is the duty of every captain to do the best for his team, and you have to remember in Test cricket that every Test is not an isolated game . . . it is part of the series. However one might disagree with that it is a fact, particularly against Australia because the Ashes are at stake. I played the game as a series such as a 30-day match, now that six Tests are being played, rather than a five-day match. It is clearly silly to get yourself one-down early in the series when you don't have to.

Frequently captains have committed their team to bat well into the second day before applying a closure of innings. Often the batting side has gone through until the afternoon tea adjournment on the second day, thus attaining a total of some 500 to 600 runs. This mostly shuts the other side out. Is/was this your approach?

Ian Chappell

Ted Dexter

CHAPPELL: If you commit your team to a score of large proportions and take nearly the first two days of a Test to do it, I would think you would have to be pretty certain the wicket was going to crumble badly in the closing stages of the game. By playing the game this way you are virtually relying on being able to bowl the opposition out cheaply and then make them follow on, and this is a very difficult way to win a Test match. It means your bowlers don't get a rest between innings, and I always feel if your own team can make 500 or 600 runs easily there is no reason why the opposition can't do the same.

DEXTER: As I said before it depends upon the state of the series particularly, but mostly on the state of the pitch. Obviously if you think the pitch is going to deteriorate and you have been lucky enough to win the toss and get first use of it, then you must make the most of it and get your runs while you can. Incidentally I think at Test cricket level it is best for the game if the fielding captain expects to field well into the second day, because if he doesn't he can then apply defensive and negative tactics in the field. If he is expecting to field for two days, unless he gets the other side out, then he has to be

5

more positive in his approach. One's tactics must be guided by trying to win the match in the quickest time possible and making the very best use of whatever conditions you happen to get. Captaincy demands positive thinking.

Clearly you had certain tactics worked out to apply to your opposition both individually and as a team. Do/did you expose these plans to your team and at all times keep them informed of your tactics?

* Note: Chappell combines his answer to this and the next question . . . in one reply.

CHAPPELL: As a team we have meetings before each overseas Test and in these we discuss the opposition and perhaps the way we will try to control the game; but these plans are not too elaborate as obviously the opposition can mess them up very quickly. I always welcome ideas from anyone in the team, as I believe that eleven heads must be better than one; however, the final decision has to be made by the captain. I also believe in having a working arrangement with the bowlers, as after all they are the ones who have to bowl to the field settings, and so these have to be worked out between you.

DEXTER: I certainly worked out tactics with my team, one of the main areas of course being bowling tactics and field placings against particular batsmen. I think this is something in Test cricket that spectators don't always appreciate. They can't understand why a batsman who gets plenty of runs in lower grade cricket comes unstuck in Test matches.

In this sphere he comes up against top class bowlers who have worked him out. As far as keeping my players informed I am absolutely certain I did that at every turn.

Do/did you seek the advice of your fellow players on the field. If not, why?

* Note Chappell has combined his reply to this with the previous question.

DEXTER: Yes. Usually on a Test match field there are many experienced players, and a captain has to be very selective in whom he listens to or goes to. Very often, in fact, advice is biased . . . for example, opening batsmen will always advise you to put the other side in when you win the toss, because they are not looking forward to facing the other side's fast bowlers.

What consideration do/did you give to the public? Does/did it take any part in your planning?

CHAPPELL: I think that by trying to win a match you are giving the public consideration enough. The main people who have a duty to the public are the selectors, who, if they pick the right style of player, have made sure there will be entertainment. It is then the captain's job to encourage each player to play his natural game and not try and stifle it.

DEXTER: Yes, I did. Where I felt I did my bit was in relation to overrate. I can't think of anything worse than a game being deliberately slowed down by the bowlers, by being slow in walking back and generally wasting time. It had happened quite a lot prior to my taking over the captaincy, and it was one area which I felt was a trap that I would not, and should not, fall into. It is annoying for spectactors when they become aware players are deliberately slowing the game down . . . it looks awful . . . it makes the game drag for all concerned and it is totally indefensible. It is a pity legislation hasn't been arrived at yet in Test cricket, insisting that 18 six-ball overs in England, or 14 eight-ball overs in Australia, be bowled in an hour. This legislation applies in English County cricket and it has proved very successful, and the sooner this can be introduced into Test cricket the better.

Do/did you consider "gamesmanship" to be necessary, and if so do/did you apply it?

CHAPPELL: If a player has any weakness I will try and take advantage of this within the laws of the game. If I didn't I wouldn't be doing the right thing by my side.

DEXTER: I am sure I did in little ways, but I don't in principle think it is either necessary or desirable. There are bound to be situations where you choose to bend things to your advantage, I suppose. For instance little things . . . there comes a great shout for LBW against you. There are ways of looking guilty as though you are out and there are ways of looking as

6

though you are not out. Clearly if you have the choice you know which one you are going to decide on. But here you have to define gamesmanship . . . if it is mean or outside the laws it is no good to anybody.

Do/did you employ "needle" and "pressure" tactics on the field?

CHAPPELL: I try and employ "pressure" tactics with my field placings, but needling is something that doesn't happen very often in Test matches because there are too many good players around who might play better if they are "needled."

DEXTER: I would not have thought so, but from watching one doesn't really know because what is going on cannot be heard. From reports from umpires and players it seems that needling and pressure, which must be a personal thing against individuals, has increased. No, I don't think it is a good thing at all, and I consider it is just as well the authorities have done something about it.

There has been, and is in the present day a good deal of "chatter" going on on the field, often directed at batsmen. This could be classed as gamesmanship and is not necessarily confined to cricket. Do/did you think this necessary?

CHAPPELL: I don't believe there is a lot of "chatter" on a Test match field, as all the players have a job to concentrate on. If there were any unnecessary talking going on, an umpire has the right to step in or

Ted Dexter hits four runs in the fourth Test against New Zealand at Old Trafford, 1958.

the batsman the right to complain to the umpire about it. I don't believe in a lot of unnecessary chatter on the field, after all it is a Test match, not an afternoon tea party.

There are one or two things which annoy me intensely on the cricket field, and if these are pursued by any opposition team, whoever they might be, I will let them know very smartly to get on with their job and allow us to do our own job.

DEXTER: No, I don't think it is necessary . . . I compare it with golf where there are some opponents who are quite successful by doing a lot of chatting to you. It is distracting and to that extent it can be effective, and I don't think it is any more gracious, or sporting or desirable for that. At the same time it would be ridiculous if everybody had to keep strict silence on the field. I can think of wicket-keepers for instance; if you weren't even allowed to pass the time of day with a wicket-keeper during a long innings it would be a pretty miserable business. Wally Grout used to keep behind me a lot, he was often quite amusing and might chat a bit, but I never thought he was unreasonable at all.

Do/did you instruct your players to "walk" when they know they are out?

CHAPPELL: Walking is purely an individual thing which I leave to the person concerned. I don't believe in walking myself, as I feel an umpire is appointed to do a job. The only thing I stress is that a player should look at the umpire when an appeal is made, and then accept the decision when it is made whether you agree with it or not.

DEXTER: No, I never did. It is a tricky subject. I've come a full circle around from county cricket in England, and I thought that the help given to an umpire by a player walking out when the umpire really couldn't possibly know and the player did know . . . I thought that was desirable, but it causes a lot of trouble in fact.

Do/did you make any arrangement with your opposing captain about "walking"?

CHAPPELL: Definitely not.

DEXTER: No . . . no I never did.

7

Some players clearly indicate they are walkers, yet do not do so when the event occurs. What is your reaction to this type of player?

CHAPPELL: I believe this to be a form of cheating and there is no place for cheating in cricket. Fortunately I think I have only seen this happen once, and even then we as the fielding side could well have been wrong.

DEXTER: That is exactly what I meant when I said it can cause an awful lot of trouble. You get a player who is genuinely a walker, a guy who reckons he will go when he knows he is out. Then the time comes when the fielding side honestly believes he is out and the batsman honestly believes he is not out. That's when you get the language flying around and people being held up as cheats of the first water. That is the sort of problem walking leads to and therefore I consider it is in everybody's interest to leave it to the umpire.

Much has been said and written about the bowling of fast short pitched balls at the batsmen, perhaps better known as bouncers or bumpers. Do/did you consider they are part of a fast bowler's equipment and do/did you encourage their use?

CHAPPELL: No one tells a fast bowler to stop bowling outswingers to a batsman because he has a weakness outside off stump and you have already given him four outswingers that over.

I believe a man who is selected to represent his country as a batsman should be capable of dealing with short pitched bowling. If he is not, he has either got to practise and become proficient or he will lose his place on the team, the same as he would with any other weakness in his game. I don't see why the fast bowler should have to suffer because the batsman has a weakness. If a bowler is obviously trying to hit a batsman then the umpire has a job to do, and of course as you get lower in the batting order so the proficiency decreases and the umpire's judgement becomes more important. No one tells the fast bowler to stop bowling

short pitched balls when the batsma... hooks him consistently for four, he doesn... have to, the bowler very smartly stop... bowling them.

I have asked bowlers to use bounce... and will continue to do so where I feel the... are going to take a wicket or perhap... contribute to this end. I have never aske... a bowler to deliberately knock a batsme... down and as a batsman I reckon it is m... fault if I get hit, not the bowler's.

With tailend batsmen I may ask for th... odd short pitched ball at the ribs, as... don't believe a tailender can expect to ju... prop onto the front foot all the time ar... have a 'quick' bowl half volleys to him. If... tailender has been in for some time and... obviously hitting them well and in n... trouble, I am not beyond asking a fa... bowler to bounce him, but I think the ma... point is that it is always in an endeavour ... take his wicket, not to take him out of th... game!

DEXTER: Yes, I did consider they we... part of a fast bowler's equipment and I d... encourage their use. Why . . . because... batsman can take advantage of a fa... bowler and by playing forward quite ear... can cancel out the bowler's pace; and th... only retaliation the bowler has against th... type of batting is to drop the ball short ar... make him play back. I think the prese... law is slightly ambiguous but nevertheles... effective. It is generally understood th... two bouncers aimed at the batsman in a... over is reasonable. More than that I fe... the umpire can start to intervene. If th... umpires were really strict on this and too... a hand early, not to wait to see if a bump... war is about to develop, then I dor... consider there is really any problem.

As a batsman, what is/was your reacti...
to this type of bowling?

CHAPPELL: I think I have already state... my case. I have had my moments... trouble with short pitched bowling, mair... because of some bad advice to give ... the hook shot, and I was silly enough ... accept this well meaning advice.

As a kid and in my early days I w... always taught to be a hooker, not ... 'ducker' or avoider of the bouncer. ...

Chappell skies Pocock
to be caught by keeper Knott
at Old Trafford in 1968

giving it away for a couple of seasons I lost the knack and got myself into more trouble by not using it as a means of defence, which I now see it to be.

My advice to young players would never be to give up the hook if you are getting out to it, but to go away and practise it until you can play it well, and it will reap you more rewards than just the runs it brings.

DEXTER: I think you have to be quite crafty. Inevitably you have to be relatively courageous because obviously you have the prospect of being hit in the teeth, or getting yourself injured. In fact if you stand your ground and watch the ball, and be prepared to be hit occasionally, you come out of it much better . . . you are hit very seldom. It is extraordinary how quick your reactions can be.

The batsman has to bide his time. He has to say, well, all right, you have had your turn, as long as I survive then I will give you some trouble in return. You have to accept it as a batsman and as I said bide your time.

What difference is there between Australian and English crowds, and is their behaviour influential in any way?

CHAPPELL: I feel crowds the world over are becoming more vocal at cricket matches, and in a lot of ways I think this is a good thing. They like to become more involved in the game, and as long as they don't do silly things which cause unnecessary holdups in play, I don't mind them letting us know when they think we have done something either badly or well. On the average the English crowd is quieter and doesn't have as many fights as its Australian counterparts.

DEXTER: Well, English crowds don't bring their ice-boxes and I am told that even the size of the ice-boxes has had to be limited to cut down on the space they occupy . . . on the Sydney Hill especially, I am told.

I think however they are becoming alike, perhaps this is due to one-day cricket in England. English spectators are becoming more volatile and the image of the old colonel with his moustache drooping, and his hat pulled over his eyes quietly snoozing in the Long Room, is not quite so any more. We get some vociferous crowds . . . we have of course some multi-racial crowds who love their cricket and make a lot of noise. I always felt Australian crowds were noisier, but I am not so sure they are now.

Do you foresee Test cricket being played on synthetic pitches in order to obtain uniformity of pace and bounce, or do you consider this to be undesirable?

CHAPPELL: I don't see a future for synthetic wickets in first class and international cricket, as I think the turf wicket and its habits are an integral part of the game. However I could see a use for them in club cricket and at school level, where players should be trying to develop their skills on reasonably true surfaces.

DEXTER: I consider it unnecessary. The only value I can see in a synthetic pitch would be to make it more readily playable after rain. The variety in pitches from one place to another helps players from different parts of the world to learn different skills and techniques. They add

9

spice and variety and it would be a great shame if they were totally uniform.

With the tension existent in Test cricket, and with television playing a prominent part in determining whether an umpire has made the correct decision . . . do you feel Test matches should be played with neutral umpires?

CHAPPELL: I feel umpires are very much like players, they have a pride of performance, and obviously they want to maintain this standard and so they are always out to perform at their best. They also, like players, have to make split second decisions, and they don't have the chance of seeing the after effects in slow motion. I don't really think they would be particularly worried what the camera showed, as obviously they give the decision thinking it is the correct one from what they saw in front of them.

I have never ever heard players discuss seriously any ideas to have neutral umpires and I would think it is not necessary. Umpires have to be looked at as you look at players, they are going to make a mistake or two as they happen to be human, it's just that the better ones make less of them.

DEXTER: I am afraid I am totally old school and totally unrepentant on this. As far as I am concerned every umpire is neutral. I am quite convinced that 999 out of 1000 umpires who ever walked out to umpire a Test match, have been quite convinced in their own minds they we going to umpire that match as well as th possibly could, and to be totally unbiase It is quite imperative for cricket that t should be so, and the players should on the field with that feeling inside the The moment you say you cannot have Australian umpiring a Test match Australia, the whole fabric of the autho of the umpire is gone.

What innings or event gave you greatest personal satisfaction wh playing against England/Australia?

CHAPPELL: The winning of the last T 1972 at the Oval gave me one of biggest thrills of my life. It was a Test were terribly keen to win and we re had to battle for victory over every one the six days we played.

When it was finally won I think realised that once again Australia was it should be, a power to be reckoned v in world cricket.

DEXTER: Well, it is an event, not innings. It was beating Australia Melbourne in 1962-63 when I was capt It was an unbelievable moment, in fa didn't really realise, I don't think, until ab an hour after that this had really happe to me. We were sitting in the afterwards and I suddenly turned somebody and said: "We've bea Australia". It was truly a remarkable th and definitely the highlight of my caree

The British Broadcasting Corporation': cricket commentator Christopher Martin Jenkins, is accompanying the M.C.C. tear during their tour of Australia and Nev Zealand.

Christopher is a broadcaster wit considerable experience and recentl covered the M.C.C. tour of the West Indie and the home series against India an Pakistan.

As a player he represented Cambridg University and has also played with Surrey i the Minor Counties Competition.

Listeners in the United Kingdom will b hearing the last half-hour of play on eac day of the Test matches and on Saturday and Sundays this will be extended to an hou or an hour-and-a-half.

Playing Times

est Matches in all States.
    11.00am — 1.00pm
    1.40pm — 3.40pm
    4.00pm — 6.00pm
    Afternoon Tea 3.40pm — 4.00pm

State Matches.

ew South Wales and Queensland.
    11.00am — 12.50pm
    1.30pm — 3.30pm
    3.50pm — 5.30pm
    Afternoon Tea 3.30pm — 3.50pm

. Australia. Victoria.
. Australia. Tasmania.
xcepting M.C.C. v S. Australia
ec. 21, 22, 23, 1974.
    11.30am — 1.20pm
    2.00pm — 4.00pm
    4.20pm — 6.00pm
    Afternoon Tea 4.00pm — 4.20pm

.C.C. v S. Australia.
ec. 21, 22, 23, 1974.
    Playing times as for Test Matches.

Country Matches.

Except in the case of the match at Canberra (playing times to be determined) the daily scheduled playing hours shall be the same as those pertaining to the State in which the playing centre is situated.

One-day (limited-over) Matches.

Melbourne, January 1st and February 5th, 1975.
    11.00am — 1.00pm
    1.30pm — 3.45pm
    4.00pm — 6.00pm

The matches will consist of one innings per team and each innings will be limited to 40 overs. (Subject to special conditions if rain or bad weather delays the start or interrupts play.)
The umpires may order extra time if, in their opinion, a finish can be obtained. Adjustments can be made to the times of intervals by agreement between the home authority and the two captains.

Test Match Grounds. (Measurements)

rom Boundary to Boundary

		(to nearest)	
		Metres	Yards
risbane	North to South	137	150
	East to West	137	150
erth	North to South	143	156
	East to West	142	155
elbourne	North to South	149	163
	East to West	173	189
dney	North to South	159	174
	East to West	154	168
delaide	North to South	190	208
	East to West	126	138

e cricket pitch at the Melbourne Cricket Ground runs approximately West of North d East of South. On all other grounds mentioned the pitches run North to South.

11

The battle of the bumpers

by KEITH MILLE[R]

THAT Peter Lever bumper which flattened New Zealand tailender Ewan Chatfield has once more raised the bumper question.

Coming right on top of the Thomson-Lillee bumper barrage, the question is high on the priority list when the I.C.C. meet later this year.

Knowing the big stick that England cricket chief Gubby Allen wields in his own country, you can bet that whatever the outcome of the bumper talk, England umpires will be briefed to clamp down on the bumper rate. Unlike the Australian umpires this series who allowed Lillee and Thomson free licence to bump, they will most assuredly get their marching tickets if they try the same treatment in England.

I have known of unofficial directions coming from the top seat at Lords to umpires. Naturally they carry them out, otherwise they are out of a job; for umpiring is their means of livelihood.

But this bumper talk is old hat . . . Ban the bumper? You may as well try and ban sex. Of course a bowler is entitled to use the bumper. The big question of course is what constitutes a fair quota.

I don't know. Nobody does.

Let's illustrate a point. Playing for Victoria against N.S.W. I once bowled a full over of bumpers at opener Arthur Morris. Yes, eight bumpers in a row. Was I spoken to? No. Morris, an expert at the hook shot, thumped almost every delivery for four. I never got booed. Morris got tremendous applause.

Now then. If I bowled the same number to, say, non-hookers Ian Redpath or Bobby Simpson, I would most certainly have been hooted off the field.

So tell me how you can frame a law to cover the bumper . . . Pure common-sense thinking by the umpire seems the only sane way, depending on the ability of a batsman to handle the short pitched stuff.

For years we saw Victoria opener Redpath ducking and weaving from

bumpers while at the other end K[e] Stackpole, a magnificent hooker, [was] having a picnic . . .

Bowling to tailenders become[s] tricky one.

But those smart aleck tailenders v[ho] deliberately plonk their front foot [way] down the pitch in front of the wic[ket] knowing full well they will not be gi[ven] out L.B.W. or get a bumper, deserv[e a] bumper or two. They blatantly flout [the] unwritten law of "no bumpers [to] tailenders".

Frankly I believe there is far m[ore] danger of serious injury to those w[ho] field close to the batsmen awaiting [a] snick from the bat to the pad catch.

A direct hit on the head from a l[usty] swipe could be fatal. Usually the m[ost] damage from the bumper is a good t[hump] in the ribs.

In my early days I was purely simply a batsman and played the h[ook]. Later, as a fast bowler, I reaped many wickets from the short pitc[hed] ball simply because batsmen [kept] attempting to hook even though t[hey] had not the remotest idea of how [to] play this most exacting, hard-to-[master] stroke. So I cut out the shot. S[ome] great players never hooked. Engla[nd's] greats, Wally Hammond and Hutton, were two.

By sharp contrast Don Bradman [was] the finest hooker cricket has known.

eight bumbers in a row.

seven wickets in the first innings. It was impossible to bat on. A half volley might skid ankle low, the next ball on the same spot stand upright, and whizz over the head or hit the body in any part. This unpredictable lift and skid made it the most dangerous pitch I have seen. It was frightening to me, the bowler, let alone the batsmen. So at times I eased my pace down only to get a gentle word from my skipper "Bowl them faster. They're harder to play".

Here were half volleys becoming wicked bumpers, with batsmen being thumped like the bodyline days. Does the umpire caution me? It was dangerous bowling. But how can you ban a delivery hurled down on the half volley? It's a headache for the law makers of the game, not forgetting the umpire.

In 1950/1 tour of Australia, Freddie Brown captained a team labelled "Brown's cows" because of lack of talent.

A born leader, Brown batted well, bowled seamers, leg breaks, fielded well. A true front line general.

Every time Lindwall or I bowled a bumper in the Test to Brown, he stood hand on hip, and scowled down the pitch at us, like some irate schoolmaster annoyed at an offending pupil.

Result was he bluffed us into keeping the ball up, and being a fine driver he thumped 62 and 79, mainly at our expense.

Lindwall and I had a talk. We realised Brown had conned us. We knew the bumper was his weakness, so we gave him a few. Brown's figures for the remainder of the Tests are interesting. 18, 16, absent hurt, 6.

So wasn't the bumper justified?

I think the most simple and common sense law to cover the bumper should come from a leaf out of the boxing game. Like a boxing referee who can stop a one sided fight because he considers one boxer is absorbing too much punishment, an umpire should be empowered to order a bowler off if he persists in "dishing it out" to a batsmen who clearly has not the ability to cope with the short pitched bumper.

Batting with him against Yorkshire at [S]mall Lane Ground, Sheffield, a [me]dium pacer named Ron Aspinall [now] a County umpire) bowled a suc[ce]ssion of bumpers which Bradman [co]lly whisked away to the leg bound-[ary]. At the end of this costly over [Br]adman, with that twinkle in his eye, [sai]d "Nugget, I hope they don't take him [off] for bowling too many bumpers".

Bradman was also my skipper in my [firs]t Test in Brisbane in 1946. After [Au]stralia had clobbered a huge score [(Br]adman 187), torrential rain turned [the] Gabba pitch into the stickiest pitch I [hav]e ever known. Like Maurice [Ch]evalier, "I remember it well". I took

15

World Cup Final: CHAMPAGNE CRICK

Almost the final run of the World Cup Final. Thomson was caught, off a No Ball, and the West Indian spectators, believing the match to be over, stormed onto the pitch.

WEST INDIES TOUR
OF AUSTRALIA **1975-1976**

1976–1980

The Centenary Test celebration coincided with the planning of a great upheaval. Not since the splitting of the atom had there been a division of such magnitude, at least in the world of cricket.

Chastened by the Australian Cricket Board's refusal to negotiate a television contract with the Channel Nine network, Kerry Packer, Nine's chairman, signed up most of the game's major personalities. World Series Cricket became a competitor of the establishment game for the next two Australian summers. Packer fought and won a restraint of trade case in the High Court in London after his players had been barred by the International Cricket Conference. On the field he guided changes that had a profound effect on the look of the game. Night cricket and coloured clothing were spectacular innovations, and the limited-overs game was re-defined by the introduction of restricted field placements.

Like colour television, first seen in Australia in 1974, these initiatives are taken for granted today, but like the first cricket reports on radio in 1924, they were momentous at the time. Bitter relations between the two competitors were mercifully resolved in 1979 when Packer was granted his wish and given the television rights to Australian cricket.

Sir Donald Bradman's contribution to the 1978–79 ABC book highlights an important revenue source for Australian cricket that is about to dry up. The largesse of the Benson & Hedges company has guaranteed the solvency of the game, assisted by the bountiful receipts from day/night matches. Pay television may develop into the new cash cow for cricket, but how demanding will its owners be in exploiting the public appetite for one-day games? They will be hoping that the appetite is insatiable.

Some television viewers could still watch the major matches free, following the ABC's pyrrhic victory in court. Channel Nine had the exclusive rights to city viewers, but the ABC took the consolation prize of showing the Test matches in the bush. It was an expensive rights deal, reportedly costing $200 000 a year, rising by $100 000 for each additional year of the ten-year contract. From here on the catchcry on national radio became 'Watch the cricket on ABC Radio'. The vivid wireless illusions continued, led by the 'game is not the same without McGilvray'.

Ray Steele

The Australian Broadcasting Commission has given unequalled support to cricket for more years than I care to remember, so I regard it as a privilege to write an introduction to the ABC Cricket Book covering the Centenary Test Match. The first Test Match was played at the MCG between Australia and England in March 1877. March 1977, exactly 100 years later, will see the greatest cricket invasion of Australia ever. The Australian Cricket Board, thanks to the generous support received from the Australian Broadcasting Commission, the Benson and Hedges Company, Qantas, TAA, and the Melbourne Hilton Hotel, hopes to stage a Centenary Test Match never to be forgotten. An intensive program of celebrations has been planned. Invitations will be issued to every living England and Australian player who has taken part in a Test Match between the two countries to come to Melbourne for the Centenary Test as our guest. What famous names this will include! The mere thought evokes countless memories of the great matches, the personalities, the skills, and the controversies, that have made Tests between England and Australia something special for 100 years. Other countries may play us, and defeat us, but somehow a Test Match between England and Australia has, in both countries, a special significance. It is the traditional challenge between cricket's oldest enemies, yet greatest friends, and there can be no doubt that this great game of cricket has formed one of the greatest bonds between our two countries.

I extend to all our visitors and spectators a very hearty welcome. What friendships will be renewed! May your visit be a truly memorable and happy one, and may the standard of play and the sportsmanship live up to this great occasion.

RAY STEELE
Chairman, Co-ordinating Committee for Centenary Test Celebrations
President Victorian Cricket Association
Hon. Treasurer Australian Cricket Board
Treasurer 1961 Tour of England
Manager 1964 Australian Tour of England, India and Pakistan
Manager 1972 Australian Tour of England.

2

CENTENARY TEST **1977**

AUSTRALIA'S GREAT CRICKET AUTHOR RAY ROBINSON LOOKS BACK OVER THE YEARS OF ENGLAND-AUSTRALIA TESTS AND SAYS . . .

Great players make great teams

RAY ROBINSON

Graph showing booms and busts on the Stock Exchange scarcely shows ?per rises and falls than the fortunes ? country in international cricket.

?eplace the bulls and bears of share ?lings with batsmen and bowlers of ? sides and similar reactions are felt ?om pleasure to panic and all points in ?ween.

?hough they make patriots despair at ?s, the cycles of successes and ?acks are as inevitable as nightfall. ?hout their dips and rallies Test cricket ?ld lack one of its greatest sources of ?rest, unpredictability.

?his was demonstrated afresh by the ?tenary Test in Melbourne, with each ? changing the crowd's expectation of ?ch side would win. Though Australia ?vailed by 45 runs in the last hour ?land's captain Tony Greig and ?ager Ken Barrington went home ?mistic about the coming five-Test ?es.

?ut, to begin, Australia's loss of seven ?ts in a row, starting in 1885, had come ? sharp surprise. The eclipse followed ?ydney victory wherein massive hitter ?rge Bonner, 6ft 6in, had battered ?land's bowlers for 111 in a session, ?first 85 minutes after tea.

?hough Australia still had the first ?vler nicknamed "Demon," saturnine ?d Spofforth, the side went from 1885 to ?8 before they broke the Englishmen's ?uence. Mostly, the Englishmen have ?n more skilful on rain-softened turf ? when Australia finally won in this Test ?ord's, 27 wickets fell in a day. The ?dliest pair were Charles Turner ("The ?ror") and left-hand spinner Jack ?ris, who shared 18 wickets in the Test.

Turner's capture of 101 English wickets in 17 Tests has been unequalled, though O'Reilly came close with 102 in 19 Tests between 1932 and 1938.

Though rain and the luck of the game — especially spilt chances — often affect results. Years of watching Tests in half a dozen countries convince me that cycles of results are chiefly governed by a team's possession of truly great players. This was evident as far back as Jack Blackham's wicketkeeping, Spofforth, Turner, Richardson and Peel's bowling, Bannerman, Grace and Murdoch's batting. Their deeds largely decided games.

11

The trend has been for England to choose specialist bowlers and batsmen, with few all-rounders of type Australia has seldom been without. One Australian all-rounder, George Giffen, was so tireless that on voyages to England he helped shovel coal in the stokehold to keep fit for the tour. This South Australian, together with swing bowler Alf Noble (a great captain) and Yorkshire left-hand spinner Wilfred Rhodes are the only three with 100 or more wickets in Anglo-Australian Tests besides totalling 1000 runs.

Giffen's faith in his off-spin was so great that team-mates once pressed vice-captain Hugh Trumble to suggest that he take himself off. George replied: "Yes, I was thinking of that, I'll go on at the other end."

Off-field changes began to creep in. "Plum" Warner (later Sir Pelham) the eighth amateur captain of England in Australia, was the first to have the professionals staying at the same hotel. His chief match-winners were amateur Reg Foster, whose 287 in Sydney in 1903 is highest English Test score in Australia, and professional spinner Rhodes, 31 wickets in five Tests.

Warner was known as "recoverer of the Ashes." The term Ashes had been coined after an Australian win by seven runs at the Oval in 1882. The Sporting Times published a mock RIP for English cricket, saying its ashes would be taken to Australia.

England brought forward more proof that a couple of incisive bowlers make the surest match-winners. They had Sydney Barnes, a swinger and spinner hailed as the greatest bowler ever. With Barnes (34 wickets) they paired left-hand paceman Frank Foster (32), the only instance of two Englishmen topping 30 wickets each on one visit.

In 65 years only four Englishmen have landed 30 wickets in a series in Australia — fast-medium swinger Maurice Tate, 38, fast bowler Harold Larwood, 33, swinger Alec Bedser, 30 and fast bowler John Snow, 31 in six Tests six years ago.

Only once in Anglo-Australian Tests has a country's cycle contained eight consecutive wins. It took a big man to command such triumphs, Warwick Armstrong, 6ft 3½in. A few taller men have played Tests — Greig is 6ft 7in — but none had the bulk of this hefty Victoria 21 stone. Besides keeping weighing machine repair mechanics in

SIR DONALD BRADMAN

12

employment in the early 1920s, Armstrong was a dominating all-rounder whose drives damaged fieldsmen's hands.

Test cricket today is showing effects of a flow-on from changes he introduced and developments that followed.

After the first World War had prevented Australia having a Test for eight years captain J. W. H. T. Douglas led the Englishmen into the field against Armstrong's Australians. Most were of middle height, including the premier batsman, Jack Hobbs. Eying them, a spectator called "Which is Hobbs?" A barracker shouted back: "The one in the white pants."

Among the wittiest shafts from Australian barrackers was one suggesting that J. W. H. T. Douglas' initials stood for Johnny Won't Hit To-day. Douglas' stand-firm batting had no effective answer to the curving flight and sharp turn of googly bowler Arthur Mailey, whose 36 wickets in four Tests are a record for an Australian in a series in this country.

In England Mailey took 10 for 66 against Gloucestershire and gave his book the title "10 for 66 and All That." In his usual deadpan manner he used to say the batting was so weak he could have taken 10 for 49, but it wouldn't have sounded so good.

As skipper in 1921 Armstrong shook England's batting with the first use of fast bowlers opening from both ends — Jack Gregory downwind and Ted McDonald into it. At Trent Bridge a Gregory bouncer top-edged by Ernest Tyldesley fell from his head to the stumps, bowling him, amid hoots.

In almost a parallel mishap 46 years later Australian opener Ric McCosker's jaw was fractured by a Willis bumper in the Centenary Test. With his jaw wired and head bandaged McCosker came in gingerly with a runner in the second innings. He pluckily partnered Rod Marsh for almost an hour and a half, enabling Marsh to become the first Australian wicketkeeper to make a Test century against England.

The long hop, that Jack Gregory did when bowling was an approach leap that made cartoonists think of kangaroos. Jack was the most spectacular all-rounder the game had seen, frightening bowler, left-hand hitter and diving slipfielder whose record of 15 catches in one series still stands. (See note under Most Catches in a Series, page 66).

He was the most eye-catching of an ex-soldier group from the A.I.F. who gave cricket its first impetus after the horrors of the first World War. A nephew of Australia's first captain, Gregory was a little early for radio, which caused a great upsurge of interest when it coincided with unprecedented deeds by Don Bradman.

Fast-medium Maurice Tate's swing, pace off the pitch and stamina enabled him to set a record 38 wickets for a visitor in a series in Australia. At the end of an over in which two wholehearted appeals for leg-before-wicket were turned down Maurice lumbered along to the batsman, Bert Oldfield, cupped his big hand by his mouth and said something in his low voice. If watchers thought he was complaining they were well out. What he murmured was "Hot, ain't it?"

BILL O'REILLY

13

Before Bradman became the only man to total over 600 runs (974) in five Tests in England in 1930, Surrey captain Percy Fender had predicted his batting would be in trouble on English wickets. Out for 252 in his first knock on the Oval, Don said "I hope Fender was at the ground today." Reminded of his forecast 47 years later, at 84 Percy said at the Centenary Test: "It was an indiscretion of youth."

The two-bowler pattern changed to flight and spin when leg-spinners Clarrie Grimmett and Bill O'Reilly bowled most of the overs and took most wickets for captain Bill Woodfull in the 1930s. It was a time when Walter Hammond's handsome batting was flourishing and Sir Leonard Hutton was developing the concentration to bat 13 hours 20 minutes to outscore Sir Donald Bradman's Test record 334 by 30 runs.

Englishmen saw their team win a series against Australia at home for the first time in 27 years when Hutton won at the Oval in 1953. Australia entered a period of having to be content with seven wins in 24 Tests against four countries in the 1950s. Fortunes touched bottom when master off-spinner Jim Laker often screwed unplayable turn to take 46 wickets in the 1956 series in England, 19 of them in a Manchester Test.

Gregory and McDonald (a Tasmanian, like Max Walker) were the fearsome forerunners of pairs who had startling impact on the game and brought cycles of success notably Lindwall and Miller, and Lillee and Thomson. England caught on with Harold Larwood and Bill Voce, unnerving in the bodyline combat in 1932-3, with Tyson, Statham and Trueman in the fifties and with Snow and Willis in Ray Illingworth's force.

Ray Lindwall and Keith Miller, backed by Bill Johnston's whiplike left wrist, were the leading phalanx in the attack directed by Bradman after World War II and by Lindsay Hassett, after his Services XI had helped English folk forget the blitz and the blackout.

As with Jack Gregory, Keith Miller was the kind of cricketer every watching boy would love to be — he could hit the longest six, bowl the quickest ball (among others) and bring off blinding catches. Miller drove or swept 31 sixes in Tests. English writer Irving Rosenwater says

SIR LEONARD HUTTON

Keith hit at least one six over seven of the nine Test grounds on which he played.

Ray Lindwall's bowling, fast and accurate, was the most telling factor in several years of post-war Tests. With a shorter run-up (13 strides) than any current Test paceman, Ray usually completed an eight-ball over in four minutes. He was first to show that a fast bowler could take 200 Test wickets and hit total 228 is third among Australians after leg-spinner Richie Benaud 248 and paceman Graham McKenzie 246.

Players nicknamed McKenzie Garth because his superb physique reminded them of a character in an adventure strip. He needed all his strength to stand up to heavy duty in the role of sole fast bowler in most of his 60 Tests. For captain Bob Simpson in England in 1964 McKenzie took 29 wickets, two more than the record for an Australian fast bowler, then shared by McDonald in 1921 and Johnston in 1948.

Dennis Lillee lifted this record to 31 with superb fast bowling in 1972, when his fellow West Australian Bob Massie captured 16 wickets in his first Test, a triumph of either-way swing at Lord's.

At the time the selectors replaced Bill Lawry as captain with Ian Chappell in 1971 Australia had not tasted victory for

RAY LINDWALL

KEITH MILLER

nine Tests (five losses and four left drawn against South Africa and England).

Television has stimulated an even greater upsurge of cricket interest than radio generated when Bradman was breaking records. Eventful cricket since Ian Chappell became captain, followed by his brother Greg, brought 30 finishes in 42 Tests, a higher proportion than in the preceding period.

I believe countless more people have been stirred by Dennis Lillee's bowling than by any other Australian in cricket history, whether they thronged to grounds for the real atmosphere or saw his arrowy rush on sets in their homes.

Just as TAB betting turnover is a truer guide to racing interest than racecourse attendances, Post Office dial-a-score calls, in addition to radio and television audiences, reveal more of the width of interest than ground attendances. The total soars highest during Australia v England cricket Tests.

On the Australians' 1975 tour of England 22 million people dialled the British cricket score service — 10 million for the World Cup and 12 million for the four Tests.

* Ray Robinson is author of On Top Down Under, a history of 100 years of Test captains.

ALEC BEDSER

The Unbelievable Centenary Test

BY KEITH DUNSTAN, ONE OF MELBOURNE'S BEST-KNOWN COLUMNISTS

IF you called on some fancy advertising agency, the sort that specialises in creating prime ministers and such, they couldn't have done better. You'd say: "Look here, we want drama every day. We want a script which will go the full five days with a situation full of brinkmanship at stumps each evening.

"Oh, by the way, Her Majesty the Queen is arriving during the middle of the last afternoon. Be a good fellow and have it brilliantly exciting then, with a decision by six o'clock."

As it turned out the real story was so improbable I doubt whether they would have dared turn it in.

I can't remember a Test match when so many pundits have been so wrong for such a long period of time.

I mean, remember those headlines after the first day.

AUSTRALIA BOUNCED OUT FOR 138
AUSTRALIA TOTTERING
AUSTRALIA IS ON HER KNEES

And there was much talk of Tony Greig's brilliant strategy.

Then England was all out for 95. A new headline read

LION SLAUGHTERED
BY THE KANGAROO

I remember sitting up the top of the Eastern stand and there was a tap on my shoulder: "I say, I've just come in. That figure on the scoreboard, 95, for England's first innings. Misprint eh?"

"No Sir, that's quite correct."

The old gentleman gasped back into his seat and didn't say another word.

This particular pundit was more astray than most. Last until Thursday? I suggested it could all be over by Monday afternoon, and it was amusing to speculate how the Victorian Cricket Association could entertain the crowd for

'Derek Randall ... small, jaunty, you could easily imagine him on a bike, delivering telegrams for the PMG'.

16

e rest of the time. They could turn on me stunts in the manner of a hundred ars ago. Why not a hot-air balloon cent, or a grand tug-o-war between the o teams?

All right, Australia went on to make 419 the second innings, declaring after nine ckets down. From my little collection of ourite headlines I can offer these:

THERE'S NO WAY WE CAN LOSE, d Melbourne's Sun News Pictorial.

AUSTRALIA HAS TEST MATCH UNDER LOCK AND KEY, rred The Australian.

As Messrs Randall, Amiss, Greig et alia ught back, by lunch time on Thursday, odness gracious, it seemed yes . . . ey had been set the impossible of 463 to n . . . by heavens, they might make it. That very English typewriter of awford White was in a state of ecstasy. wrote: "Glory, Glory, Glory, the Poms e not taking it lying down."

When it gets past 5 p.m. the radio mmentators at the MCG never fail to y "The seagulls have all come down m the tops of the stands and the adows are lengthening across the ound." That's how it was when Knott ally succumbed to Lillee and it was all er. This was another downright probable line in the script. England just ed to make it by 45 runs, exactly the rgin by which Australia won the ginal Test match 100 years ago.

Please forgive me if I just let loose the od of memories from that marvellous eek. In the Members' Stand there was s beautiful benign atmosphere engen- red by old times; ex-Test bowling Hans eling had this idea of bringing together ery ex-Test player from either side.

Sometimes it was a delicate exercise nnecting the old image that was in e's mind with the present-day ntleman who was sitting in the stand. at balding greying chap with the bare me. Yes, yes, it is . . . Sir Leonard tton. Or that portly chap with the tton chop whiskers straight out of ckwick Papers. It couldn't be. Yes, it's dfrey Evans. And that squat stern oking chap, in his sixties I'll be bound. e'd be a director of British Leyland or mething like that. It's Cyril Washbrook. And those two chaps, incredible, ey're putting on their old vaudeville act

of 25 years ago, same shirt, same tie, same suit, same shoes — you still can't tell them apart and they haven't changed a whit — Alec and Eric Bedser.

The biggest shock was Harold Larwood, such a little chap, quite thin, under 11 stone. His old colleagues Voce and Bowes towered above him head and shoulders. Could he really have been the fastest bowler in the world?

At first he refused utterly to come to the Centenary Test, and only after intense persuasion did he agree. When it was all over I asked him about this: "I was shy," he said. "I thought I was too old to meet all these people. Now I wouldn't have missed it for worlds. What I didn't realise was everybody else had grown old too, and we were here together."

I asked him what he thought of the boozy predatory crowds of the 1970s. "They're nothing," he replied. "You should have heard what they did to me in 1932. They weren't cheering me like they do to Lillee. They were hooting and jeering. And if the cheers inspired Lillee, the hoots certainly inspired me. It made me work just that much harder."

Jack Ikin had grey hair, but he hadn't changed that much. Now what was that

'Or that portly chap with the mutton chop whiskers straight out of Pickwick Papers. It couldn't be. Yes, it's Godfrey Evans'.

17

famous incident in which he was involved with Bradman in 1946?

"It was during the First Test in Brisbane," he said. "I was fielding at second slip and I caught Bradman when he was 28. Oh, he was out, there's no doubt about it. Everyone in the English team thought so, but the umpire gave him not out. Bradman then went on to make 187.

"This was Bradman's first return appearance after the war, you see. He was wondering whether he still had his old powers. He said later that if he had gone out then when I caught him, he would have retired and never played again."

The most vivid memory of that match, the one that will last for ever, is of Dennis Lillee on the second morning, on Sunday, when we all should have been at matins. There he was with that extraordinarily long run, hair askew, shirt unbuttoned down towards the waist and a strange similarity to the ancient pictures of the 'Demon' Spofforth. It was a picture of relentless, controlled action. As he came in his elbows were high and he changed the ball from his left hand to the right, first three or four little steps, then giant strides.

All the time the crowd chanted **LILL-EE, LILL-EE, LILL-EE,** an awe-inspiring sound. If you stood under the concrete stands in Bay 9 it actually hurt the ear drum. When the time came to bowl to Amiss, this war cry was quite terrifying. One Lillee bouncer was the most vicious I have seen. Amiss hopped awkwardly aside on one foot and his cap fell to the ground.

The crowd worship of Lillee was greater than anything I have witnessed in 30 years of cricket watching. Even when Lillee came in to bat the crowd went berserk. For him to lift his bat was worth a wild cheer, for him to actually make contact with the ball was marvellous, but for Lillee to make a run was pure heaven and any fieldsman who stopped that ball was justifiably hooted.

The Lillee chant never stopped. Even when I was going home in the train at 6.45 p.m. the lads in our carriage were still chanting **LILL-EE, LILL-EE.** They got their money's worth: 6/26 in the first innings, 5/139 in the second.

My next vivid memory is of Derek Randall, voted the man of the match. What an unlikely fellow he seemed for the hope of England. Small, jaunty, you could easily imagine him on a bike, delivering telegrams. During the entire past Test series in Australia we witnessed what can only be described as the weak collapse of England against Lillee.

Well, this PMG-looking bloke outrageously taunted Lillee, grinned at him,

'That balding, greying chap with the bare dome. Yes, yes, it is . . . Sir Leonard Hutton'.

18

he crowd worship of Lillee was greater than anything I have witnessed in 30 years of icket watching'. Chaired by Gary Cosier and Greg Chappell.

19

sang, whistled, pointed to the part in his head when a bumper whistled over his head.

One time he pointed at the wicket and suggested that Lillee might try bowling at it. He earned a screaming bumper the very next ball, but he didn't appear to mind. He scored 174 runs, more than he scored in the entire four Tests in India.

One remembers too the courage of Amiss, the defiance of Tony Greig, Rick McCosker taking a ball full in the face then returning in the second innings, jaw wired, face like a pumpkin, so many bandages that he couldn't hear, and still managing to make 25 runs.

Oh, I tell you, it had everything. There was the century by Rod Marsh, the first century ever by an Australian wicket-keeper against England. And remember when England was four down for 320 and we were just beginning to think, by golly, they could make it. Greg Chappell was bowling, Randall flashed and it appeared that the ball went straight into Marsh's gloves, a spectacular catch. The crowd hollered and Umpire Brooks raised his hand.

Marsh then ran forward to signal that it wasn't a catch and Randall wasn't out. You couldn't have any lack of sportsmanship in a centenary Test. Marsh put his arm around Chappell's shoulders and said "Sorry Greg."

It goes on and on. Remember the brilliant fielding, the catching of Greg Chappell, the glorious throws of Walters from the boundary and the sensational debut of David Hookes. If Randall looks like a messenger boy, then the fair-haired, 21-year-old Hookes looks as if he should be in the front row of the Trinity choir.

He doesn't smile like Randall, but his determination is something to see. No one will forget his style after he was taunted by Tony Greig. The choirboy hit him for five consecutive fours in the one over.

Oh yes, what a Test. What a Test. It makes a man wonder what they can possibly do for an encore in England. And another thing, stand up all those who were saying a short time back that cricket was finished.

'Rick McCosker . . . jaw wired, face like a pumpkin'.

20

*ere was the century by Rod Marsh, the first century ever by an Australian
ket-keeper against England'.*

21

AUSTRALIA TOUR
OF ENGLAND 1977

Cricket,

past, present and future

SIR DONALD BRADMAN REFLECTS...

Don Bradman captained Australia in 19 Test Matches against England. He won the toss 6 times ... 5 in Australia and once at Lord's (1948 England Captain Norman Yardley). The late Walter Hammond won the toss in all Tests in the 1938 series, in which Bradman captained.

Don Bradman's successor Lindsay Hassett won 9 out of his 10 tosses against England, including all five in England in 1953.

Bradman called 'Heads' and when Hassett was asked whether he called Heads or Tails he replied 'as far as I can remember I called "Heads" at all times. I may have been working on the principle that after the Don's experience "Heads" were due for a run'.

Bernard Kerr, Director of Sporting Programs at the Australian Broadcasting Commission, has asked me to contribute an article for the ABC book covering the visit of the Englishmen in the 1978/9 season.

There are many subjects I could write about but it seems opportune for me to help clarify an issue concerning which there is a great deal of misunderstanding in the community.

Last year, conventional cricket went through the convulsions of having to compete with a private promoter. In some respects it was a case of history repeating itself, though modernity brought a different slant.

Any student of the game will know that the first English cricket team to visit Australia was brought out by a firm of caterers, Messrs Spiers & Pond, who allegedly made a handsome profit out of the venture.

In the early days of English cricket, professional teams dominated the scene,

and we can all read about George Parr's 'roving band of mercenaries' (as they were dubbed) in the middle of the 19th century.

Wealthy patrons of the sport organised matches and tours, one of the most notable being Lord Sheffield, whose 1891/2 team to Australia marked his presentation to this country of the magnificent Shield which bears his name and for which the States have proudly competed ever since.

Some teams were a mixture of amateurs and professionals. One would normally assume that the professionals would be the most skilled and highly paid, but this was not always the case. Dr WG Grace, the greatest name in English cricket history and the finest player of his day, came to Australia as an amateur and was paid a sum far in excess of that received by any professional member of the party. Understandably this differential was scarcely welcomed by the pros.

Australian players dictated the terms for

Dr WG Grace, the finest player of his day

One can only assume from history that the gradual development of cricket, both nationally and internationally, brought with it the absolute necessity of creating an accepted management and/or controlling body at each level.

Early this century the Australian Cricket Council was formed, to be followed by the Australian Board of Control for International Cricket (now called The Australian Cricket Board), only to have it's properly established authority challenged by six of the leading players in 1912.

They were promptly replaced for the tour abroad that year, and for most of the 'rebels' it was the end of their test careers.

From then on, despite minor problems, the system of State Association and Board management was accepted as the best in the overall interests of cricket.

I have been involved at every level of cricket, from the country boy who was invited to perform before the selectors, to the rank and file of grade players, and ultimately to Captain of Australia, Chairman of Selectors and Chairman of the Board, a progression which in our democratic system is open to every boy in the land irrespective of his background or status.

My experience has given me an intimate knowledge of how the system works.

It would be absurd to suggest that all the Board's decisions have been correct — or that all the causes I espoused were the wisest, but there can be no doubt that the Board has administered cricket honestly and conscientiously in a sincere effort to do what was best for the game.

I have heard and read the most unjustified criticism of the Board and often found it hard to discern whether the cause was bias, ignorance, or even occasionally a more sinister reason.

One sometimes hears that not enough former players are administrators.

I agree with this view but the former players are themselves to blame because our democratic set-up makes it possible for anyone with ability and energy, and who is prepared to give voluntary service, to gain access to an administrative post.

It is a great pity that more players don't aspire to become administrators because (a) it would enable them to put something back into the game and (b) they would

their early tours of England and it is well documented that in 1899 when Victor Trumper was first invited to tour England, the other players only agreed to him going if his fee was a half share of the sum which each of the others would receive from their split up of the tour profits.

His success on tour caused the decision to be changed but I make the point, and I believe it is a most important point, that in all teams under the auspices of the Australian Cricket Board, either at home or when touring, the most humble performer is paid precisely the same as the most illustrious.

The Australian Cricket Board publicly discloses the remuneration of the players coming under its jurisdiction.

We are not told what the most recent private promoter is doing in this regard but I would be surprised if there were not wide differences between the amounts being received by the participating players.

14

learn at first hand more about the problems.

Take the State Cricket Associations as examples. How many people, players or members of the public, bother to ascertain what it costs to run an Association, or where the money goes.

For First Class cricket to have an existence there must be an organisation running a competition such as our Saturday grade club matches.

Players for these clubs are fostered through schools, junior bodies and Country Associations and at great expense the system provides them with opportunities to develop their skills and so gravitate to Sheffield Shield and Test status.

That is the training ground. What of the cost?

The briefest look at the sort of expense involved discloses that in South Australia alone for the year ended 30th June 1978, direct Cricket Association costs included in round figures —

Grants to Clubs	16 000
Competition expenses	31 000
General cricket expenses	9 000
Schoolboy competition	3 000
Coaching	12 000
Country cricket	6 000
	$77 000

Donald Bradman — 1932

In addition, to run the organisation, there must be an office, a secretary and his staff, together with the many resultant expenses.

All of this merely to give the players opportunities, and long before you get to the First Class ranks.

At Sheffield Shield level the expenses continue. To send the South Australian teams on interstate tours last year cost more than $31 000, with no off-setting income, because gate money is retained by the home State.

The South Australian matches at home produced losses exceeding $22 000.

A similar pattern would doubtless emerge from perusing the figures of each of the competing states.

It is crystal clear that you must get to the Test level before there is any hope of making a profit. And not all Test matches are profitable either.

The expense structure has materially worsened in recent years due to inflation and other factors and from the foregoing it can be seen how essential it is for money to be ploughed back into the game to keep it viable.

It is perfectly true that until fairly recently the remuneration of cricketers has been at a low level. But the Australian scene was one of predominantly amateur sportsmen normally working at other jobs who took pride in representing their State or Country at sport and who regarded any monetary return as mainly a reimbursement of out-of-pocket expenses.

Nobody was compelled to play. You were invited and were always free to decline at any level.

That is still the case, though one detects in some quarters an almost incredible belief that if a player, having taken advantage of all the facilities provided at the expense of others, has thereby managed to develop special talent, he now has a right to be chosen and to virtually name his own fee.

On the English scene, I am not aware of

the precise emoluments paid to professional players, but even if they have been on the low side, one needs to see the complete picture before forming a judgment. For instance it is the custom for leading players to be allocated a benefit match (many have had more than one) after a period of service and I have written dozens of articles for inclusion in the booklets prepared to boost the players' receipts.

I am given to understand that the income from such benefit matches has always been adjudged as free of tax and it takes little imagination to deduce what a $25 000 benefit would be worth on a tax paid basis.

Good luck to the players. They deserve to be rewarded and they and their friends work extremely hard to make a success of these matches. My sole aim in mentioning the matter is to indicate that the basic pay of a player is not the only way in which he may be rewarded for his services.

It has been claimed that the entry of a modern private promoter into the field was responsible for bringing financial rewards to the players which otherwise they would not have received.

The Chairman of the Australian Cricket Board has published in full detail how the Board had previously embarked upon a policy of paying the players the maximum it could afford after taking into consideration it's over-all responsibility to Australian cricket at all levels.

This policy decision was made and was operating before any modern private promoter entered the field. Moreover the player's representatives were informed of the Board policy and had expressed satisfaction with it.

Better payments were made possible by revenue coming into the game from sponsors, a medium that was virtually non-existent until quite recently.

If anything should now happen to kill that sponsorship revenue there is no possible way the receipts from gate money or previous conventional sources could sustain the current level of payments to players and the structures at lower levels which are essential if the players are to develop their talents to a point which will attract worthwhile audiences or enable them to compete successfully at international level.

Occasionally the old fallacious argument is trotted out that other sportsmen, golfers and tennis players for instance, are much better paid than cricketers.

Protagonists conveniently ignore the essential comparisons which must go with such a contention.

Except on rare and special occasions, golfers and tennis players pay their own travel and accommodation costs. They compete as individuals and the big money goes to the winners.

They are able to compete in the big circuits of the USA, Japan and Europe, vastly different areas from some of the cricketing regions.

A great American professional can fly to England, win the British Open, and be

Bradman Stand — SCG

home again in a matter of days, whereas to compete on an English cricket tour, an Australian must travel in a party of about 18 for some 4 to 5 months, all travel and accommodation costs paid by the administration, and, as I said earlier, with every player in the party getting the same remuneration.

One is sometimes regaled by stories of how players have finished on the scrap heap because of having followed a sporting career.

No doubt that has happened. Why? If a fellow lacks enough balance and intelligence to make a choice which will be in his best interests, or succumbs to the temptations which can intrude, then he can scarcely blame the sport.

What about the myriads of individuals whose lives have been brightened, enriched, and lifted onto a higher plane because of what sport has done for them in terms of health, opportunities, personal

16

development and human relationships?

I get rather irritated listening to 'my rights', and I hear too seldom of 'my responsibilities'. And the same criticism is not by any means confined to sport.

There are thousands of cricket lovers in Australia voluntarily putting many hours a week into the game they love without thought of financial reward.

But they derive enormous satisfaction from their labours.

It would be difficult to name a sport where the intangible rewards are so great.

It is fifty years this year since my test career started and I must very shortly vacate my active administrative posts to make way for someone younger and more vigorous.

Despite the trials and tribulations, many heartaches and even moments of despair, they have all been far out-weighed by the intangibles I referred to, and for which I remain most grateful.

I think that would be the verdict of all those who have conscientiously tried to serve the wonderful game of which they were privileged to be a part.

I share the view expressed by the late Sir Robert Menzies when he said 'if I reach Valhalla I hope to find cricketers sitting on my right and left because I am happy in their company'.

During the luncheon adjournment of the second day's play in the 200th Test played between Australia and England at Lord's, the late Sir Robert Menzies visited the BBC's Broadcasting Box to talk with our Editor Alan McGilvray about some of the past Australian and England players he had seen. Sir Robert talked about several players including Sir Donald Bradman. In extending our best wishes to Sir Donald for a happy and healthy 70th year it is appropriate that Sir Robert Menzies' comments about him should be included. This is an extract taken from the recording made in June 1968.

'I saw Don Bradman bat the first time he batted on the Melbourne Cricket Ground and some of his strokes, you might say, were agricultural and some of the people sitting around me were not impressed, but I felt then there was something about him and I said "we will be watching this fellow for the next 20 years because he's got it" . . . of course he had.

'The whole point about Bradman, which perhaps has not always been understood is that Bradman hit every ball on it's merit and to where it ought to go. If a ball called for a shot to the covers it got it and went to the covers. It was the inevitability of Bradman's batting which perhaps deprived him of the ultimate praise of some of the onlookers because many thought there was nothing inevitable about Napper McCabe who was a beautiful batsman, nothing inevitable about Charlie Macartney . . . he was magnificent . . . nothing inevitable about Frank Woolley, and so you could go right around the circle. There was always a chance with these batsmen that something might happen, but with Don Bradman there was an inevitability about his play.

'And you know one of the reasons for that is it has not always been understood that Don Bradman was not only a superb producer of batsmen's strokes . . . a magnificent captain . . . a first class field. He happens to have been a highly intelligent man in anybody's language.

'He seldom ever discussed cricket with me, why should he . . . you know you don't discuss cricket with the incompetent.

'But he used to discuss with me International finance, the economic movements in the Country and I used to say to myself, if I was so satisfied that I knew more about these things than Don I would be rather proud, in fact, I might almost be kept as Prime Minister. He is a great man.

'Like Jack Hobbs he has a place amongst the immortals . . . you know Alan, I say among the immortals for as you know I am bigotted. I think that in all the sporting arenas the immortals will be produced by cricketers.

'Cricket has been my greatest joy, but Alan to come around here to have this talk with you I have had to go without my poached salmon, which our mutual friend the President of the MCC Arthur Gilligan, who has so many friends in Australia, promised me.'

Ed. — As can be imagined Arthur did not allow Sir Robert to go without his poached salmon.

17

The 1980s

1980–1984

The restoration of Australian cricket after the World Series upheaval was painful and acrimonious. During the great divide, forty-one-year-old Bob Simpson was recalled to the captaincy, leading a weakened Australian team to victory over India, led by the patka'd Bishen Bedi.

In the Caribbean the West Indies was far too strong, until its World Series Cricket players were stood down and the series ended with Australia, almost victorious in Jamaica, denied by a riot. Alan McGilvray gave a graphic account of this bottle throwing, bullet buzzing drama which can be heard on the audio tape, *More Cricket Flashbacks*.

The 1978-79 Ashes series was a disaster, a callow Graham Yallop proving no match for the shrewd Mike Brearley, and England won 5–1 against inexperienced opposition. Kim Hughes successfully took over at the end of the summer against Pakistan and led young teams to the World Cup in England and then to India for six Tests. Both tours underlined Australia's lack of experience and when peace was restored in 1979 the captaincy reverted to Greg Chappell, who appeared refreshed after the tough competition of World Series Cricket.

Over the next five years Chappell and Hughes shared the leadership, Chappell opting out of the 1981 Ashes series and the 1983 World Cup due to family and business responsibilities. Physically the demands of playing and leading had taken their toll. Hughes never appeared to have the total support of the senior players Marsh and Lillee, and the team performance may well have improved had the more respected Marsh been in charge during Chappell's absence.

Hughes's task was difficult. Unlike his successor, Border, the strain of the captaincy ultimately affected his batting. Having won the first Test in 1981, a combination of Botham's brilliance and injuries to key bowlers Lawson and Hogg turned the series and Brearley seized the moment. Chappell resumed control, levelling series with the West Indies and India in 1981–82 and regaining the Ashes in 1982–83, scoring two centuries. Pakistan's 1983–84 visit was the curtain call for Chappell, Marsh and Lillee.

The focus on limited-overs cricket sharpened after the reunification. Big crowds attended the day/night matches, guaranteeing the financial success of our summer's entertainment.

Stuff of centuries
not always great

by John Arlott

t was of moment to me when John Arlott accepted my invitation, during the Centenary
est at Lord's, to contribute to the ABC Cricket Book. John and I have enjoyed a long and
pleasant association in so many commentary
boxes . . . our first combined commentary was
at Trent Bridge Nottingham in the 1948 Austra-
ia-England Test. I shall forever remember the
reception he received when it was announced,
over the Public Address system, that John
Arlott had just given his last Test Match broad-
ast. There was a momentary silence, as
though it could not be believed, then a
crescendo of applause, of lengthy duration,
rom the thousands of spectators who at-
ended Lord's. I watched him throughout this
moving occasion and I know it all meant so
much to him. Play stopped as the players
urned to face the commentary box and add
heir applause. Surely a moment of history, as
 truly great contributor to cricket . . . to
players . . . and to millions of listeners, ended
n incomparable career. Well done John Arlott
 . . very well done. — Ed.

The simple, but conclusive, difference be-
ween the two Centenary Test Matches was
he weather. At Melbourne, in 1977, the sun
hone for a series of happy and absorbing
ays of meaningful cricket which pro-
ressed to a healthy and well received out-
ome. Even the detail of the result — a win
or Australia by 45 runs — was a felicitous
cho of the match it celebrated, the first
est, played on the same ground in 1877
when the home country also won by 45
uns.

To be sure, no other stadium in the world
ould match the generosity and suitability
f the facilities of the greatest cricket
round in the world with all its modernisa-
ons carried out for the 1956 Olympics.
ord's, though, had adequate space for its
lustrious visitors — all who had taken part
 Anglo-Australian Tests in England — in Q
tand; and the marquee afforded satisfac-
ory catering facilities. Their hotel — the

Russell — was not within such convenient
walking distance as the Melbourne Hilton of
the MCG — but well organized transport
was provided. The TCCB dinner on the Saturday night could hardly have been a better
or less trammelled occasion. Their fellow
guests fully understood the situation and
the players were not harassed.

Those privileged to listen to the conversations there heard the sound of cricket history, relished in contemplation, the edge of
old hostilities rounded by mature understanding. The photographs taken by Patrick
Eagar of the Test players of the two
countries who gathered at Lord's on the
Saturday are historic records. The autograph hunters had never had such an opportunity and those with an eye for history
— or even adequate checking facilities —
had a splendid haul.

Because the sun shone at Melbourne, the
cricket ran smoothly and according to the
captains' reasonable expectations. Strategy could be defeated but it was never dis-
torted. At Lord's, too much was rendered
shapeless by rain and bad light which cost
the match ten hours of playing time.

Thus was a finish prevented; and the late
start of play on Saturday led to some un-
pleasant scenes. Such was the anger of
certain MCC members sitting in front of the
pavilion at the delay that the English captain
was struck; one umpire seized by the
throat and the other jostled to the ground in
behaviour which Greg Chappell described
as 'the worst I have seen by members anywhere in the world'. Ironically, that recalls
the fact that the Test marked by this match
— that of 1880 at The Oval — was delayed as
far through season — and, indeed, almost
did not take place at all — because of ill-will
caused by crowd rioting in the match between Lord Harris's English XI and New
South Wales at Sydney during the previous
winter.

43

Finally, by depriving the players of the time in which a clear cut result might have been achieved, the weather pitched the end of the match into a frustrating draw.

The Australian players had made the trip out of season and, hence, completely lacking in match fitness. The savage English summer — the worst within human memory — gave them little chance of serious play, and when they lost to Nottinghamshire by an innings in the weekend preceding the Centenary Test, and England took the two one-day internationals with relative ease, they seemed to many English eyes, ripe for the killing.

Those who know the Australian cricketing character realized that nothing could be more dangerous than offering them pity. They soon confirmed that opinion. This was always going to be a good toss to win and Chappell duly won it and gave first innings to Australia. From that moment the issue was never in real doubt. England had no one of more than honest fast-medium to bowl on a slow, easy pitch which gave bowlers no real help but, while granting the batsmen relative security, did not encourage stroke play.

Athey bowled Lillee

The start was delayed by almost an hou and in the rest of the day Wood, the le handed Australian opening batsman with front foot bias, scored a steady and com petent century which virtually made Austra lia safe. Laird stayed with him in a firs wicket partnership of 64 and Chappell wa beginning to blossom when, playing his ha bitual flick off the pads, to general surpris placed it straight into Gatting's hands a square leg. Hughes stayed to 227 for tw by the close of play. In the hour and a qua ter of cricket possible on Friday, Wood an Yallop lost their wickets but Hughes struc the ball most handsomely and Austral were 278 for four when the rain came.

The rain of Friday had dried out and ear in the morning the Lord's staff believed start might be made on time at 11.30 b then a two-hour storm soaked the u covered old pitches at the ends of th square and made them, in the opinion the umpires — supported by the captains too dangerous to be played over A parac of 16 former captains in England-Austral Tests temporarily diverted attention fro the lack of play to recollection, salute an nostalgia. The crowd's frustration at the de lay was aggravated by alcohol: the umpire and captains were jostled as they came i and when the umpires went out to resta play, they were escorted through the men bers by four policemen.

Eventually, at a quarter-to-four, O bowled the first ball of the day and Hughe pulled it spectacularly over midwicket f six, to declare Australia's strategic pu pose. In the hour-and-a-half possible f play Hughes, Border, and Marsh hoiste Australia to 385 for five — safe from defe — Chappell declared, and Gooch and Bo cott received two balls before bad lig closed yet another day.

After the time lost on Saturday it wa agreed to extend play to 11 to 7 on Mond and 11 to 6 on Tuesday: on Monday th was possible and the players made muc headway. Lillee, sharp, resourceful, movir the ball late and varying his pace with co siderable skill, deceived Gooch into mistimed hook and bowled Athey with fine breakback. Gower, still extreme popular despite some poor Test inning was cheered in to join Boycott. Betwee them they scored 107 of England's 20 and their partnership was the only stab phase of the innings. As Lillee tired, Gow punished him for four fours but, rested after lunch, he returned to attack an England apparently secure at 137 for two, to bowl Gower; have Boycott caught at the wicket and reduce them to 151 for four, needing 35 to escape the follow-on. Then, however, Pascoe at his fiery best chopped the innings down to 173 for eight — another 13 wanted to escape following their innings. This was the decisive moment of the match. If Chappell had had another pace bowler, or if he could have called back the weary Lillee opposite Pascoe (five for ten in his savage spell), he might have knocked down Old's wicket, attacked the England batting a second time that afternoon and won the match. In the event Old heaved Bright's slow left arm for four and six and England escaped.

When Australia batted again, Old, by far the best of the English bowlers in the match, accounted for Laird and Wood to leave the innings 15 for two; but then Hughes and Chappell proceeded to make batting look simple as they set up a declaration. On the last morning Hughes stepped up to Old, bowling at honest fast medium

and drove him straight to the top deck of the pavilion; a prodigious blow. Chappell, Hughes and Border scored 83 from 14 overs before Hughes was lbw to Botham and Chappell declared, setting England 370 to win in 350 minutes. On such a wicket where batsmen could stay but had positively to take risks to attack, it was a pragmatic calculation.

Discussion afterwards centred round how hard, and how riskily, England should have gone for the win. There was little doubt that Gooch saw the win as a possibility. He struck handsomely but was frustrated by some brilliant stops in the field and by hitting the stumps at the bowler's end. Still he had scored 16 of the first 19 runs before he, yet again, walked across his stumps and was lbw. What ought England to have done then? That was, and remains, the centre of debate. Athey, coming in first wicket down, was playing for his Test life. He knew it; and it was confirmed by his eventual omission from the party to tour West Indies (though surely he must become for long an England player). Should Botham have come in him-

Geoff Dymock

Graeme Wood

self at first wicket down when his thruster, Gooch, was out? That would have been his opportunity to demonstrate the policy of attack he had advocated. He, probably alone, could have set up an English win by a fast scoring innings; and Boycott would have been a reassuring end-man. If Botham had attacked and failed, there were still plenty of men who, at need and on instructions, could have played for time. In the event Athey came, strove slowly to establish himself and went, caught bat-pad. There was never again any sign of an attempt by England to win. Gower played initially at his most felicitous and was promising to dominate when he violated the old maxim 'never cut an off spinner' and was bowled off the under-edge by Mallett. Boycott, the deputed anchorman, never deviated from his purpose: he ensured that England did not lose and in the process scored his sixth century against Australia, his nineteenth in all Tests. Gatting seeking to establish his place on the tour, stayed with him until, at the unexciting end, England, still 126 short of their objective, achieved a draw in a match they never deserved to win — and, to be frank, never seemed to believe they could win.

MCC announced that 'investigations are continuing and will be rigorously pursued with a view to identifying and disciplining the culprits' which is the least that could be done to meet the indignation of those many members who deplored the incident. The two umpires were distressed as well as shocked by their treatment at the hands of the members. They are both thoughtful and conscientious men who take their duties seriously. It was a happy gesture that the Australian Cricket Board should have invited 'Dickie' Bird to go out there and officiate during four months of their coming season.

Among the guests, officials, ex-players and players, there was an unmarred atmosphere of cordiality. Cornhill were excellent and generous hosts and, in general, arrangements were efficient and unobtrusive.

Despite the magnificent bowling of Lillee and the determined defensive effort of Boycott, the Man of the Match award went to Kim Hughes whose batting, above anything else, brought a celebratory air to the game and, indeed, proffered a gallant start to the second century.

Greg Chappell

Dennis Lillee

47

NEW ZEALAND, INDIA TOUR
OF AUSTRALIA **1980-1981**

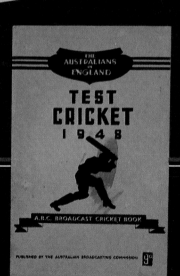

A.B.C
CRICKET
BROADCAST
BOOK

TEST SEASON
1950-51

PRICE ONE SHILLING
PUBLISHED BY THE AUSTRALIAN BROADCASTING COMMISSION

ABC CRICKET BOOK

SOUTH AFRICANS TOUR 1952-53

2/-

CONTAINS STORIES,
PICTURES OF PLAYERS,
FIELD PLACINGS,
SCORE SHEETS

A.B.C Cricket BOOK

WEST INDIES TOUR 1951-1952

PUBLISHED BY THE AUSTRALIAN BROADCASTING COMMISSION

2/-

ABC Coronation CRICKET BOOK
ENGLISH TOUR
1953

PUBLISHED BY THE AUSTRALIAN BROADCASTING COMMISSION

2/-

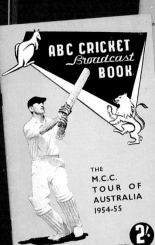

ABC CRICKET Broadcast BOOK

THE
M.C.C.
TOUR OF
AUSTRALIA
1954-55

PUBLISHED BY THE AUSTRALIAN BROADCASTING COMMISSION

2/-

A.B.C CRICKET BOOK

2/-

TOUR OF ENGLAND 1956

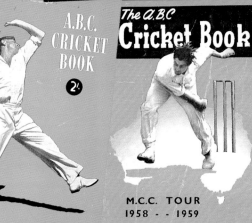

The A.B.C Cricket Book

M.C.C. TOUR
1958 - - 1959

PUBLISHED BY THE AUSTRALIAN BROADCASTING COMMISSION

2/-

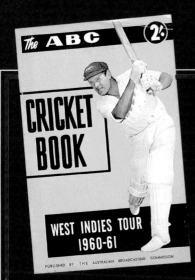

The ABC CRICKET BOOK 2/-

CRICKET BOOK

WEST INDIES TOUR 1960-61

PUBLISHED BY THE AUSTRALIAN BROADCASTING COMMISSION

THE ABC CRICKET BOOK

2/-

AUSTRALIAN TOUR OF U.K. 1961

PUBLISHED BY THE AUSTRALIAN BROADCASTING COMMISSION

ABC CRICKET BOOK 2/-

MCC TOUR OF AUSTRALIA 1962-63

PUBLISHED BY THE AUSTRALIAN BROADCASTING COMMISSION

THE ABC CRICKET BOOK 2/-

SOUTH AFRICAN TOUR 1963-64

PUBLISHED BY THE AUSTRALIAN BROADCASTING COMMISSION

THE ABC CRICKET BOOK 2/-

AUSTRALIAN TOUR OF ENGLAND 1964

PUBLISHED BY THE AUSTRALIAN BROADCASTING COMMISSION

THE ABC CRICKET BOOK 2/-

AUSTRALIAN TOUR OF WEST INDIES 1965

PUBLISHED BY THE AUSTRALIAN BROADCASTING COMMISSION

ABC CRICKET BOOK 2/-

MCC TOUR OF AUSTRALIA 1965-66
PUBLISHED BY THE AUSTRALIAN BROADCASTING COMMISSION

THE ABC CRICKET BOOK
PUBLISHED BY THE AUSTRALIAN BROADCASTING COMMISSION
20c

THE AUSTRALIAN TOUR OF SOUTH AFRICA 1966/7

THE ABC CRICKET BOOK

THE AUSTRALIAN TOUR OF ENGLAND, 1968

25c

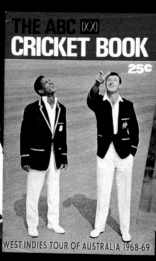

THE ABC CRICKET BOOK
25c

WEST INDIES TOUR OF AUSTRALIA 1968-69

ABC CRICKET BOOK

AUSTRALIAN TOUR OF SOUTH AFRICA 1969-70
30c

CRICKET BOOK

MCC TOUR OF AUSTRALIA 1970-71
30c

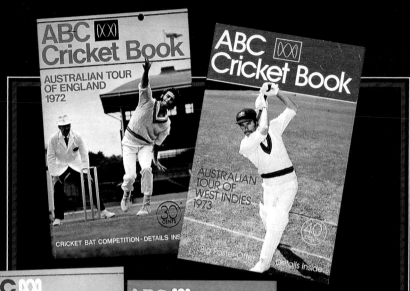

ABC Cricket Book
AUSTRALIAN TOUR OF ENGLAND 1972
30 CENTS
CRICKET BAT COMPETITION - DETAILS INS

ABC Cricket Book
AUSTRALIAN TOUR OF WEST INDIES 1973
40 CENTS
Big Poster Offer Details Inside

ABC CRICKET BOOK
1974-75 MCC TOUR OF AUSTRALIA
CRICKET BAT COMPETITION DETAILS INSIDE
50 CENTS

ABC CRICKET BOOK
AUSTRALIAN TOUR OF ENGLAND 1975
50 cents

ABC CRICKET BOOK
WEST INDIES TOUR OF AUSTRALIA 1975-76
Colour pin-ups inside
60 CENTS

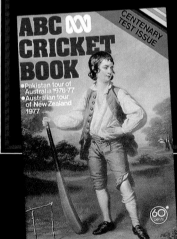

ABC CRICKET BOOK
CENTENARY TEST ISSUE
• Pakistan tour of Australia 1976-77
• Australian tour of New Zealand 1977
60 cents

ABC CRICKET BOOK
AUSTRALIAN TOUR OF ENGLAND · 1977
60

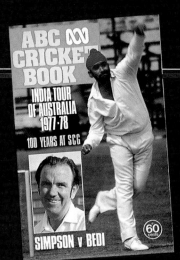

ABC
CRICKET
BOOK

INDIA TOUR
OF AUSTRALIA
1977·78

100 YEARS AT SCG

60 cents

SIMPSON v BEDI

ABC
CRICKET BOOK

AUSTRALIAN
TOUR OF
WEST INDIES
1978

SIMPSON REMEMBERS

PROFILES:
W.I. and Aust. players

60 cents

ABC
CRICKET BOOK

England Tour
of Australia 1978·79

FOR THE FIRST TIME
FULL STATISTICS
1877·1979

· Sir Donald
Bradman
CRICKET'S
FUTURE

England's
Team
FULL DETAILS

80 cents

ABC
CRICKET BOOK

ENGLAND, WEST INDIES
in Australia, 1979·80

ABC
Radio
covers
all the
Tests

$1·00

Unique Australia · England · West Indies
STATISTICS

ABC
CRICKET
BOOK

NEW ZEALAND, INDIA
IN AUSTRALIA 1980-81

· A TON OF CRICKET
· INDIA'S TESTING TIME
· THOSE SEASONED KIWIS

$1·00

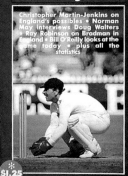

ABC CRICKET BOOK

Australian Tour
of United Kingdom 1981

Christopher Martin-Jenkins on
England's possibles • Norman
May interviews Doug Walters
• Ray Robinson on Bradman in
England • Bill O'Reilly looks at the
game today • plus all the
statistics

$1·25

PAKISTAN
WEST INDIES
IN AUSTRALIA 1981·82

$1·25

· Full Team Details & Statistics
· McGilvray on England
· Man of the Series Competition
· 15 Full Colour Pin-ups

We're 50

ABC
1932-1982

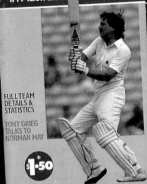

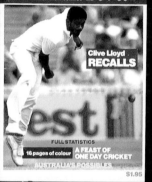

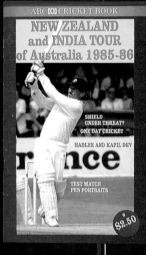

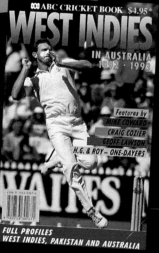

ABC CRICKET BOOK $4.99*

PAKISTAN and SRI LANKA
NEW ZEALAND IN AUSTRALIA
1989-1990

FULL STATISTICS
PLAYER PROFILES
RISE OF PAKISTAN AND
SRI LANKA
— DAVID FRITH —
ASHES FROM ASHES
— PHILIP DERRIMAN —

ABC CRICKET BOOK

ENGLAND TOUR OF
AUSTRALIA 1990-1991
— THE BATTLE FOR THE ASHES —

• GREG CHAPPELL ON
ALLAN BORDER
• ENGLAND,
HOPELESS OR SERIOUS?
Matthew Engel

• RAY BRIGHT'S ELEVEN
HG and Roy
• STATE BY STATE SHEFFIELD
SHIELD PREVIEW

$4.99

COMPREHENSIVE STATISTICS, SCORECARDS, PLAYER PROFILES

ABC CRICKET BOOK

INDIA TOUR
OF AUSTRALIA
1991 - 1992

$4.95

COMPLETE
FIRST CLASS
AND WORLD CUP
PREVIEW
INCLUDING
SOUTH AFRICA

ABC CRICKET BOOK $4.95*

WEST INDIES
IN AUSTRALIA
1992 · 1993

Features by
MIKE COWARD
CRAIG COZIER
GEOFF LAWSON
H.G. & ROY — ONE-DAYERS

MATES

FULL PROFILES
WEST INDIES, PAKISTAN AND AUSTRALIA

ABC CRICKET BOOK

the
AUSTRALIAN TOUR
of
ENGLAND
1993

AUST $4.95
UK £2.50

ABC CRICKET BOOK

AUSTRALIA
NEW ZEALAND
& SOUTH AFRICA
93-94

AUST $4.95
NZ $6.95

Doug Walters talks about the greats and says 'Dennis Lillee under all conditions is by far the best bowler I've played with or against.'

IAN FOR CAPTAIN, LILLEE AND VIV RICHARDS TOP THE LIST

Doug Walters, in his benefit year, with a great season behind him but dropped for the tour of England, talks to Norman May about himself and the players he has known. Photography by Gary Johnston.

Norman May: *Doug, you were a regular member of the Australian team throughout the summer but you were dropped for the tour of England.*

Doug Walters: I'm very disappointed about it. I was hoping that the selectors would pick the touring team on current form rather than past reputations. On the other hand I'm very happy about the selection of young Dirk Wellham, and one of my fondest memories of the season was our century partnership for NSW in the last match before the team was announced.

But from the personal point of view, I think I'd enough to be selected.

On your performances in the Tests and the one-day Internationals, you could be rated as second only to Greg Chappell. Were you surprised by the results you achieved?

I was very surprised. I thought I had no chance of getting back into the Australian side, and probably the 186 against South Australia had a big bearing on the selection of that first team. I was quite pleased with my overall form and I was consistent throughout the season. Probably, I'm not playing as many careless shots these days, and obviously I'm not helping the gully fieldsman quite as much as I used to.

Have you altered your batting technique to cover up those apparent weaknesses of the past?

I tried to work on it 2 or 3 years ago. Ross Edwards and I got together; we had a similar problem — every time we went to the wicket we had extra gully fieldsmen waiting

15

for us, and I was caught there more often than not. So we realised that we had to do something about it, and we tried to get our bat coming through a little straighter, and if the ball did deviate, we would try to let it go and not follow it across.

But you came in to bat with Australia in real trouble against Perth and you played a series of square cuts from the word go.

Perth is such a good wicket that you can afford to play your shots far earlier than perhaps a lot of other wickets around Australia. The bounce is so true and I guess that helps a lot, not only square cuts, but I think you can drive if you're not quite to the pitch of the ball.

What about your attitude? It appears now that you want to stay out there in the middle.

I know that I have given my wicket away on a number of occasions in the past to bowlers who probably didn't deserve it, and over the last couple of years, I have decided that I'd like to make the bowlers earn it.

Is this the wisdom of experience as opposed to youth?

Yes, I think so. But there are certain situations, particularly in one-day cricket in which you don't have time to do that. I don't regard myself as a good slogger of the ball anyhow, and I think if you look for singles, and try to pick the gaps in the field, you can keep the score rolling without lofting the ball or playing too many careless shots.

On the subject now of one-day cricket; feature of the season has been the ir creased interest in the one-day Inter nationals and the decline of interest, in sense in the Test matches. Has your att tude to one-day cricket changed?

One-day cricket is something that the Aus tralians are only just beginning to accept. thought for quite a while that we were on playing it because the crowds were comin in and that's where the money was. W didn't really care too much if we won c lost. All of those attitudes have changed Now we're going out and trying to win eve game. I think all of our players have ac cepted that, and we're a better one-da team now than we ever were in the past.

And what of Test matches? Are they s as important to you as they were, say, the 1960s?

Oh, very much so. There's nothing lik playing in a Test match and I believe that of the other players agree with me. I thir that we attack just as much as we alway did, even though the bowlers may get in the habit of playing defensively, but I'm su that they welcome the chance to bowl to field with 3 or 4 slips.

Personally, I'll take the Test match eve time.

he batsman's natural enemy is the fast
owler, and you've just finished a season
ith only one real pace man per team
gainst you, Hadlee for New Zealand and
apil Dev, perhaps, for India. Was it an
asier season batting mainly against me-
ium pace and slower bowlers?

 sure it was. I don't think there's any
mparison between the attacks we've just
ed and, say, a West Indies attack or an
glish attack or a Pakistani attack for that
tter. It's far easier if you've only got one
t fellow against you.

ver the years, you've faced some beaut-
s in the fast bowling field. Who do you
te as the best during your playing ca-
er?

nnis Lillee under all conditions is by far
 best bowler I've ever played with or
ainst. Of course there are other great
es, the current West Indians Andy
berts and Michael Holding are tremen-
us bowlers and what about Wes Hall and
arley Griffith in the earlier days?

has been said that you personally have
een worried by fast bowlers, in particular
 John Snow in the early 1970s.

on't think I was scared of John Snow, but
 was easily their best bowler, and there
re other bowlers in that team I should
ve preferred to face. We had gone
ough a couple of seasons without really
ch fast bowling, and it was the first occa-
n that we struck a fellow with the ability
Snow to get the ball up off a good length.
 was into the rib cage all of the time and
was very awkward to handle.

Andy Roberts

17

From what you are saying, can you condition yourself to fast bowling by facing it consistently?

Yes. The only way to overcome the problem is continual practise against it. As I said, we hadn't faced any fast bowling for a couple of seasons prior to that tour and Snow hit us with a vengeance.

During your career, you've had many pluses and some minuses, and one of the minuses would be your Test record in England.

Well, I feel a little disappointed about that. I've played some of my best cricket in England, but unfortunately not in the Tests. My failure was a combination, I think, of the wickets and the bowlers realising my weakness around that gully area and concentrating on it. If you do have a weakness, the English players will pounce on it as quick, if not quicker, than anybody else.

Let's talk now about behaviour on the field. You can get yourself fined these days if you say something nasty to an umpire. Have you been involved in any incidents of this type?

No, I can't remember any. I must talk under my breath a little bit on occasions. I probably get annoyed much the same as anyone else but some people like to show it but others don't. I can't remember being involved in an incident with an umpire; I don't think there's any sense in it.

Doug drives at Trent Bridge ▶

A few years ago, in a match against Pakistan in Adelaide, you made headlines when the opposing captain stated that you should have walked. What's your opinion on walking?

I don't believe that anyone should walk. The umpire is out there to do a job and he does it to the best of his ability. You get mistakes that go the other way, and if he occasionally gives you 'not out' when you might have touched the ball, then they sort of even themselves out over a period of time. So if a player doesn't want to walk, then that's fine.

Do you remember the incident against Pakistan in Adelaide?

Yes I do, and I still believe that I didn't hit the ball. I hit the ground, and I didn't think my bat made any contact with the ball.

What about 'sledging'? There must have been times when opposing players have had a chip at you out on the field. Do you answer back or just ignore them?

I like to pretend that I haven't heard the comment. Obviously I've heard it, but, if you answer back, it only annoys the bowler and probably makes him try to bowl an extra yard quicker. I don't believe that there's too much value in answering back.

Yet there are men in your own team who seem to enjoy it.

Well, yes there are, but I can't really see any sense in doing it because you know you are only going to make the bowler try harder to knock you over.

What about your opinions of other players? Who do you think is the best batsman in the world?

I think Viv Richards is probably the best, the most dangerous batsman in the world. He has played some fantastic innings. Greg Chappell obviously ranks a very close second and Geoff Boycott is playing as well as ever; all different styles of batsmen. But the player I'd least like to bowl at would be Viv Richards.

And what about captains?

I think Ian Chappell certainly was the best captain I've played under, and that probably would include against. A captain, to a certain degree is only as good as the side under him and Ian had a strong side for the later part of his captaincy period. He had the ability to get the best out of his players and that's where good captaincy comes in.

Ian got 100% out of his players all the time and no one could bludge on him. If he felt that someone wasn't playing well, or had a weakness, then he would try to help him. If someone had a problem to talk over he would go out to dinner with the bloke, and he went out of his way to make sure that the team was happy. I don't know really about opposing captains, because I think you can only judge captains in your own team.

Ian Chappell

The point you're making is that captain is not just a matter of being out on field.

That's right, captaincy is really a 24-hc job. There may be problems away from t cricket field and he has to know what's g ing on. He has to maintain a certain amou of team spirit. I believe that this is all i portant and most of it happens after o'clock.

Doug, this is your benefit year and yo whole career has received a great dea publicity. What has been your great moment?

I don't think there's any greater mome than first getting chosen to play for yo country. I think that's something that ev cricketer wants to do and they dream o when they're a kid. When it really happe. it's a fantastic feeling. I guess to follow it and score a century in my first Test mat that was the biggest thrill.

And the best innings you think you played.

The most satisfying innings was proba that hundred in Perth in 1974 again England, hitting a six off the last ball. As y said earlier, my record in England had been all that flash, so scoring runs agai England here in Australia gave me a p ticular thrill.

One thing we haven't touched is s bowling. Do you like playing against sp

Well, I guess I play the spin a little bet than the faster bowling so I'll have to sa prefer it, but if you get the spinners un difficult conditions they can be just as a ward. I remember Bisham Bedi bowling t mendously during our tour of India in 19 Derek Underwood would have to come i consideration. He bowls magnificently some of those English wickets, and a faster pace than most spinners. Lar Gibbs could be another one. They're good that they can even tie batsmen do on good wickets.

Let's finish on bowling, Doug. It see now that you can't get that elusive 5 Test wicket.

Well, I thought I might have to blindf someone to get it, I've been sitting on t 49 for so long. I'm very pleased to have F the opportunity to come back this year a pass the 5000 run mark but I don't think lose any sleep over that 50th wicket.

20

The lure of krugerrands destabilised Australia's rebuilding process in 1985. Sixteen players were recruited for two seasons of 'rebel' South African cricket, led by Kim Hughes, who had made a tearful exit after another defeat by the champion West Indies. Without retirees Dennis Lillee, Rod Marsh and Greg Chappell, Hughes went to the Caribbean in 1984 on a mission impossible. Tenacious draws in Georgetown and Port of Spain raised hope, but a savage Clive Lloyd innings in Bridgetown was the cue for more splendid pace bowling, and the West Indies won the series 3–0. On Lloyd's farewell tour in Australia the champions triumphed again, 3–1, and secured the one-day trophy for the fourth consecutive time.

Allan Border reluctantly assumed the leadership after Hughes's resignation. It was the start of the longest captaincy career in Test history. The initial years were beset by disappointments and defeats. England conclusively regained the Ashes in 1985, and New Zealand, inspired by Richard Hadlee, beat Australia 2–1, repeating the success at home 1–0 in 1986. India had the best of a drawn series and in the reciprocal Tests on the subcontinent Dean Jones played one of the great innings of the era in a remarkable tied Test. England showed up Australia's comparative inexperience in 1986–87, to retain the Ashes, 2–1.

The appointment of Bob Simpson as national coach in 1986 lifted commitment and improved discipline. The 1987 World Cup selections revealed that the selectors would not tolerate any idiosyncratic behaviour. Throughout this period Border remained single-minded and even if the losses hurt it did not affect his batting.

In the first 26 Tests of his leadership Border averaged over 57 per innings.

The featured interview with Clive Lloyd in 1984 includes his observations on possible improvements to the game. Yes, almost a decade later an international panel of umpires is in place, and maybe Clive's wish to see small children at big matches outside Australia is being granted, judging by the appreciative young audience who watched Australia in South Africa.

1985 marked Alan McGilvray's swansong Ashes tour and the tributes flowed. Alan broadcast over 200 Test matches during six decades from 1938 to 1985. His confidential style warmed cold nights listening from afar, the analysis blending with precise descriptions of play. As editor of the *ABC Cricket Book* Alan had an eye for detail and encouraged fresh ideas, notably the interviews with key personalities.

CLIVE LLOYD
RECALLS HIS INTERNATIONAL CAREER

INTERVIEWED BY
ABC CRICKET COMMENTATOR
JIM MAXWELL

JIM MAXWELL: *During your career cricket has been transformed from a semi-professional game into multi-media international entertainment. What have been the benefits and the demands for the players?*

CLIVE LLOYD: Well I can say that a lot has been demanded of the players, for instance travelling. There are a lot more tours, there is a lot more promotional work and a lot more one day games. It has been rather demanding but I still think that it is for the betterment of cricket really. Years ago you went on tour for six months in a place like India and when you won a Test Match you got nothing out of it. The same thing happened in England and I thought as the years went on, with the introduction of one day games and a much heavier work load generally that it was only right to get some incentive and some money out of cricket. It is now excellent, especially in Australia. You make a lot of money if you win Test Matches. England was the first to start the one day game and we got a lot of money from winning competitions if our County sides were good enough. This carried over to Test Matches

6

Clive Lloyd

with money for winning Test Matches and Series, as well as Man of the Match awards. Cricketers are giving so much these days, there is a lot of training, and a lot of time with their families is lost. What is wrong with having some sort of monetary gain?

If you compare today with your earlier days, how much tougher was it then when you were touring?

It was much tougher in the sense that we didn't stay at these luxurious hotels and travelling was a little bit primitive. You didn't get much meal money and the mode of travel was not as extravagant as it is these days so a lot of changes have taken place and I am quite happy about them.

What about the amount of international cricket. Is there too much now?

Looking at our schedule for this year and last

Viv Richards

year it was a bit hectic. We left England whe we played County Cricket, we went to Indi then from India we went to Australia for a or day series then we came back here and playe Australia again, then in the summer we will t playing against England and in the winter, month or a month and a half after we have le England we will be playing Australia again un March. So there is a lot of cricket, there is r doubt about that. I suppose the cricketer need the cricket and the salaries that they w derive from it but still I think that if they con tinue to be as hectic as they have been the they will not be able to give of their best. The will become rather stale.

One of the West Indies great strengths in th years that you have been captain has bee fast bowling. Can your fast bowlers susta their dominance over opposing batsme given the frequency of Tours?

We've got a lot of young fast bowlers comin up. I think if you look at the make-up of th team at the moment, we have the right ba ance. We have three quick, one medium pac and a spinner. If we had a spinner of the ca ibre of Roger Harper years ago, we might hav played him because it would have given us different blend. The make-up of the side woul have been excellent. I doubt whether w would go back to four fast bowlers. At th moment I would like to keep what we have.

Cricket has been exposed dramatically in th last few years, particularly since World Serie cricket. Is there a danger of too much ex posure for International Cricket?

It is entirely up to the Cricket Board to monito the system. It is obvious that cricket is a gam that needs exposure. When the Packer thin came in, a lot of people started to watc cricket because of the promos which wer excellent. I don't think they have over exposed it as yet.

International Cricket has for many years bee played between top national teams. Can yo see the game continuing in that way or coul we see a reversion to something like th Rest of the World against the West Indies?

No, we will still have national sides becaus there is a little bit more pride involved wher you are playing for your Nation. I doub whether the Rest of the World qualificatio against England and Australia could ever tak the place of national sides.

Does a player's national identity lose muc by him playing County Cricket, Shell Shiel Cricket and his country?

Yes, Vivian Richards plays all year in Count Cricket for example and then you see hir playing again next year. The English have seen him for the last eight years in England so a little value is lost in contrast to touring only once every four years. By playing County Cricket however, our players become better. Their technique has improved especially where bowling is concerned.

As captain you have had a tremendous run of success with a very good side. Who has been your inspiration?

Many people have inspired me. Some of them are not that well known as Test cricketers. Of course, as Lance Gibbs is my cousin, I watched every move he used to make. But he didn't really captain teams very much. He might have captained Guyana once or twice. I was impressed with a fellow called Fred Wills who was more or less my mentor when I was playing for the Demerara Club in Guyana, the same club that Lance played for. He was my captain and I watched him quite a lot. Berkeley Gaskin helped me as did Clyde Walcott to a lesser extent. Jackie Bond from Lancashire was excellent. I played probably the majority of my years in England under him with Lancashire and I learnt a lot from him. I had a cross-section of people to watch. Gary Sobers too was somebody that I idolised as a player. I played under him for a couple of years before Rohan Kanhai took over.

What is the most important aspect of captaincy?

I think basically it is the trust that you have with your players. You have got to be somebody that has knowledge of them, you have got to be a friend to your players. Over the years we have become very good friends. Your players must want to play for you. If you ask them to bowl an extra couple of overs, even if they are tired, they must want to do it. You have got to be able to have good public relations with your players and you must impress upon them that cricket is not only played on the field but off the field where they are all ambassadors. These are just minor things. They must believe that you think a lot of them as cricketers and as people because that is very important. Once you have got that situation, you will get the best out of your players.

How much work off the field have you done in your career to make the West Indies a great team?

Quite a lot. You have to mix with your players. It is important that you sit down at times and you iron out faults that they might have. You have to spend some time with them and that can be done privately in their rooms or at a team meeting where you pin-point their good and bad points. Once you are respected by other people your players automatically respect you. I think, off the field, it is just as important as on the field.

What about discipline? Have you been much of an enforcer as a captain during your career in that regard?

Yes, but I was never regimental in things that I did. I believe in the old adage, "Man know thyself". If you know that you can have four drinks and still perform the next day, don't have eight. I believe that every player will know exactly what is expected of him and how important cricket is to the West Indian nation and to himself. If you are a Test player, or any player, you would like to know that when you finish playing, you will be recalled with a very good record on and off the field.

There must have been times during your career when injuries almost finished you. What is it that has kept you going, that has enabled you to maintain the desire and the will to want to be a Test Cricketer for all this time?

I think it is a sort of determination. I really didn't think that I had done enough. I wanted to continue because I still thought that I had a part to play. The point is that I just decided that I would not give up. I was just strong-willed enough to decide that I would continue, play as long as possible and try to keep myself fitter than when I was much younger.

Your batting, in the last few seasons, has been better than at any stage during your career. Can you put your finger on the reason why you have played so well?

I have become more confident. I have nothing to prove to people as I have already done that so now I just play my own game. As captain, I know I am good enough and I don't have to think about having to compete with anybody. I just enjoy myself. But at the same time, the work is harder as you get older so I have to put a little more effort into keeping myself fit. That is the important thing.

What have been the pressures of captaincy? Have they at any stage affected your performance as a player?

Strangely, I had never played better since I started as captain in 1974. I've always either topped the averages, or been number two or three so captaincy helped me because it helped me to be more responsible. You get out there and you realise that you are the captain and that you have got to put your best foot forward. You have just got to stay in there and make as many as possible and give the other fellows some incentive.

How deep is the reservoir of talent in the West Indies?

Last year when India was here, I was a little bit worried as far as batting was concerned as we didn't have many batsmen but after this year's Shell Shield, I think that we have a great depth of batsmen. We have a lot of good players who with the right guidance will become world class players. Where bowling is concerned we have adequate reserves too. We will always continue to produce cricketers because it is the only well organised sport and it is something that is revered. Cricket is like a religion in the West Indies. We have done so well over a long period, people just want to play cricket and we have a lot of youngsters who are just waiting to get in to play for the West Indies. That is a good sign.

If we look back to the World Cup defeat last year, that seems to have been a spur to the West Indies to play magnificent cricket because you haven't been touched since. As the West Indies captain, did you regret losing that match?

Yes, I regret it in the sense that we were complacent, we just decided that we could beat anybody and that we would not have a bad day. But it can happen in one day games. In Test Matches you can make up lost ground but in a one day game you have to concentrate for that day and I don't think that we were thinking. Unfortunately, we kept our worst cricket for last.

Who in your opinion is the world's best cricketer?

If you are talking about batsmen, I would think that Vivian Richards would have to be the world's best batsman, but if we are talking about bowlers, I would think there is no doubt that Dennis Lillee has got to be the greatest cricketer of my period because of the injuries that he had and has come out of, and he has 350 test wickets as a fast bowler. The best all-round cricketer would easily have to be Sir Garfield Sobers. There is nothing that he couldn't do. He is at the top. He is on a different level to everybody because he was a genius. Garfield Sobers definitely would have to be the greatest cricketer I have ever seen or played with.

What effect did the leadership style of Sir Frank Worrell and Sir Garfield Sobers have on you?

I never played under Frank and never saw him as captain but listening to him, he was a person that understood below the surface like a psychoanalyst. He was always thinking what

Sobers — there is nothing that he couldn't do

was coming hours ahead. He was a deep thinker and I presumed that he could get the best out of his players which is very important. I would think that he was one of our greatest captains.

Gary Sobers was flamboyant and at times he did things on the spur of the moment. I don't think that he was as deep a thinker as Frank Worrell. A lot of you might think that he wasn't the best captain that we had but still I thought that at times he did some marvellous things. He too, would have to rank among those who have done a great job for us.

Looking at Pitches, how have they changed in the period that you have played the game?

There is no doubt that over the years the wickets have become worse. From 1968 to 1975 I thought that the wickets were excellent throughout the world but they have since deteriorated. The surfaces are not the same. Bounce is very uneven. There is a lot of patchy grass so the wicket becomes two paced. Years ago we had some very very well organised wickets. I presume that these days they are just playing so much more that the square is just wearing a little quicker than normal.

Wherever we have been, the wickets have gone bad. Old Trafford at one stage was the best ground in the business. There were good wickets at the Oval, at Lord's, then coming to the West Indies we had Sabina Park and Trinidad. In Australia, Melbourne and Brisbane had very good wickets, I think they are now trying to work on them and bring them back to their previous level and I hope that they do it as quickly as possible.

What effect is this having on the quality of cricket?

It is obvious that it will deteriorate. If you have the best players playing in the world then you have to have the best surface. You can't get the McEnroes and the Llendls to play on bad tennis surfaces. They wouldn't come. The same thing should apply to cricket.

What about artificial surfaces, can you ever see the day when cricket will be played on synthetic pitches?

I don't see anything wrong with that for one day games because it means that everyone will have the same surface to play on. Probably in years to come, they might have one where it is probably quick for two days or three days and then they put one down where it slows a bit. I would like to see a little bit more preparation going into wickets. That is the most important thing.

Looking at your career, could we go back a little bit and see how it developed from childhood?

I was influenced by Lance Gibbs and we played in our backyard. I played a lot of cricket in the grounds of Demerara Cricket Club. I used to go to practice, but I couldn't take part because I was too young and I would field. I suppose that is why my fielding developed. All I did was field in the afternoon when they were practising and probably had a little knock up with somebody bowling. Lance would bowl to me when everybody was finished. Then I graduated from that and it took me a couple of months before I got a bat at the nets because all the senior players had to bat first. But I was quite happy to be a member of the club and we helped out with teas, going for ice, scoring, all sorts of things. We did anything to be among the cricketers. We just idolised them, we wanted to be like them or even better than they were. Then I graduated and played for my club, for Guyana and then for the West Indies, only because of hard graft and wanting to get to the top. I haven't re-

gretted any one day in my life where cricket was concerned. I would do it all over again. The friends I've made, the places I've seen. The memories that I have will be with me for the rest of my life and will be cherished.

What influence has World Series Cricket had on your cricket and your life?

For the first time I was able to take my wife and kids on tour with me, and I was quite chuffed about that. We were very grateful to Kerry Packer in the sense that he made us aware of what we were worth. He brought in all sorts of different innovations. Night cricket, white ball, soft clothes and the promotional side of cricket was excellent and now it has caught on everywhere. To me that was the great turning point in my cricketing life and I am grateful to Mr. Packer for it.

There was a period when you wore a helmet, you are not wearing one now, why is that?

Well, I think at one stage I thought that some of the wickets were not the best and you put a helmet on. But then again I used to perspire which would cloud my glasses. They used to steam up with condensation. But you never know, I might still put one on one of these days.

What would you do to improve the game, either for the players or for those who love to watch it?

For one thing, I would like to see us playing in all cricket centres where there are proper facilities for everyone; spectators, players, commentators and writers, especially in the West Indies. I would like to see a panel of umpires officiating in Test Cricket throughout the world. I would like to see better coaching facilities for cricketers, more coaching schools. I would like to see small school children at cricket. Only in Australia do you see a lot of school children. You hardly see them anywhere else. Prices must be well within their reach. I think that would promote cricket a little bit more throughout the world.

What about the influence of the media on the game. Has it been even handed during your career?

I think it is getting better. I like the way it is run in Australia. Here, we don't have as much media coverage as we would like. I would like to see the system in Australia and in England, taken to other parts of the world. I think that the media has a very important part to play in cricket.

Have you a preference between One Day and Test Cricket?

Test Cricket without doubt. There is nothing like making a test century or a double century

10

Clive Lloyd

in a Test Match. That is what it is all about. Thinking about what you are doing with fellows trying to work on you for hours. In One Day cricket you can't set the fields that you would like to because it is a faster game. It's a good spectator sport and I hope it stays around for quite some while because it is bringing revenue to cricket.

How much more demanding is the one day game compared to Test Cricket?
You are batting and bowling in the One Day so you are much more tired than in a Test Match. As captain, I find that One Day is very tiring because you have to be on the ball for five hours or you could lose that game. But in a Test Match you can have a little laugh and still make up. I find it very, very demanding.

It's strange to ask this question because you're getting near the end of your career, *but what sort of final ambitions do you have as a player?*
I've covered about everything I would like to as captain. I would be quite happy to leave the scene at the end of the year when I think I'll be leaving behind a very good squad of young players. A squad that can be developed and perhaps continue at the top for another couple of years.

Are you concerned about handing over the captaincy?
I don't think you want to give somebody the captaincy for two years or three years. A captain must have a long stint. Thus whoever is chosen must be good enough to carry it on for a while. There are quite a few candidates. Viv Richards, who has been vice-captain for three years or four years, would be the logical choice.

11

A TRIBUTE TO ALAN McGILVRAY

by Norman Tasker
Sport Editor of THE SUN, SYDNEY

Alan McGilvray made his first cricket commentary for the ABC about the time King Edward VIII decided to do his own thing and give up the throne of England. At the same time a young Joe Louis was starting to show the form that made him the world's greatest fighter, and British shipbuilders were putting the finshing touches to their new superliner, *Queen Mary*. It was an age in which radio itself was still something of a new-fangled luxury.

Fifty years and 225 Test matches later, Alan McGilvray is about to declare stumps on an innings unique in Australian radio, and unique in cricket. The 1985 Australian tour of England will mark his farewell to broadcasting after a career in which his commentaries have provided a staple diet for three generations of cricket lovers. As the Australian

Prime Minister, Bob Hawke, said at McGilvray's final Test match in Australia, it is difficult to nominate any one figure who has given so much pleasure to so many people over so long a period.

Allan Border's team is the tenth which McGilvray has accompanied to England. He has also toured the West Indies three times, South Africa twice and New Zealand once, and has been on hand for every Test match played in Australia since Walter Hammond's team took on Don Bradman's side in 1946. His contribution to cricket, and to the Australian way of life, has been honoured by the award of the MBE (1974) and the Australia Medal (1980), and is reflected by the respect in which he is held by the public at large and, importantly, by generations of international cricketers with whom he has come into contact.

5

McGilvray's career as a cricket broadcaster was built on a very deep-seated love of the game. He is essentially a cricketer first and a broadcaster second. A handy batsman and medium-paced bowler with Sydney Grammar School in the late 'twenties, he quickly asserted himself in grade cricket with Paddington and won a place in the NSW Sheffield Shield team of 1933-34.

'I remember my first meeting with them so well,' he recalls. 'We were going off to Adelaide and Melbourne on the southern tour. I had to report to the captain when we got off the train and when I went to his compartment he was in conference with Stan McCabe, Don Bradman, Bill O'Reilly and Bertie Oldfield. I've never been so nervous and overwhelmed in my life.'

McGilvray's introduction to Shield cricket was on the Melbourne Cricket Ground, where he played his debut innings in partnership with the great Bradman. 'I managed to hang about for a couple of hours while Don did all the batting,' he recalls. 'There were about 40,000 people at the MCG and they were all there to see Bradman. Every time I was at strike, they were yelling at me to "get out of there and let Bradman have a go". Don got 187 that day. It was a wonderful experience just to be part of it.'

Through those early days in Shield cricket, the shrewdly analytical McGilvray mind that later became so familiar to radio listeners all over the world was already in evidence. He was an almost obsessive student of the game, keen to learn from every experience, and keen to heed and to analyse whatever he could glean from the great names with whom he mixed. It was this quality that earned him the captaincy of NSW in the summer of 1935-36 — only his third summer in the NSW team. The retirement of Alan Kippax, the switch to South Australia of Bradman, and the absence in South Africa of Stan McCabe provided the opportunity for the young McGilvray. But he made such a good fist of it that he retained the captaincy when the Australian players returned from South Africa, and he had men like McCabe, O'Reilly and Jack Fingleton in his team.

McGilvray was fortunate through his days in the NSW team to have had the support of some very well-respected people. One of them was the former great Australian captain M A Noble, who had taken an interest in McGilvray's career from his school days. McGilvray would confer with Noble before each game, studying the opponents and considering tactics. It was such a conference that worked out an intricate plan to probe what they considered the most minute flaw in the Bradman armoury. They reasoned that he so often got off the mark by flicking the ball behind square leg, they might just pick him up at leg slip if they harassed him a little. McGilvray sat on his bat at square leg, forcing Bradman to play a little more fine. The ball kicked, the catch came, Bradman was out for a duck, and McGilvray's reputation as a captain was entrenched.

McGilvray's time as a first class cricketer was short. His personal success with bat and ball did not fulfil the early potential, and there was a little official discomfort, too, because he had agreed to an ABC proposal that he do radio summaries at the end of each day's play. He led NSW against England in 1936-37, and was dropped.

But the seeds had already been sown for a career in cricket broadcasting which has taken him from the pioneering days of the middle 'thirties to the present, where sport on radio is a very slick operation indeed.

McGilvray's original 'break' in radio came as a result of his association with M A Noble. Radio itself, and sport on radio in particular, was in its infancy. Since there were few professional sports broadcasters as such, the trend was to encourage experts in their field to deliberate on events as they unfolded. Thus men like Noble, Vic Richardson and Halford Hooker became the hub of early ABC commentaries. Noble knew McGilvray had a sharp cricketing mind and it was his recommendation to the then sporting director Charles Moses that won McGilvray the early chance. As captain of NSW he had the ideal platform to give authority to the reports he made on the NSW team's fortunes.

Once his career as a first class cricketer had come to an end, the McGilvray career in radio quickly accelerated. Its greatest fillip came with the audacious 'synthetic' broadcasts which Moses contrived to cover the 1938 tour of England.

6

Don Bradman

in many ways the pioneer group who dictated the shape of cricket broadcasting which followed.

Later there were Johnny Moyes and Lindsay Hassett and, more recently, Norman O'Neill and Max Walker. With all of them McGilvray developed a sense of teamwork that made commentaries engrossing conversation pieces. In that sense, he did much to shape the style of modern commentary both here and in England. In his early tours to England McGilvray was strikingly different, because his commentary was more direct, concentrating on describing each ball and recording the score at least two or three times an over. The English commentary teams were more prone to let the cricket go on without them, providing all manner of peripheral information about the fashions, the bird life or the quality of their lunch, turning back to the cricket only when something significant took place. McGilvray's style caught on, and by the 'sixties the commentators of both countries adopted pretty well the same patterns.

Much has changed in cricket in McGilvray's time at the microphone. 'Times change and standards change,' he says 'but the quality of cricket doesn't alter much from era to era. It's more athletic these days, and there is so much more of it played. But good players are good players in any era, and there are plenty of them around today'.

McGilvray rates Don Bradman's 1948 team the best he has seen, a shade better than Clive Lloyd's West Indies team of 1984-85 and Ali Bacher's South African team of 1970. He has a soft spot for Ian Chappell amongst the most successful of Australia's leaders. His one regret about the modern game is that it is losing a touch of its dignity. His traditional values, he concedes, are a little offended by some of today's more histrionic players. But to McGilvray, that is a small scar on cricket's enduring character.

McGilvray has spent several months working on a book to recount some of the great moments and great people of his fifty years in cricket commentary. It will be launched at the end of the 1985 tour. When the end of the tour comes, and Alan McGilvray calls his last Test, a significant era in the history of Australian broadcasting will have come to a close.

'That remains the greatest experience I had in radio,' McGilvray recalls. 'We manufactured the commentaries from telegrams we received from England. Each over, we would get a cable which would tell us in code what happened to every ball. We had a picture of the ground in front of us, a scorer and a sound effects man. We made the sound of bat hitting ball by banging a pencil on a block of wood. In the end it almost felt like we were there.'

Those 'synthetic Tests' laid the foundation for cricket broadcasting as it is today. They were accepted with such enthusiasm in the community that there was little doubt thereafter that the broadcasting of Test cricket would have a high priority in ABC thinking.

McGilvray has been at the centre of the ABC's commitment to cricket ever since. His first live Test commentaries were in 1946-47 when Bradman's team greeted England after the war with a spanking. In the nearly forty years since, he has seen some marvellous cricket, experienced many historic days and worked with some great names of radio. In the early part he teamed up with the former Australian captain Vic Richardson and the former England captain Arthur Gilligan. That was a legendary team, and

1988–1990

Facing the perennial world champions again at home, Australia's batsmen floundered against Marshall, Ambrose and Walsh, losing the first three Tests. Allan Border took eleven wickets in a fourth Test victory, but the series was over. The West Indies were also decisively victorious in the one-dayers, after rain ruined Australia's hopes in the third final. Bill O'Reilly's lengthy association with the SCG was officially recognised when the former Hills Stand was re-christened, and Bill wrote nostalgically of his SCG experiences in the 1988–89 book. Peter McFarline's search for characters was amplified by Australia's meek batting against the West Indies.

The Frank Worrell Trophy disappointment behind them, Australia set off for England, their team almost universally written off. Terry Alderman's deceptive movement and the plundering bats of Taylor, Boon and Steve Waugh regained the Ashes triumphantly, 4–0, and Allan Border returned to a tickertape reception and the honour of being named Australian of the Year. Merv Hughes's moustache featured on every London bus and his hostile bowling proved he was not just a good-looking Aussie tourist! Elaine Canty delves into the psyche of a cult hero.

Sent on a goodwill one-day tour to India, Border's bowlers struggled, without a proper break, at the start of 1989–90. New Zealand drew a one-off Test in Perth thanks to Mark Greatbatch. Australia were hammered by Sri Lankan pocket rocket Aravinda de Silva in a Brisbane draw, and only won Hobart's inaugural Test in the final hour of the fifth day. Pakistan's challenge was lbw'd by Alderman in Melbourne, and although Dean Jones scored a hundred in each innings in Adelaide the game was drawn, and then the series was washed away in rain-plagued Sydney.

The *ABC Cricket Book* reappeared in 1988-89 after a fallow season. Jim Maxwell became the new editor, and if you can cope with working in the third person the story continues. Perceiving that the core market for the publication enjoyed the traditional pocket book size and layout, the editor, in consultation with Stuart Neal of ABC Enterprises, did some corrective surgery while looking to vary the scope of featured contributors. The statistical section was rationalised and more emphasis was placed on one-day records. Throughout, the quality of Patrick Eagar's photography stands out like the Sydney Cricket Ground lights, and much of the credit for the layout goes to Howard Binns-McDonald.

In 1987 Australia surprised its opponents by winning the World Cup in Calcutta. The Simpson work ethic and a committed approach were paying off, victory over England in Calcutta rewarding the dogged perseverance of Allan Border. David Boon developed greater consistency in the home series against New Zealand, won by Australia 1–0 after surviving for a nail-biting draw in the third Test. Boon continued his solid form in the Bicentennial Test, ensuring a draw with 184 not out when Australia followed on. Sri Lanka played its first Test in Australia at the end of a successful one-day series for the home side. Beaten by an innings, there was more concern about the whole team disappearing down the cavernous cracks in the Perth pitch. Later that year in Pakistan, controversial umpiring decisions and pitch protests precipitated a diplomatic disaster when Australia's management threatened to abandon the tour. Beaten by an innings in the rancorous Karachi Test, Australia recovered and almost squared the series in Lahore.

CHARACTERS

WHERE HAVE ALL THE CHARACTERS GONE?

Peter McFarline

CHARACTERS. PERSONALITIES. PEOPLE. More than flashing drives, rearing bouncers and diving catches, they are the game of cricket.

Those of us who are hooked on cricket remember the first big match we ever saw not for the result but for the names — the personalities — who played in it.

The names and faces that flood the memory of my first game are hardly a cross-section of Wisden's honor board . . . Hedley Keith, Ken Funston, Geoff Noblet, Gil Langley, Ian Craig.

My father, whose passion for cricket was only thinly disguised by the conservatism demanded of a country pharmacist of the time, always claimed it was a coincidence that we were in Melbourne at the same time as the Fifth Test between Australia and South Africa in February, 1953. And to my absolute delight, we were staying at The Windsor Hotel, in those days the headquarters of touring cricketers in Melbourne.

In the lounge after dinner, the players mingled and relaxed. Today, such behaviour would probably be construed as a breach of the code of behaviour. Hedley Keith, a left-handed batsman who was about to play in his first Test, took my autograph book and returned with five pages of precious South African signatures.

Craig, who at 17 was about to become the youngest of all Test players — until Mushtaq Mohammed took the honor from him a decade later — gathered the scrawls of his Australian team mates. The balding wicket-keeper Langley took me on his knee and made funny faces. Funston and Noblet let me listen in while they had a drink and a chat. And then, oh rapture! Sir Donald Bradman — the legend — came in, and spoke a few words to me. His signature went on a page of its own.

For the next few days, I watched in awe and fascination, as the tiny Lindsay Hassett made a double century, Craig a more than satisfactory debut with scores of 47 and 53 and the South Africans achieved a famous and unlikely victory to draw the series 2-all.

This wasn't just a cricket match I was watching . . . it was the ultimate contest be-

Who are these cricket characters?

Answers, page 38

WEST INDIES TOUR
OF AUSTRALIA 1988-1989

tween larger-than-life sportsmen I had actually met, wonderful men of superior talent who were humble enough to sign their names for, and spend a few moments with a whipper-snapper from the country.

After that, every Test match took on, for me, the significance of a summit conference. Every name that was chosen to represent his country was as important as the monarch. Thirty five years ago, without the monster of television, cricket was a way of life for many Australians. The sweeping national dependence on the radio and the gruff yet lilting commentaries of John Arlott during a tour of England have been well documented.

In 1956, the magazine *Sporting Life* offered 500 pounds to any of its readers who could correctly nominate the 17 players to be selected for the tour of England. By then I was at school in Brisbane where cricket fever was a powerful tropical disease and names not widely known in the rest of the country — Grout, Mackay, Archer K, Archer R, Bratchford, Raymer — were worshipped with a fierce loyalty.

Hundreds of us entered the competition; there was wild speculation about how we would spend the money if we won. Late one Monday afternoon the selected side came through on the ABC news . . . radio, of course. I wrote the names down quickly — the expected ones — Miller, Lindwall, Benaud, Davidson, Harvey, Johnson — and then the surprises. All touring teams have at least one surprise. This one had three — Jack Wilson, the South Australian spinner, John Rutherford, the Western Australian opening batsman and Pat Crawford, the tall fast bowler from New South Wales. And, by Jupiter, I'd got them all. No-one else in my school had. I must have been the only one in Australia to pre-empt the selectors.

Five hundred pounds! Soon everyone in our suburb knew about it. The arguments about what I would do with the money raged through the house. Wait until you get the cheque, said father. Invest it in government bonds — mother. Run away — me. Go away — sister.

Every afternoon for three weeks I sweated on the arrival of the postman. All the while my excitement grew. I half expected a congratulatory telegram. When it didn't come I consoled myself with the words in the magazine . . . "the winner will be advised by mail and the result published in next month's edition".

Finally, the great moment arrived. The postie, who was well aware of my jubilant optimism, smiled benignly as he handed me the envelope bearing the Sporting Life trademark. I tore it open, saw the contents and immediately wished to be a long way away — on my own. Inside was a postal note for ten shillings and a note from the editor explaining that there had been more than 1500 correct entries — out of 10 000 — and to keep faith with the successful readers, it had been decided to give them each ten bob. This magazine went out of circulation shortly after — permanently. So did I — temporarily.

A psychologist of the eighties might say that it was one of life's salient lessons. I suppose it was. More importantly, it exemplifies just how big a part cricket and cricketers played then in Australian life.

For all sorts of reasons, the import of the game has been reduced dramatically in recent times. Simple evolution has made sure we have no control over most of them.

But I often fear that this withering of the influence of cricket has been accelerated by a desire of authorities to negate the characters, the personalities of the game.

Not long ago, I returned to Australia after a period working overseas. During a Test match, a well-meaning official offered to introduce me to a group of players from the national team, whose personnel had changed substantially in my absence. I accepted the offer gladly — we were in a bar at the time. Five minutes later, the introductions had been made and the players had faded fast, from sight and from mind. 'Aren't they great?' said the official. 'They don't drink in bars after nine o'clock, they don't swear, they don't make any trouble'. They also didn't win many Test matches, although it took me some time to work out there was some significance between the two.

Keith Miller left his stamp on the game as a player and a personality. Yet he continued to have a large influence on sports lovers after his playing days simply because he behaved in exactly the same way as he had when he was a national idol. The Miller I have been privileged to know is, like Bill O'Reilly, one of the great rewards of sporting journalism.

I wonder in this age of cricket automa-

tons whether Miller and O'Reilly, Denis Compton and Bill Edrich, Arthur Mailey and the other legendary characters would have been able to blossom.

Would the boy from Dungog, Doug Walters, have had the same impact in the late eighties as he did in the late sixties? How could the heavy emphasis today on fitness, discipline and behaviour have handled a genius who chain-smoked, was an inveterate card player and needed only the minimum of practice to hone his skills? The answer is, I suspect, that it wouldn't.

Just as it wouldn't have allowed the wise-cracking practical joker Gary Gilmour to make it to Test level. Or Wally Grout, the finest 'keeper I have seen, who regarded laughter, cigarettes, and a bet as necessary ingredients of everyday living.

Sometimes when I see David Boon returning, poker-faced and emotionless, to the pavilion after a big innings, I wonder if he really enjoys his job. Of course, that's the difference. For many of these players, cricket is their job. For their predecessors, it was a hobby. Times have changed but not for cricket lovers. We still go to the cricket for enjoyment. Our expectations haven't changed but those of modern players have.

We all remember Ken Mackay as one of the country's best all rounders. Today he would have made a fortune. But when he held Queensland together through the fifties before the selectors finally gave him to the nation, he battled through as a door to door insurance salesman. He never complained ... selling insurance gave him the change to meet cricket lovers and talk cricket.

Hardly any player made monetary profit from the game then — yet so many invested so much of themselves in it. The investment these days is much greater in terms of hours and effort — but has the game turned so far that it is killing its very heart?

The characters are — *page 36, Left — top to bottom* — Neil Harvey, Keith Miller, Ray Lindwall, Wally Grout. *Right — top to bottom* — Arthur Mailey, Richie Benaud, Alan Davidson, Bill O'Reilly. *Page 38, left,* Doug Walters, *right,* Gary Gilmour

WEST INDIES TOUR OF AUSTRALIA **1988-1989**

O'REILLY'S OLD MATE

Bill O'Reilly's legendary association with cricket and the Sydney Cricket Ground was officially recognised following a change of government in NSW earlier this year. His name now appears on the stand built to replace the old 'Bob' Stand, subsequently resited at North Sydney Oval, where the name O'Reilly has also been perpetuated on a new stand.

Bill O'Reilly, regarded as the greatest bowler of his time, and revered for his forthright comments on the game, recalls the formative experiences of his SCG association.

I feel it running strongly though my veins already — a stirring sense of clansmanship between that old sacred site on the Hill and me. We have been on close terms of intimate friendship since that first shivery afternoon I walked out there to the deep square leg boundary to nod my head and say good-day.

I took up an unaccustomed fielding post at the behest of my legendary captain, Alf Noble, whom I had met for the first time in my life a few moments before as he handed out his fielding portfolios with a majestic wave of his strong right hand. 'Good-day', I said, 'I'm a new boy, my name's O'Reilly, and you'd better keep your eyes on me for I've never fielded so close to the fence before.'

I'm sure I received a friendly nod and heard a homely chuckle. 'Old Alf's never heard of you before. Perhaps he's been reading of your performances with Botany Harriers.' We became friends.

I didn't get close to the middle of the ground. Alf never did ask me to have a bowl.

And just in case his 'MA Noble' stand over there wishes to speak up in his defence, I'll get in first.

The game was a 'spur of the moment' reaction by the Cricket Association to a dreadful accident in a suburban cricket fixture wherein a young man named Proud had been permanently blinded in an early round of the 1926-27 season.

That explains why the great man Noble, then 53 years old, had been persuaded to make one of those gallant reappearances simply to boost the gate for a good cause.

The game had barely begun when one of those long streamlined dirty black clouds full of fire and brimstone landed a deluge of hailstones, a foot deep, so it seemed, right over the ground and our first meeting was brought to a disappointing close.

But there were plenty to follow and with each succeeding interview, so to speak, our mutual respect grew.

Now that we two have become clansmen I'm sure that it has been easy for me to recognise an affinity that allows for the discussion of personal secrets dear to the hearts of both of us.

I'd already proudly made him aware that our allegiance to each other stemmed from a courageous red-headed 23-year-old policeman who took this great country on singlehanded as he stepped ashore from the SS *Hornet* at Circular Quay on Wednesday, January 25th 1865 — all the way from Cavan's Ballyconnell.

Not to be outdone, my mate hurriedly informed me that just thirteen years after young Peter O'Reilly set foot, he himself was closely involved in one of the most historic events of his own career.

It happened in 1878 when the 28-year-old Lord Harris, with a pedigree unparalleled in this land, led his team of English amateurs (bar two or three) against NSW, in a match which the locals were heavily backed, by people from the opposite side

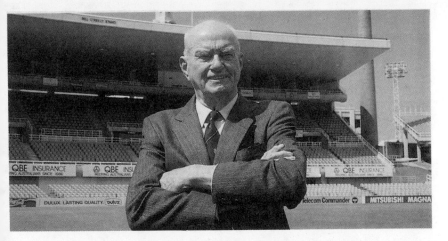

Bill O'Reilly's association with the SCG is now secure for all time

of the ground, my mate interpolated, to win easily.

When Billy Murdoch, the local hero, a solicitor from Cootamundra, was given run out at a vital stage, bedlam erupted.

The result was that Harris, having aired the event to the very last swipe in the London *Telegraph*, vowed never again to have anything to do with wild colonial boys like us.

And here my mate dropped his voice a decibel or two, as he said, 'Do you recall the sequel that took place more than 50 years later?'

Well, our Australian Board, in one of their moments of contrition, had invited Lord Harris to accompany his friend Plum Warner as an official visitor with Jardine's 1932-33 side, with an eye no doubt to smoothing the rift that began at Sydney here in 1878.

But you will know of course that the Supreme Umpire on High gave his Lordship a beckoning signal and closed his innings for him in March a few months before the team was scheduled to sail from Tilbury.

Strange isn't it, how obituary notices can often fortuitously clear the deck.

Had Harris attended the first Test here in Sydney and been forced to listen to the uproarious welcome the local boys gave to the first unhappy onslaught of the bodyline tactics, perhaps this great ground of ours would have been held historically responsible for the demise of one of England's most illustrious cricket sons.

Apart from those 'core of our hearts' se-crets, there are many brilliant memories that bind us close together.

Easily the most inspiring bowling performance I have seen there was the glorious display of big lumbering Englishman Maurice Tate when he wiped the floor with the NSW expert batting line with an unsurpassed exhibition of brilliantly controlled swing bowling in 1924.

That performance not only left me spellbound but more importantly set met thinking deeply about the real significance of the bowling art.

As for batting — like bowling — only one name comes lightning-like to my mind.

No one who was blessed by God to have been present at that bodyline baptism already mentioned, at the SCG would hesitate for a fleeting second to nominate Stan McCabe's fabulous exhibition of incredible courage and incomparable skill as the greatest, the most thrilling and the proudest Australian exhibition of batsmanship our magnificent old SCG can remember.

As we both turned away with tears in our eyes resulting from our trip together down memory lane, my old mate on the square leg boundary gave a quick glance across his left shoulder and said, 'Hey! don't let us forget our old mate over there hiding miserably behind the Doug Walters stand. He's the best score board the world has ever seen. Every time I look at him I could cry'.

'Yes, mate', I said. 'I fully agree. I feel like having a weep myself.'

BIG MERV

18

HERO AND MATCHWINNER

Elaine Canty

MERVYN GREGORY HUGHES conducts the country's most popular calisthenics classes.

One of the enduring memories of last summer is the sight of the cheerful holiday crowd in Bay 13 at the MCG, stretching and bending behind its idol as he sombrely went through his warm up routine on the fence.

For Australians, starved of a charismatic cricket hero since the departure of the Chappells, Max Walker, Dennis Lillee and Rodney Marsh, big flamboyant Merv with the barrel chest and quite the most splendid moustache in Australian sport has emerged like a desert flower.

Making the team to tour England has finished the season on the highest possible note for the Footscray and Victorian paceman who's had what he calls 'a jagged year'.

The 88-89 season mirrored his Test career where he has played only eleven Tests in four years. He's therefore desperately keen to establish himself as a regular in the Australian team.

The Perth Test against the West Indies in which he reached a personal peak, taking thirteen wickets including a remarkable 8-87 in the first innings, was followed by a trough during which he took only one wicket in the remaining three Tests.

Hughes nominates as his other personal triumphs of the summer his unbeaten 72 in Adelaide in the fifth Test, and making his debut for his country in the One-Day games.

But typically, he considers the team's successes, such as the Australian victory in the fourth Test, more important.

Big Merv's extraordinary crowd appeal is due in no small measure to his magnificent handlebar moustache ... generous and black ... in the fine tradition of those earlier quicks like nineteenth century Fred 'The Demon' Spofforth.

19

Hughes has something of a Samson complex about his machismo moustache. In a frank admission which may surprise Northern Territory Magistrate Barrett (who cast aspersions on the manliness of the Australian team), Merv says he owes his image to a visit to Darwin: 'Four years ago I came back from the Northern Territory with a full beard. I decided to get a cleanup and shave most of it off. I left the moustache to see how it looked'.

'Right after that' he says, 'my cricket took a dramatic turn for the better'. Not one to tempt fate, and unable to decide whether his good fortune was due to the extra work he'd put in or the extra hair he'd put on, Merv has decided to stick with the moustache.

He admits that he might just be forced to reassess the situation should he receive a tempting commercial offer to shave in public.

As for Magistrate Barrett's remarks suggesting that it's improper to show emotion on the cricket field, Hughes is blunt: 'I can't see what my behaviour has to do with someone dropping his daks in a Northern Territory food store'.

For a man who claims to be 'not all that superstitious', Hughes has some intriguing habits.

'I do like to be last out of the dressing-room so I'm last on to the oval' he says, and 'when we (the Victorian team) travel for a game interstate, I have to have a cappucino and a sausage roll at the airport cafeteria . . . that's a must'.

He shrugs off a well deserved reputation as a locker room clown. 'If the team you're playing with is batting well, you can spend 6 hours confined to one spot. You'd go a bit silly if you didn't get up to some antics to break the monotony'.

Apart from his capacity for sheer hard work, it's Merv's unabashed joy at the fall of an opposition wicket which has endeared him to the crowds. 'I come from a school where you show your emotions' says a deadpan Hughes.

The big man seems genuinely at a loss to explain his new status as a cult hero. 'Bowlers have been doing warmups in front of Bay 13 for as long as the game has been played' he puzzles. 'It could have happened when the Australians were doing well with Thomson, Lillee and Max Walker fielding down there. I sit back at times and think . . . why me? Why all of a sudden are they making me look good?'.

His Victorian teammates would agree with Hughes' self assessment as 'a battler who works pretty hard at his game, enjoys his cricket and has a bit of fun with the crowd'. They would also add that he is quickwitted, popular and a dedicated team man.

Regarding the forthcoming tour, Hughes says 'It's not going to be a holiday. We're over there to play cricket and try and win back the Ashes'. He's hoping for a couple of early wins with 'everyone keeping the pressure on everyone else for their spot in the team'.

For Merv Hughes, cricket is not only his job but his hobby. 'It's a business I enjoy,' he says 'I really couldn't see myself doing anything else'.

20

The 1990s

England's 1990-91 Ashes venture stumbled on Alderman's swing in Brisbane and the enigmatic Bruce Reid's angled bounce in Melbourne. By the end of the series, won 3–0 by Australia, Mark Waugh had made a century on debut and Craig McDermott was re-established. Greg Chappell examines Allan Border's extraordinary career in the tour lead up.

For the first time the annual book seriously embraced humour—Matthew Engel on England's plight, and the irreverent HG and Roy selecting Ray Bright's Eleven. The nostalgia theme is taken up by Scobie Malone's inventor Jon Cleary, and Geoff Lawson eases into retirement with a few bumpers.

Australia didn't win the Frank Worrell Trophy in the Caribbean. They were beaten by hungrier and more skilful opponents. Australia's victory in the one-day series roused the champions and it was Ambrose, Patterson, Marshall, Walsh, Greenidge, Richardson and Richards all over again. McDermott bowled superbly but the batsmen were worn down by unrelenting pace.

The 1991-92 series against India also found some holes in Australia's batting, Kepil Dev and Prabhakar swinging them out. India in turn were denied by disciplined bowling and fielding, a 4–0 result eventuating.

The 1992 World Cup, staged in Australia and New Zealand, was a popular event despite the wearying travel program. Australia lost its opening match to tournament bolters New Zealand and struggled to find form, losing to England, South Africa and Pakistan. The mercurial Pakistanis won the final, maintaining the record of teams batting first being victorious— and not just in finals.

In 1992-93 the West Indians, looking weaker than in previous years, played unconvincingly until Brian Lara swung their confidence with 277 in the Sydney Test. Australia had the best of a Brisbane draw and Shane Warne produced a match winning effort at the MCG. In Adelaide, another epic contest ended in the closest margin of Test victory, 1 run. Alas for the beleaguered Australians and Border, the West Indies triumphed, and Ambrose celebrated his success with a devastating performance in Perth, carrying his side to a huge win inside three days. Dean Jones, dropped from the Test team, tactlessly sparked Ambrose's ire in the one-day finals by indicating that Curtly's white wrist bands were a distraction. The rest was destruction, and another Windies' one-day cup. A battle-weary Australian team re-focussed for New Zealand and, after winning the Christchurch Test by an innings, lost momentum and the Auckland Test, hanging on for a 3–2 win in the one-dayers.

Returning to England for his fourth tour and third as captain in 1993, Border gained renewed inspiration from Warne's bowling. Warne, May, Hughes and then Reiffel shared the spoils and everyone made runs. McDermott was injured and returned home, but from the moment Warne bowled Gatting with his huge debut leg break, England went from disbelief to disaster. Slater, Taylor, Boon, the Waughs and Border slaughtered some of the most inept English bowling in history and the Ashes were retained. England recovered respect in the last Test at the Oval, where a new combination of bowlers discovered a consistent, penetrative length.

The highlight of the 1993-94 season was South Africa's return to the Test arena against Australia. A weakened New Zealand team was convincingly beaten prior to Christmas and then rain ruined the Boxing Day Test. In Sydney, Shane Warne continued his mesmerising summer of havoc, taking a record twelve wickets. South Africa showed extraordinary spirit to stay in the contest, and having lost it for four days snatched an incredible five-run victory on the last day.

The new stars were de Villiers, Donald, Rhodes and Cronje. Australia squared the series in Adelaide, Warne again, with Steve Waugh, producing the first of several all round efforts at home and then on the veldt.

The toss was becoming a major factor in the one-dayers—bat first, win game—and Australia duly did that in the finals after South Africa drew first blood.

In South Africa Warne was rarely collared but, with McDermott injured and Hughes out of form after recovering from a knee operation, Australia did well to square the series and the one-dayers. In the third Test South Africa seemed more intent on playing safe than pursuing victory. Steve Waugh's Man of the Series achievement reflected his maturity and the hope of continued consistency under the new captain, Mark Taylor. Allan Border retired with a stupendous record— most Tests, most runs, most catches, most one-dayers, arguably the most durable player in the history of international cricket.

THE EXTRAORDINARY CAREER OF ALLAN BORDER

Greg Chappell

Allan Border is the first of the modern generation of Australian cricketers. A generation able to devote their life to the pursuit of a cricket career without the need for a 'real job'.

Allan gained his opportunity in the New South Wales and Australian teams, due to the split in cricket created by the advent of World Series Cricket.

With a unique blend of talent, desire, courage and a contrary nature, he has fashioned a remarkable record-breaking career which has become the bench-mark for following generations of Australian cricketers.

I expect Allan to captain the Australian team through this season's series with England and on the tour of the West Indies before relinquishing the reins to either Steve Waugh or Mark Taylor. Allan would then continue as a senior player for another season or two, or until the desire to play at the highest level and to his own high standard runs out.

By that stage he will have captained Australia a record number of times (62), played more Tests than any other Australian (125), and made more runs than any other Test cricketer, as well as hold the world record for Test catches. A remarkable achievement.

I first saw Allan Border bat on television during his second Test against England at the SCG in January 1979 where he took on the England spinners so confidently that he remained not out in each innings. Wisden recorded that Border was in a 'lonely class of his own' and I was aware I was witnessing the beginning of the career of an exceptionally talented individual.

5

The following season I played alongside Allan for Australia and again witnessed his batting prowess, but it wasn't until I played against him in a Shield match at the 'Gabba that I fully appreciated his talents. Allan scored 200 for New South Wales against Queensland in that game and I was one of the bowlers who suffered at his hands. The qualities which I most admired during that innings, and ever since, were Allan's ability to take full toll of deliveries only marginally short or full of a good length or slightly off line and his marvellous powers of concentration.

These talents were on view again in Pakistan a few months later when Allan scored 150 not out in each innings of the Lahore Test match. Of the many innings I witnessed him play these are the two which I rate as his most accomplished. On display in these two innings were all of the above qualities plus quick footwork, deft placement and a cheekiness which suggested someone who was enjoying his work.

Allan was a reluctant captain having witnessed at close quarters the pressures of the job and this reluctance handicapped him in the role until he threw off the shackles against England at Headingley on the 1989 tour. Part of Allan's reluctance was due to his belief that the team he was leading was inferior to previous Australian teams and outmanned by the West Indies and England.

This belief underlined a side of Allan's character which has always intrigued me. To have achieved such personal success at the highest level of the game would suggest an unflagging belief in one's own ability and yet Allan was amazingly doubtful of his.

Most of us have our own doubts and fears, at least from time to time, but rarely express them publicly and often try to deny them privately lest we find it impossible to walk through the gate, but Allan continually amazed me by making public the doubts he had. Once he walked through the gate he forgot all those fears and doubts however, for they were rarely, if ever, visible when he held a bat in his hand.

Doubts occasionally arose in the field with his catching for he was one of the first to volunteer for outfield duties to get out of the slips cordon. His confidence has grown in that area in recent times also, to the extent that he is only shaded by Mark Taylor in the current Australian team.

This lack of confidence may explain the contrary side of Allan's character which has landed him with a long list of nicknames such as Grumpy, Puggsley and Angry Anderson among others. Cricketers, like overgrown schoolboys, can be cruel to each other in the area of nicknames. Allan has earnt every one of his over the years, but his grumpiness may well have been his strongest ally during the troubled years of his early captaincy. Having inherited the captaincy of a side which he perceived to be inferior to his main opponents, Allan captained it tentatively and contributed to some of its difficulties which led to some of the anger which he occasionally unleashed on his team mates.

But the anger which he took to the wicket with him when his side was up against the odds made him an opponent to be reckoned with as he retreated into his cocoon of dark concentration and impregnable defence. This frame of mind produced some magnificent rear guard actions which were truly courageous, but would have given Allan little satisfaction for he prefers to take the game to the opposition bowlers in the manner he did at Headingley last year. To me the Headingley Test was the watershed for Allan's captaincy as he went on to lead the side with flair, imagination and confidence.

If he continues to lead in this manner for the remainder of his captaincy term I have no doubt his team can reclaim the title of best team from the West Indies in the Caribbean in early 1991. I am equally convinced that Allan will recapture some of the instinctive flair which marked his early Test innings and thus appropriately cap one of cricket's most extraordinary careers.

6

CRICKET IN ENGLAND — HOPELESS OR SERIOUS?

Matthew Engel
(*The Guardian*)

AN OLD, WISE AND VERY DRUNK Irish rugby union man summed it up once in a Dublin bar late at night. 'The state of English rugby,' he slurred, 'is serious, but not hopeless. The state of Irish rugby is hopeless, but not serious.'

Can we say the same about English and Australian cricket? And, if so, which one is serious and which hopeless? Or vice, indeed, versa.

It is easy to get depressed about the state of our great, shared national game. Test matches are afflicted by dwindling attendances, slow over-rates, the disappearance of spin bowling, the decline of chivalry and the whole set of dreary attitudes that can all be lumped together under the name 'professionalism'.

Many of these are particular phenomena of the 1980s. But the principle is not new. Cricket is a game which exists in the belief that everything is always getting worse. In every human sport in which performance can be measured, we know that standards have improved consistently throughout the century. No one would try and argue that Herb Elliott was a faster runner than Sebastian Coe. But try sitting among the members at Lord's or the MCG and suggesting that Border is a better batsman than Harvey, or Gooch better than Hutton! You could get lynched.

It was always like this. I discovered a piece in the *Manchester Guardian* of 1883 casting a critical eye on the players of the time and looking back wistfully to the Yorkshire bowlers of the 1850s, Freeman and Emmett. 'Truly there were giants in those days,' said the writer sadly.

In 1893, *The Guardian* had a report of the traditional match between the ancient universities at Lord's when the teams included many of the most famous names of early cricket in England: including CB Fry, FS Jackson and Ranjitsinhji. What a game that must have been. Not according to the man who was there: 'the most uninteresting Oxford v Cambridge match seen for years — perhaps the most uninteresting ever.'

This phenomenon of imaginative nostalgia has always been worse in England than in Australia. After all, you have a country that always likes to tell itself that things are going better. The English are different. 'She'll be wrong, mate,' ought to be the national motto.

The cricketers of the 1950s have been the chief exemplars of this. In the '50s — for a few, brief years — England was unchallenged as the best team in the world. And several of the players of that time have spent the '60s, '70s, '80s and the start of the '90s making sure everyone else knows it.

Fred Trueman, whose radio summaries are regarded by many listeners as having the force of holy writ, inadvertently created a national catchphrase when he would say, with an almost audible shake of the head as his successors in the team committed some almighty blunder: 'I don't know what's going on out there' or sometimes, 'I don't know what's going off out there'. The use of this was discontinued when the BBC suggested to him that he was actually being paid to know what was going on (or off) out there.

Dear old Alec Bedser, who was a con-

ientious chairman of selectors for what
eemed like forever, always picked the
am with an air that suggested he would
r rather be naming himself, his twin
ric, Trueman, Statham, May, Cowdrey
c rather than the poor youngsters he
as obliged to choose instead.

We await with confidence the moment
hen Sir Ian Botham, the universally re-
ected grand old man of the England
am, starts clucking these days that
ese dreadful kids of the 2010s and 2020s
e no good and, what's more, have no
ea how to behave.

The other thing to remember about the
nglish is that, deep down, we actually
refer losing. If we start winning a Test
ries easily, we assume that this is noth-
g to do with the brilliance of our own
nd of heroes but entirely due to the in-
mpetence of the opposition. When
ngland regained the Ashes in 1985,
ere was far more ink and paper used up
scussing the uselessness of Australia's
wlers than there was praising the bril-
ance of England's batsmen. In 1989,
hen the tables were turned and we had a
od old crisis to talk about, somehow
eryone seemed to feel a great deal more
mfortable.

This is not to say we like losing all the
me. What goes down really well is a re-
lt like Headingley 1981 or Kingston
90 when, against all the odds, our boys
anage to overcome an apparently
perior enemy. But this is a piece of
stalgia too. It reminds us of the war.
sually someone will use the phrase
unkirk spirit' — not El Alamein or D-
ay or any battle we actually won but
unkirk, a successful evacuation and re-
eat.

Australians, it seems to me, like to see
posing cricket teams beaten into the
ound and then stamped on. We would
el uncomfortable with that, if we could
er do it. In 1959, the last occasion on
hich England won a series 5-0 (against
dia), attendances plummeted.

In 1978-79, when Brearley's team
ushed the WSC-weakened Australians
der Yallop, we all felt uneasy and
ought it would be nice if the Aussies
uld do a bit better. Do Australians ever
el that about us? In 1984, when the
est Indies staged its first 'blackwash'
d beat England 5-0 attendances actual-

ly rose throughout the series. We were
like rabbits caught in a car's headlights,
mesmerised by the force that was about
to crush us. Australians, in similar circumstances, generally head for the beach.
On the day England regained the Ashes
at the MCG in 1986-7, the Melbourne *Sun*
did its best to ignore the whole nasty
business and concentrated on the Davis
Cup instead.

There is also the matter of selection. In
this matter, cricket followers on both
sides of the world take an identical view
since it is agreed by everyone that, by
definition, selectors are idiots.

The most dramatic evidence of this also
came on that last Ashes tour when the
Australians named one Peter Taylor for
the Sydney Test match.

It was widely believed that they had in
fact got it wrong, had intended to pick
Mark Taylor but got confused. As it happened, Peter won the Sydney Test for
Australia and the selectors had to be
given credit for a particularly imaginative
and inspired choice. But the fact that so
many people thought the selectors could
be daft enough to get the names muddled
up was instructive. (Actually, subsequent
events suggested they should have picked
Mark as well but no one's perfect.)

In Australia, then, abusing selectors is
quite a popular pastime. But here again,
the English are different. With us, it's an
obsession. Indeed, it is often more fun
than the actual cricket. In 1988, England
used 23 players in six Tests against the
West Indies and Sri Lanka. Everyone
agreed this was farcical. Peter May, the
chairman of selectors, resigned. Ted Dexter came in, promising a new policy of
continuity. The selection panel was cut
from five to three. In 1989, in five Tests
against Australia, they used 29.

To be fair to Dexter, he had an appal-
ling set of injuries and the added problem
of a large chunk of the team, including
those who always proclaimed their patri-
otism most staunchly, announcing that
they would rather ply their trade in South
Africa, thank you. And in 1988, May's
committee managed the magnificent feat
of using four different captains. To lose
one captain (as Oscar Wilde might have
said had he followed cricket) is a misfor-
tune, to lose two smacks of carelessness,
to lose three makes you think that the

21

Emburey, Cowdrey, Gatting and Gooch — all recent captains.

people in charge have not got a clue what they're doing.

I am writing this before the end of England's series against India; anything can happen yet. But so far this northern summer, England have only had one captain and a reasonable number of players. It all seems to be going jolly well. This is very disconcerting. It is against all tradition.

One particular custom has been discarded. England Test teams always used to be picked on a Friday night and announced on a Sunday morning. For as long as I can remember, part of the fabric of an English summer has been switching on the Sunday lunchtime news and then getting in a flaming temper because of the latest act of selectors' lunacy.

But it is of course unreasonable to ask three people to keep a secret for 36 hours. So now the team is announced haphazardly, generally on a Saturday morning. An no one even takes much notice because the selectors have been proceeding with a boring policy of rationality and continuity.

Where are the stupidities of yesteryear? I don't know what's going off out there. Hopeless.

But still not really quite serious — which is why, in spite of it all, we love this crazy game so much.

HG Nelson and Roy Slaven
ABC Sport's Irreverent All-rounders

RAY BRIGHT'S ELEVEN

T HE SUCCESS of any cricket team is based on balance. Only an idiot would think of selecting the five best batsmen, the five best bowlers and a cricket-keeper and send them out through the gates at 11 am and expect them to bat. As Mike Brearley said to us over a meal in the St John's College Chichester common room after retaining the Ashes, quote: 'Look at my record chaps. On paper I'm a cricketing dill, an abberration, at best indifferent. Not only do I hate the game but I've never even rolled the arm over in the nets. I've never held a catch — in fact, to be frank, the moving ball scares me — and I've never consciously tried to play a shot with the bat, yet history singles me out as the greatest English skipper of the post-war era.' Unquote.

Australians, we should never forget

that England invented the game and the traditional English selection process is still an eye-opener. They always used to select a Captain first, a moulder of men, a thinker, a welder of skills, a master craftsman who can, on his intellectual anvil, forge genius from dross. Just look at some of the English skippers. Lord Ted Dexter — an absolute duffer with the willow but, by gee, when playing for a draw on the morning of the second day, a dead-set genius. Ray Illingworth? Sure he could bowl donkey drops a bit, but for directing traffic out in the middle he was without peer. There is a lesson in looking at the modern era where the MCC brains trust has begun to adopt the Australian tradition of selecting the best players to lead the side out. Players-turned-captains like Boycott and Gower and Botham and Gatting have simply led England into oblivion. Players are made, captains are born.

And so, applying the tried and tested traditional English model to Australian conditions we have selected Ray Bright to lead what will generally be regarded as the finest Australian team of the modern era. Now the selection of Ray as skip might raise a few eyebrows but just look at the record. Ray Bright was a permanent fixture in the Test team for many seasons and while his contribution on the field was one which took few wickets and made even fewer runs, he was obviously in the side for other reasons. It was simply the vicious inter- and intra-state politics of the period that locked him out of the top job, though the players themselves knew he was well-credentialled, and even on occasion called him 'Skip'.

His overall contribution in that period during the so-called Chappelli-led renaissance was second to none. It was Ray who took charge in the nets and it was Ray who was obsessed with the scientific approach to players' fitness levels. As Ray often said 'A fit team will always beat a fat team.' It was Ray who ensured the slips cradle followed the team to the motel each night. It was Ray who organised the dawn practice sessions and introduced the spontaneous midnight marathon. It was Ray who insisted on arm wrestling sessions to advance the wrist flexibility of the team and Ray who pioneered the revolutionary training tech-

nique of, when in the nets, having batsmen bat and bowlers bowl. It was Ray who championed the radical concept of fielding to the bowler rather than bowling to the field. Ray is fondly remembered by the players and the public for all of these things.

Ray Bright is captain of the team if for no other reason than for reviving the old fashioned belief of having pride in the baggy green — a baby-like notion thrown out so cruelly with the bath water by Benaud and Simpson. Captains who were interested solely in themselves and their own feeble records, and who gave not a jot for their country.

Ray would have insisted on the opening pairing of Keith Stackpole and Rick Darling. Stacky was a big burly bloke capable of bludgeoning the ball square of the wicket in either direction. Who can forget the methods Stacky used to dispatch the fearsome poet John Snow? Stacky simply stood and delivered. But while cruel with the bat, Stacky was a slug between wickets. If it wasn't a boundary it was a dot ball and this could be a problem when the outfield was damp and rotating the strike paramount. Who better to put the rocket up Stacky than the mercurial Rick Darling, arguably the fastest man in the world over the measured chain? One would have learned from the other. Ray used to dream of a slim, swift Stacky and a stout, stoic Darling.

The perfect first drop was Chappelli — the Charles Bronson of the caper. He was a man to place the willow in the mouth and let his pants do the talking. A man of colourful words and crude actions who'd rather lose his wicket than let the ball get on top of him.

Ray would have elevated Paul Sheahan to second drop. Paul saved Australia between forty and fifty runs per innings with his hands at cover but, more than this, Paul was the most elegant and pretty right handed-batsman the world has ever seen. A man with a technique straight out of the copybook. Why he wasn't given more time at the crease is post-war cricket's greatest crime. To follow Sheahan, Allan Border, the finest player of spin in the world. AB is a pudgy, pugnacious, grafting player who values his wicket more than his life. Like Sheahan, he was prepared to take on the Windies quicks without a protector and would proudly leer 'If you're good enough have a shot'. At Port of Spain this attitude was enormously distracting to players and fielders alike. In Trinidad and Tobago the deeds of Sheahan and Border have been incorporated into local legend and reggae songs.

In Doug Walters, Ray had an enigma. He was a comfort zone player. A player who would rack up a double-ton when Australia had an abundance of runs but, when the chips were down, forget him; play him as a bowler. However, Ray would have got the best out of Doug by expecting nothing and supplying him with a new deck of cards and a packet of smokes at the beginning of each day. Doug was at his best when Ray tricked him into thinking that a large crowd had turned up to watch an elaborate five day practice session.

Wayne Phillips was Australia's Farouk Engineer. A freak capable of standing behind the stumps all day, yet willing to open the batting in that difficult last twenty minutes of play. A perfect night-watchman.

And so to the bowlers.

Ray would have paired Rodney Hogg and Jeff Thomson. While Hoggy was the finely tuned rapier, the poisoned dart in the blowpipe, the single shot derringer at point blank range, the brain surgeon with the laser and the microscope, Thommo was Captain Blood, a Rommel led Blitzkrieg, a broadsword wielded with brutal passion in a crowded dance floor where the only music was the sweet smack of the ball hitting the pommie batsman's skull. While Hoggy would hide behind the palm leaf with an arrow at the oasis, Thommo would back up the truck and poison the well. While Hoggy was prepared to sit patiently at the negotiation table and suggest economic sanctions, Thommo would have all red buttons pressed and the big one out of the bomb bay doors and eleven cities in rubble with the surviving populace begging for peace. It was Ray who encouraged Thommo never to think, so in delivery, because Jeff had no idea where the ball would go, neither did the batsmen. Hoggy and Thommo — the perfect new-ball combination for cricket.

At first change, Gary Gilmour. A man blessed with an abundance of skills that matched his ampleness of stature. A man who had that rare quality: he could bring the ball back in to the right hander. And he could bat. Sure he had dicky ankles, but Ray could have farmed his work load in such a way that his ankle strength would have increased. The sad truth is that Gary was never used enough. As a lefty, Gary would have been the perfect foil to Hoggy and Thommo.

And then to clean up the tail, Ray slips the leash and brings himself on into the breeze holding down one end while Doug Walters darts and drifts big out and in swingers from the other, with sleeves rolled up. Ray loved to bowl to the end from which Hoggy had been bowling because he could gain enormous purchase from the pitch where Rod had stumbled and fallen cutting the turf to shreds.

On paper an unbeatable combination. Had selectors stuck to the English model by choosing skipper first and team second, then Australian cricket would have been the envy of the world.

39

EDITORIAL

CRICKET FACES NUMEROUS CHALLENGES today, rivalled as it is by other sports for our children's playtime, your entertainment dollar and everyone's televiewing enslavement. Were it not for the one-day game, cricket would be struggling for survival, and as time passes one wonders how long Test match cricket can survive when the one-dayers are paying its bills. By the year 2000 only England, Australia, and perhaps South Africa, are likely to be able to justify regular staging of Test cricket. Even the three-match Test series will be under threat as the demand grows for more instant gratification cricket and its accompanying financial guarantee.

In Australia, the Cricket Board is working hard to maintain and expand the game's profile. The World Cup generated tremendous interest, and its success can be gauged by the increased number of children involved in the upsurge of school cricket. The expansion of cricket development officers within each state association initiated this resurgence, but a focal point such as the World Cup has served to ignite interest, rousing children to imitate their heroes. Now the task is to create a greater link between school cricket and that historical base, club cricket.

As our working lives continue to reshape, so the opportunity grows for more part-time employment and greater recreational time. For cricket it's twilight time, cool shades of evening for boys and girls to play alongside the oldies and not just within their own age group.

But what about the fans, the viewers and the listeners: how are they being treated?

The facilities at most grounds where there are reserved seats are pleasurable enough. Brisbane's periphery is overdue for bulldozing—a stark contrast with the superb playing conditions—but Brisbane, and Perth, have a bigger problem. Their Test match crowds fail to rate alongside one-day attendances. (And that probably can be said of the other venues outside Boxing Day in Melbourne, opening day in Sydney and the long weekend in Adelaide).

It all comes down to price. Should fans pay the same amount for a day at a Test as they do for a one-dayer? There seems to be a reluctance to reduce reserved seat charges for Test matches for fear that the game will be sold short. Hopefully, a change in pricing policy is afoot, because the listening and viewing audience is enormous. At the same time, an education campaign on the merits of Test cricket should be aimed at the television audience during match coverage. Too much of the marketing emphasis is about confrontation, which might explain those occasional anarchic moments in the middle when umpires are derided and captains forget that they are responsible for the conduct of the game.

1

The necessity for a match referee will be further examined this season, as the perception lingers that unless someone actually strikes a blow, no action other than a slap on the wrist is likely. Again, it comes back to the captains and their capacity for disciplined leadership.

Jumping off my horse and on to the season ahead, you may see and hear about some of the greatest bowling in the recent history of the game. And that should ensure plenty of decisions in the Test matches. For Australia the worry is that the West Indies pace attack will again be dominant, overcoming the declining capabilities of their batsmen. Last year's poor batting performance by Australia, apart from Boon and, at times, Taylor, was a signal that new blood is required. Marsh's decline opens the door for someone, but also threatens to destabilise the line-up unless the replacement is successful. Be it Moody, Hayden, or even Boon, Australia needs to bat with more authority to be sure of giving its bowlers dependable totals. Dean Jones, Mark Waugh and Allan Border batted unconvincingly last season when it mattered. One of Martyn, Lehmann, Langer or Bevan could force their way in if Australia is under the hammer. A fit McDermott and a refreshed Reid and Hughes will be a handful, supported by a trim Shane Warne's improving wrist spin.

In the one-dayers, the appearance of the deadly duo, Waqar and Wasim, adds rare quality to the spectacle. Is there a better combination than these two rampant Pakistani fast bowlers? I cannot recall a pair of bowlers able to consistently deliver the unplayable ball. Recalling Australia's vulnerability to Kapil's swing makes you wonder what will happen. And with two white balls!

While the internationals are pacesetting across the country the other sometimes overlooked competition reaches a landmark. The centenary of the Sheffield Shield will be celebrated throughout the season, highlighted by a special celebration in Adelaide from December 19, when South Australia meet New South Wales. The value of the Sheffield Shield as a nursery for Test players is now underlined by the fact that most of the games are played without the top names. It is important that the focus is on achieving national selection, unlike English domestic cricket, which is more of a separate entity than an exclusive breeding ground for Test players.

That says as much about the difference in cricket structure between the two old rivals as it does, conversely, about the difference in umpiring standards. At least independent umpires will create a perception that justice is being done, even if it isn't. Of course, the independents have not yet been impanelled, because the International Cricket Council says it needs a sponsor to fund them. The Australian Cricket Board's stated opposition to independents seems paradoxical in view of their commitment to a sponsor whose slogan attests that 'only the best will do.'

£150 well spent — THE SHEFFIELD SHIELD

2

WEST INDIES TOUR
OF AUSTRALIA **1992-1993**

DOWN IN THE PIT
Who Wants to Bowl Fast?

by Geoff Lawson

CRICKET HAS ALWAYS been looked upon by foreigners (especially the Yanks) as a dubious, complex, time wasting game. The game attracts criticisms of being slow moving and slow to move with the times.

However, there is no doubt that in the past 100 years or so the game has undergone a massive evolution. Underarm bowlers of the nineteenth century soon found that they could no longer compete with the 'round-armers' and then the 'over the top' deliverers. As wicket preparation became more exacting so too did the accuracy and speed of the bowlers. An improvement which kept the challenge up to the batsman. F R Spofforth was a curlier customer when bowling into the deep footholes he had created at the other end of the pitch than when that practice was outlawed. Unlimited fieldsman behind the square-leg umpire convinced Douglas Jardine that there indeed was a plan to contain the greatest batsman of all. That ploy too was quickly erased. Greg Chappell forced the legislators to move on the process of limited-overs cricket by turning the clock back. Those fast men with long back foot dragging actions forced the no-ball interpretation to change.

The latest round of ordinations have been once again directed at fast bowlers—that honest, hard-toiling, downtrodden, pit worker whose only mistake in life is to require a longer run-up than Colin Cowdrey. Over rate limitations and short pitched bowling have been the latest points of conjecture. Much of the criticism has been directed at the West Indians but other teams and individuals are also a target. Is it because those teams and individuals are so much better than the rest and need to be cut down to size so that mediocrity becomes the yardstick by which all cricketers are measured? (Why wasn't Bradman made to use a narrower bat in that case?). Or is it because they truly flaunt the laws or more importantly the basic moral philosophy that makes cricket the much admired and durable contest that it is?

There can be no doubt that fast bowling regularly wins matches, no matter what standard you are playing. It just happens that such bowlers take longer to get through their overs than slow bowlers. That is a fact that no rule, law or statute will ever affect. Fast bowlers take more wickets at less cost than slow bowlers—100 years of statistics show that conclusively. Why then have these new rules been introduced to limit the fast bowler?

The back foot no ball rule should be brought back . . .

Most administrators don't want to watch *any* team bowl 70–75 overs in 6 hours of cricket. I don't, and more importantly, the spectators don't. On the other hand they do want to see genuinely skilled, fast bowlers plying their trade. A gaggle of military medium seam bowlers with short run-ups dominating a day's play would be mind numbing.

Bouncers. The law on intimidatory bowling was always sufficient for intuitive umpires to use effectively in stopping excessive short pitched bowling. The umps won't like this . . . but their lack of action more than anything else has led to the introduction of specific limits on bouncers. I haven't heard one umpire who likes the new rule and so called 'umpiring by numbers'. It is just another artificial constraint on a game that has developed far more as an art than a science. The Pakistani's on their recent tour of England stated publicly that 'the one bouncer rule was destroying the effectiveness of Akram and Younis'. If a batsman is continually allowed onto the front foot two things are guaranteed: 1. Plenty of runs ('you beauty' cry the purists). 2. More draws ('it stinks' moan the fans).

36

Over the years I've found that if you don't bowl short the batsman can't play the hook shot. The hook must be one of, if not the most dramatic, crowd pleasing stroke in the game and here we are trying to eliminate it!!! You're only allowed two fieldsman behind square leg as it is.

Other factors in the past 15 years have indirectly led the legislative charge. The preparation of pitches that don't deteriorate as the match wears on has led to spin bowlers being less and less effective. If the ball won't deviate I don't care how good your slow bowlers are they aren't going to bowl sides out. So what does the skipper do? He bowls the seamers who are less expensive and the fast bowlers who have more penetration. World cricket in general, and Australian cricket in particular, is suffering a dearth of spin bowling at all levels. Captains won't bowl them, curators won't give them a chance, and umpires refuse to give front foot lbws regardless of what line the pads are struck or where the ball is going. The fast bowler has become dominant for many reasons (that ascendancy has not been restricted to the contemporary game).

There is no more fascinating contest than watching a slow bowler parrying with a quality batsman on a turning pitch. Variety and balance are the keys to great cricket. Variety of batsmen and bowlers. Who can blame any selector or captain for picking four fast bowlers when he knows they will tip the scales in his favour.

The legislators will most likely continue to furtively tweak the dials on the control panel in search of the best wavelength but they need the assistance of everyone in the medium not just those who live to bowl fast.

Over rate problems could be easily solved (bearing in mind always that quality is more desirable than quantity) by penalising teams say 10 runs per over not bowled. This will effect outcomes of matches and not just the hip pockets. Imagine finishing 10 overs short as some international sides have done recently. A Test could be decided either way by a team with a full complement of quickies cynically abusing the laws. The back foot no-ball rule dispensed with in 1962 should be brought back to ease the burden on bowlers and umpires. Unfortunately many officials believe it is more important to get a no-ball millimetre perfect than to get a good look at lbw calls. The back foot rule allows far more time to observe, make a call, then look down the pitch while giving batsmen a true free hit they currently are denied. Everyone wins with this change. Short pitched bowling is simply a matter for insightful umpires. Intimidation varies depending on batsmen and situations; it is a matter of assessing each situation, not relying on the numbers.

Geoff Lawson will join the ABC Radio Cricket commentary team this summer. Geoff retired from first-class cricket with a record of 666 wickets, including 180 in Test matches. In his testimonial season Geoff created two new career records for New South Wales—115 matches and 395 wickets, 367 of them in Sheffield Shield.

NOSTALGIA:

EVERYONE'S TWELFTH MAN

b y J O N C L E A R Y

Nostalgia is what turns the past into myth; or sometimes into downright lies. It is what turns the slog to long-on that lands twenty feet short into the beautiful skyer that cleared the fence by ten feet. I am probably the only man in cricket history who opened an innings with Fingleton, Hutton, Morris and Simpson (all in Authors v Publishers matches in London), but in the telling of those matches time and distance has convinced me I really didn't need those hacks at the other end. The past was always golden, wasn't it?

I first landed in Britain in the summer of 1946. The country was still recovering from the war years. Food was rationed; petrol was doled out as if it were twelve-year-old Scotch; there was a dreadful shortage of fast bowlers. England was looking for someone to replace Kenneth Farnes, killed in the war; while back in Australia lethal weapons were still being forged, marked Lindwall and Miller. Cricket, like all other sports except love-making, was trying to get up off its knees.

The revival, I was told by English friends, was beginning at club and village level. Pitches that had been parade grounds for Dad's Army were levelled again, watered and rolled. I joined a club called London Australian, founded in 1919 by World War I Diggers who had married English brides and stayed on. In my first match I learned the difference between Australian and English attitudes. The other side was batting and as I ran (ran? Walked: I was a slow tweaker) up to bowl, I noticed the batsman at my end was backing up two or three yards down the wicket. I stopped, removed the bails and in that dulcet voice we are noted for, yelled 'Howzat?' There was dead silence and a horrified look from the umpire. I repeated the question, in case he didn't understand my accent. Then, in a tone that I recognized years later when I heard Mrs Tatcher ticking off a Labour speaker, he said—no, he *uttered*: 'It is out—but *gentlemen don't play like that.*'

I looked around: everyone, including the expatriate Australians, who obviously had been in England too long, was looking at me as if I had just raped the batsman's sister. Where was Vinoo Mankad when I needed him? (He still had to come). Or Ian Chappell? (He was still at school in Adelaide). I crawled on my hands and knees all the way to the pavilion, pleading with the batsman to come back, that I hadn't meant it, that being from the Colonies I didn't know any better, but he didn't even look at me. I spent the rest of the innings at extra-long long-on (which is just the other side of Swindon), pondering the discovery that cricket actually was a gentleman's game.

From playing with London Australian I moved down to play with a village club in the Thames valley. At that time there was a bestselling author named Angela Thirkell, who wrote novels stuffed with upper class county types and village 'characters'. I think she had a hand in the selection of the team I played with. There was a peer, a rear-admiral, a RAF flying-officer, the village constable, the blacksmith and various other odds and sods, including the expatriate Aussie writer who was still learning to play a gentleman's game.

The peer and the policeman would open the innings. The peer would push the ball to mid-wicket, call, 'Come, Entwistle,' and the copper would respond, 'Coming, m'lud.' The first time I heard it I fell over laughing—something else I learned a gentleman doesn't do.

While I was discovering aspects and attitudes of the past, the future was on its way from Australia. True, there were elements of the past in the team, notably Bradman, Barnes and Hassett, but the 1948 touring team was to show hints of the professionalism that gradually was to take over in the years to come. Not in terms of financial reward but in the approach to the game.

Speaking of financial reward: in 1948 the English players were paid £75 per match and umpires £50 per match. Today an England player gets £2200 per match plus a bonus of £70 for every ten Tests in which he has played. The umpire receives £1900 per match plus a bonus of £70 for every three Tests in which he has stood. Nostalgia, even allowing for inflation, cannot make those 1948 figures appealing. I asked a couple of the Australian tourists what they were paid, but their memories were a total blank. Back then one did really play for one's country and the baggy green cap—there was precious little else to play for.

Where was I before those facts and figures intruded on the pitch? Oh yes, the 1948 team. There was the fast bowling combination of Lindwall and Miller, a combination once or twice equalled but never surpassed; Miller was also the most naturally gifted of the batsmen but was too cavalier for the record books. There was Bill Johnston, one of the best left-arm fast-mediums Australia has produced. And there was Ern Toshack, left-arm, who could put the ball on a penny five times out of six; he once bowled a long hop and almost had a nervous breakdown. Today, of course, his manager, his sponsor, the team psychologist, the trainer and Alan Jones would all be working on him through the tea interval, trying to motivate him out of his trauma.

Among the new batsmen were Morris and Harvey, two of the finest ever; Harvey was also the best all-round fieldsman I have ever seen. Then there were Tallon and Saggers, neither of them ever bettered as 'keepers; and first class batsmen into the bargain. It was a team worth queuing through the night for—which I did for the Lord's Test.

We started queuing at the gates at 10 the previous evening. At 4 a.m. the first buskers arrived. A Geordie stand-up comic from Durham who was totally imcomprehensible to anyone south of the River Tyne; we didn't know he was a comic till he started to laugh at his own jokes. He was followed by a strong-man who bent iron bars with his teeth and challenged all us wimps in the queue to do the same. After lying all night on the pavement, I couldn't have raised the strength

25

to bend a length of spaghetti. Then the sun came up, they let us into the ground and Morris scored 105 and all the aches and pains disappeared.

The series went on, to be won by Australia. There was some brilliant batting, not least by some of the Englishmen; Comptom was as cavalier and entertaining as Miller. Harvey established himself, at nineteen, as a Test batsman; Morris topped both the Test aggregates and averages. In the fourth Test at Leeds Australia were set 404 to win on the last day—and achieved it. Bradman was bowled for a duck in his last Test appearance at The Oval, but it did nothing to dim his glory, only dimmed thousands of pairs of eyes who saw him walk from his wicket for the last time. There were cold days and wet days, but somehow in memory it was a long golden summer.

The game has changed since then. It is no longer played 'as gentlemen play it' (but did they *always* play it like that? Were there no cheats and bounders back in the days when the game was played in top hats and bets were taken on the result?). Today there is sledging: sometimes I think a 'keeper is chosen as much for his mouth as for his gloves. There is the dreary over rate, as if bowlers think inaction is part of the entertainment. No batsman ever 'walks' these days; if he did, the selectors would accuse him of treason. Yet there are still those flashes that light up the game, the innings or a bowling spell that wins an almost-lost match, the catch in which the fieldsman's arm moves quicker than a hummingbird's wing. It is still cricket, of which nostalgia, as in love and all sports, is a part. There are kids today storing memories for the future.

Don Bradman going out to bat prior to his world record innings of 334 at Leeds

Top Bill Johnston, Don Tallon, *Middle* Ern Toshack, Arthur Morris, *Above* Neil Harvey, Keith Miller

26

the CHANGING COLOUR of South African cricket

By Marius Benson

The policy of segregation of old-style South Africa has given way to radical new ideas.

From the time South Africa joined international cricket in 1889 to the time it was thrown out in 1970, only one non-white player was ever chosen to represent his country. Charles Bennet Llewellyn, a coloured man from Pietermaritzburg, was an all-rounder. He batted right-handed but bowled spin with his left and played fifteen Tests between 1895 and 1912.

With that single exception, for eight decades South Africa never chose a player who was not white and refused to play any team that was not entirely white.

For seven years now South African cricket has been opening its ranks to black and coloured players. And, unlike other sports, it is backing its noble, non-racial rhetoric with actions and with cash.

In the mid-eighties Doctor Ali Bacher, the managing director of South Africa's United Cricket Board, had a change of heart experienced by many South Africans.

'We all woke up with a bump; everyone realised that there was something wrong. Was the world right? Some of the cricket administrators and cricketing people started to realise for the first time the hardships that the black people in this country have suffered.'

I spoke to Ali Bacher in Atteridgeville, a township of 250 000 people on the outskirts of Pretoria. It has produced some famous sons and daughters, but they've been black liberation leaders rather than batsmen and bowlers.

'About two and a half million dollars a year is being spent on the township programs - in the South African context a lot of money.

'The objective is to obviously broaden the base of cricket, but at the same time it's there to give opportunities to disadvantaged people and to improve race relations in this country.

'The money comes from commerce and industry primarily. But last summer for the first time my board accepted the principle that fifteen per cent of the gate money should go into a central fund which we use to develop sports facilities in the disadvantaged areas.

'The same principle will be adopted when the Australians tour South Africa, so in some ways Allan Border's team will help us to promote further disadvantaged sport in South Africa.'

Seven years after the township program was introduced there are about fifty coaching centres training nearly five thousand children around the country.

The equipment is minimal, none of the wickets are turf and full-size fields are hard to come by. But in the townships, which were deserts for cricket or any recreational facilities, the progress is tangible.

The man responsible for running the network of coaching clinics in the townships is Khaya Majola, the United Cricket Board's Director of National Development.

'We have two teams in Soweto, we have one team playing in the Transvaal regional competition and that team has reached the heights of 'reserve two' now. So it's happening.

'If you want to compare it with sports

like soccer, it is still a minority sport. But it is the fastest growing sport in the black communities. Four hundred thousand black people are today involved in cricket; by the end of the century we hope to have one million players and watchers.'

And Khaya Majola says the heroes that are inspiring the township kids are local heroes.

'We thought the kids would be saying we want to be Curtly Ambrose, we want to be Brian Lara. But strangely they are identifying themselves with South Africans. They want to be Allan Donald, they want to be Jonty Rhodes. And it's one way of saying that cricket is moving faster than politicians in that we identify ourselves as South Africans.'

Already four black players have won selection in the squads of two provincial teams, Transvaal and Eastern Province. Khaya Majola is confident that the coaching clinics will see black players reach the highest level of cricket within the next few years.

One of the rising black stars in South African cricket is Jacob Malao. At twenty, the whip-thin off-spinner from Soweto looks like the reincarnation of Lance Gibbs, who carried the West Indies spin attack through the 'sixties and beyond.

A gentle run-up and a bowling action of liquid grace delivers a ball which bites and spins at the Transvaal training nets at Johannesburg's famous Wanderers ground. Under the bespectacled gaze of coach Eddie Barlow Jake Malao is becoming an increasingly accurate and dangerous proposition for batsmen.

At the Wanderers nets he stands out as much as any of his team mates would if they found themselves in his Soweto home. Skin colour aside, he stands out because his training gear of scruffy track pants and a T-shirt with the sleeves torn off looks a little less state of the art than his team mates' mix of cricket whites and lycra shorts. And where they are wearing silver or gold chains around their necks, he prefers a leather map of Africa in the yellow and green identified with the black freedom movement.

Jake was one of twelve boys from his school who tried cricket, but he's the sole survivor of Soweto's cricket class of '83. He found his vocation in spin after an early brush with pace.

'At that time we had five bowlers. I was the sixth fast bowler, so I didn't get a chance. So when I started turning the ball I started to get a chance to play cricket.'

For a boy who was drawn to the game by a desire to dodge homework Jake Malao is now a model of discipline and dedication.

'I want to work very hard to be a permanent player for Transvaal. And I want to show other black players coming up that it's very important to represent a squad like Transvaal like I do.

'That comes through discipline and working hard.

'I enjoy being with them, they just treat me like their brothers and I'm glad. In some sports they don't do like that but with cricket it's different.

'The guys, they give me well welcome. They enjoy to be with me.'

And as for the prospect of being the first black chosen for South Africa, Jake Malao replies with a self-deprecating chuckle.

'I don't know with that…I don't know with that. But being black, I mean I'm proud to be black, to give example to black cricketers that if you work hard you'll come to the top.'

With that Jake Malao returned to the nets to practise, bringing his long left arm through the wide arc that brings the ball down with increasing accuracy and menace. It's a sight likely to become familiar to provincial opponents over the coming seasons. It could become familiar to Australia and other touring teams.

Certainly the all-white face of South African cricket is gone and a bold new look is ready to take on the world.

17

WHEN DELAYS

The joy of cricket is shared by many, and all cricket followers are familiar with the peaceful moments that precede every adrenalin surge. Long run up interludes and rain stopped play conversations are always nostalgic, mainly discursive and occasionally controversial.

The temptation to compare Trumper with Bradman, or Headley with Richards, or O'Reilly with Warne, is a fantasy land we have all been to. No other game can linger so dreamily and, for the devotee, flashes of brilliance, of emotion, of drama, are the reward for patient attention.

For sixty years the *ABC Cricket Book* has been stronger on fact than fantasy. That is why this final chapter is sheer indulgence, full of baubles for your dreamtime discussions during the next navel contemplation while absorbing a cricket match.

The following team selections are based on the period covering fifty-two editions of the *ABC Cricket Book*. Each team contains an unnamed twelfth man whom you can choose, depending on the venue, the pitch, the year, the opposition, the condition of your liver or the likely result of the toss!

RAIN

PLAY . . .

ENTERTAINERS

AUSTRALIA		CAREER RECORD	
Don Bradman	CAPTAIN	6966 runs	Avge 99.94
Richie Benaud	VICE-CAPTAIN	2201 runs	248 wkts
Greg Chappell		7110 runs	47 wkts
Neil Harvey		6149 runs	Avge 48.41
Merv Hughes		212 wkts	S/R 57.95
Dennis Lillee		355 wkts	S/R 52.01
Rod Marsh		3663 runs	355 dismissals
Keith Miller		2958 runs	170 wkts
Arthur Morris		3533 runs	Avge 46.86
Norm O'Neill		2779 runs	Avge 45.55
Jeff Thomson		200 wkts	S/R 52.67
Doug Walters		5357 runs	49 wkts

The Entertainers are the crowd pullers of Australian cricket, and there are many other names that can be added to the list.

Bradman drew more crowds to cricket than anyone in history, and his record boasts consistent domination of the opposition. As a captain he never lost a series. Benaud toiled for many seasons before establishing his record as a match-winning leg spinner. He smashed several Test hundreds and became an inspirational leader, figuring prominently in the renaissance of 1960-61. Greg Chappell has the distinction of scoring hundreds in his first and last Tests, making the on drive a signature stroke during a classically elegant career. Neil Harvey drove bowlers crazy with his nimble footwork and dashing strokes. He was never stumped in 137 Test innings. Merv Hughes has been the personality player and performer in the current era. His bristling bowling intimidates batsmen and he has been an outstanding strike bowler. Dennis Lillee is arguably Australia's greatest bowler. Averaging five wickets per Test, Lillee developed from a tearaway to a master of swing and variation, the voluble showman. Rod Marsh became Lillee's accomplice, a pugnacious character behind the stumps and a bludgeoning batsman. Keith Miller's extroverted personality was magnetic. Spontaneous, explosive, powerful and athletic, he made the game worth watching, bowling bouncers or hitting sixes. Arthur Morris, like Harvey, was a brilliant player of spin and thundered his strokes with rapture. Norm O'Neill crashed back foot drives more powerfully than most, an exciting batsman prone to nervousness at the start of his innings and a spectacular fieldsman. Jeff Thomson had two outstanding seasons when his javelin-like action speared opponents with ferocious speed. His contribution alongside Lillee was electrifyingly lethal. Doug Walters played innings that could swing a match. The archetypal laconic Aussie, he cut and pulled in the old-fashioned tradition of the bush-bred batsman.

Should anyone break down in the fantasy contest there are plenty of standbys: Favell, the Waughs, Ian Chappell, Jones, Slater, Burge, Shepherd, Warne, O'Reilly, Davidson, McCabe, Martin. Just thinking of their deeds and zestful approach is inspiring. Promoters would relish the chance to arrange a match between this team and any of the talented teams from the world around us. Here are a few combinations to dream about.

ENGLAND   CAREER RECORD

David Gower _____ CAPTAIN _____	8231 runs	Avge 44.25
Ted Dexter _____ VICE-CAPTAIN _____	4502 runs	Avge 47.89
Bob Barber _____	1495 runs	Avge 35.59
Ian Botham _____	5200 runs	383 wkts
Denis Compton _____	5807 runs	Avge 50.06
Alan Knott _____	4389 runs	269 dismissals
Peter May _____	4537 runs	Avge 46.77
Colin Milburn _____	654 runs	Avge 46.71
John Snow _____	202 wkts	S/R 59.50
Fred Trueman _____	307 wkts	S/R 49.43
Frank Tyson _____	76 wkts	S/R 45.42
John Wardle _____	102 wkts	S/R 64.68

WEST INDIES   CAREER RECORD

Frank Worrell _____ CAPTAIN _____	3860 runs	Avge 49.48
Clive Lloyd _____ VICE-CAPTAIN _____	7515 runs	Avge 46.67
Curtly Ambrose _____	219 wkts	S/R 53.84
Gordon Greenidge _____	7558 runs	Avge 44.72
Wesley Hall _____	192 wkts	S/R 56.88
Michael Holding _____	249 wkts	S/R 50.92
Malcolm Marshall _____	376 wkts	S/R 46.77
Viv Richards _____	8540 runs	Avge 50.23
Andy Roberts _____	202 wkts	S/R 55.12
Gary Sobers _____	8032 runs	235 wkts
Clyde Walcott _____	3798 runs	Avge 56.68
Everton Weekes _____	4455 runs	Avge 58.61

SOUTH AFRICA   CAREER RECORD

Dudley Nourse _____ CAPTAIN _____ 2960 runs Avge 53.81
Eddie Barlow _____ VICE-CAPTAIN _____ 2516 runs 40 wkts
Neil Adcock _____ 104 wkts S/R 61.45
Colin Bland _____ 1669 runs Avge 49.08
Alan Donald _____ 70 wkts S/R 52.19
Denis Lindsay _____ 1103 runs 59 dismissals
Roy McLean _____ 2120 runs Avge 30.28
Graeme Pollock _____ 2256 runs Avge 60.97
Peter Pollock _____ 116 wkts S/R 56.22
Mike Procter _____ 41 wkts S/R 36.93
Barry Richards _____ 508 runs Avge 72.57
Hugh Tayfield _____ 170 wkts S/R 79.81

NEW ZEALAND   CAREER RECORD

John Reid _____ CAPTAIN _____ 3428 runs Avge 33.28
Martin Crowe _____ VICE-CAPTAIN _____ 5230 runs Avge 47.89
John Bracewell _____ 102 wkts S/R 82.38
Lance Cairns _____ 130 wkts S/R 81.75
Martin Donnelly _____ 582 runs Avge 52.90
Sir Richard Hadlee _____ 3124 runs 431 wkts
Andrew Jones _____ 2898 runs Avge 46.00
Danny Morrison _____ 120 wkts S/R 62.77
Bert Sutcliffe _____ 2727 runs Avge 40.10
Bruce Taylor _____ 898 runs 111 wkts
Glenn Turner _____ 2991 runs Avge 44.64
Ken Wadsworth _____ 1010 runs 96 dismissals

INDIA   CAREER RECORD

Nawab of Pataudi jnr _____ CAPTAIN _____	2793 runs	Avge 34.91
Sunil Gavaskar _____ VICE-CAPTAIN _____	10 122 runs	Avge 51.12
Mohammed Azharuddin _____	4020 runs	Avge 47.29
Bishen Bedi _____	266 wkts	S/R 80.31
Bhagwat Chandrasekhar _____	242 wkts	S/R 65.96
Kapil Dev _____	5248 runs	434 wkts
Farokh Engineer _____	2611 runs	82 dismissals
Vinod Kambli _____	965 runs	Avge 80.42
Erapally Prasanna _____	189 wkts	S/R 75.94
Ravi Shastri _____	3830 runs	151 wkts
Kris Srikkanth _____	2062 runs	Avge 29.88
Sachin Tendulkar _____	2023 runs	Avge 50.58

PAKISTAN   CAREER RECORD

Imran Khan _____ CAPTAIN _____	3807 runs	362 wkts
Hanif Mohammad _____ VICE-CAPTAIN _____	3915 runs	Avge 43.98
Abdul Qadir _____	236 wkts	S/R 72.56
Asif Iqbal _____	3575 runs	Avge 38.85
Fazal Mahmood _____	139 wkts	S/R 70.75
Javed Miandad _____	8832 runs	Avge 52.57
Majid Khan _____	3931 runs	Avge 38.92
Mohsin Khan _____	2709 runs	Avge 37.10
Waqar Younus _____	166 wkts	S/R 36.64
Wasim Akram _____	222 wkts	S/R 54.20
Zaheer Abbas _____	5062 runs	Avge 44.79

AUSTRALIA DEBUT PERFORMANCE

Greg Chappell _____ CAPTAIN _____	108 v England 1970-71
Terry Alderman _____	4/68, 5/62 v England 1981
Wally Grout _____	6 catches v South Africa 1957-58
Rod Hogg _____	7/74, 1/35 v England 1978-79
Bruce Laird _____	92, 75 v West Indies 1979-80
Dennis Lillee _____	5/84 v England 1970-71
Bob Massie _____	8/84, 8/53 v England 1972
Paul Sheahan _____	81, 35 v India 1967-68
Peter Taylor _____	6/78, 2/76, 42 v England 1986-87
Doug Walters _____	155 v England 1965-66
Mark Waugh _____	138 v England 1990-91
Kepler Wessels _____	162, 46 v England 1982-83

Researching debutant performances has uncovered a new trivia source. Almost fifty players debuted successfully in the 1934-1994 period. Among the omissions are Wayne Phillips, Dirk Wellham, Jim Burke and Gary Cosier, who all scored hundreds; Wayne Clark, Ian Meckiff and Laurie Mayne who each took eight wickets. The trouble spot was number three and Paul Sheahan emerged as the most significant scorer in that position. Invariably batsmen begin their careers as openers, or at five or six. Greg Chappell scored his century at number seven which is coincidentally the same position Bradman batted on debut. Bruce Laird made a belated Test entry after the disbandment of World Series Cricket, and in the context of the West Indies pace barrage of Roberts, Holding, Garner and Croft, this was an outstanding effort.

Few spin bowlers have initially excelled. Taylor's effort was remarkable after just one first-

class game in the 1986-87 season. His innings of
42 was as significant as his bowling. Rod Hogg
and Dennis Lillee grabbed the headlines with
express bowling, while Bob Massie's performance
was bewilderingly brilliant. Terry Alderman
began his love affair on English grounds and,
were it not for the legendary exploits of Ian
Botham, Alderman's 42 wickets would probably
have won the series. Wally Grout took a world
record six catches in South Africa's second
innings at Johannesburg in the first Test of the
1957-58 series; the beginning of a remarkable
career at the mature age of 29.

Kepler Wessels is unique in the present era
for his dual nationality, and debuted for Australia
after serving a qualifying period before returning
to South Africa and leading them on their return
to international cricket in 1991. Doug Walters
and Mark Waugh started their attractive Test
careers stylishly, and Walters repeated his effort in
his second Test.

Most of the exceptional debut performances
were against England, so here is an opposing team
to contemplate.

ENGLAND DEBUT PERFORMANCE

Peter May _____ CAPTAIN _____	138 v South Africa 1951
Alec Bedser	7/49, 4/96 v India 1946
Bob Berry	5/63, 4/53 v West Indies 1950
Ken Farnes	5/102, 5/77 v Australia 1934
Paul Gibb	93, 106 v South Africa 1938-39
Tony Greig	57, 62, 1/21, 4/53 v Australia 1972
Alan Knott	7 catches v Pakistan 1967
Jim Laker	7/103, 2/95 v West Indies 1947-48
John Lever	7/46, 3/24 v India 1976-77
Peter Richardson	81, 73 v Australia 1956
Phil Sharpe	23, 85* v West Indies 1963
David Steele	50, 45, 1/1, 1/19 v Australia 1975

England's high turnover of Test cricketers and the relatively poor debut performances of many subsequent top players added to the selection puzzle. For example, Ken Barrington, Len Hutton and Graham Gooch (a pair) failed to score, and Peter May was the only major batsman to score a century. Alec Bedser, Jim Laker, Alan Knott and Tony Greig started exceptional careers, but other names on the list would be less familiar.

Ken Farnes had a reputation as the fastest bowler of his time in England and took 30 wickets in 15 Tests. He was killed in a training plane crash during World War II.

Paul Gibb played in eight Tests, five as an opener and three as a wicket-keeper/batsman. He also scored a century in the extraordinary 1939 Durban Test. After nine days' play England were 5/654 chasing 696 for victory when the match was called off; otherwise the tourists would have missed their ship home.

Diminutive Bob Berry appeared in only two Tests, bowling left arm spin. He joined the group of spinning occasionals despite a match-winning effort on a turning pitch at Old Trafford, where Alf Valentine took 11 wickets on his debut in the same match. Berry later established a reputation as a publican and a pigeon breeder.

Likeable John Lever bowled fast left arm, bagging 73 wickets in 21 Tests, one of the fortunate celebrants at the 1977 occasion in Melbourne.

Left hander Peter Richardson scored five Test centuries but struggled to repeat his consistent record in Australia against the left handers Davidson and Meckiff in 1958-59. His brother Dick played one Test, the last instance of brothers appearing for England in the same match.

Phil Sharpe appeared in 12 Tests, a tough Yorkshire-bred batsman and brilliant slip fieldsman. He put England into a position where they could force victory after his undefeated second innings at Edgbaston. Sharpe sang in amateur opera and became an England selector in 1983.

The bespectacled David Steele was 33 when the selectors called on him, and he maintained form against Lillee and Thomson with 73 and 92 in his second Test, then 39 and 66 at the Oval. He made one century in eight Tests, 106 against the West Indies in 1976. He also dismissed Ashley Mallett with his fourth ball in Test cricket.

WEST INDIES   DEBUT PERFORMANCE

Frank Worrell ____ CAPTAIN ____	97, 78* v England 1947–48
Colin Croft ____	3/85, 4/47 v Pakistan 1976–77
Gordon Greenidge ____	93, 107 v India 1974–75
Conrad Hunte ____	142 v Pakistan 1957–58
Hines Johnson ____	5/41, 5/55 v England 1947–48
Lester King ____	5/46, 2/18 v India 1961–62
Clive Lloyd ____	82, 78* v India 1977–78
Deryck Murray ____	6 catches v England 1963
Patrick Patterson ____	4/30, 3/44 v England 1985–86
Lawrence Rowe ____	214, 100 v New Zealand 1971–72
Collie Smith ____	44, 104 v Australia 1954–55
Alf Valentine ____	8/104, 3/100 v England 1950

The undisputed world champions since 1978 have produced the greatest combination of attractive batsmen and aggressive fast bowlers in the game. Not all the lustrous names shone on debut. Richie Richardson and Larry Gomes scored ducks, Viv Richards made 4 and 3 and Michael Holding's figures were 0 for 127.

The first twelve contains the usual mix of West Indian explosiveness, nurtured by the graceful Frank Worrell, who made his debut on the jute matting in Trinidad. Worrell led the West Indies on the famous Australian tour in 1960-61, and after receiving a knighthood for his services to the game died tragically of leukaemia in 1967.

Colin Croft became a menacing bowler, using the extremities of the return crease to fire out 125 victims in 27 Tests. Gordon Greenidge murdered bowlers when possessed, in a career spanning 108 Tests and 7558 runs. Conrad Hunte is remembered in Australia for that brilliant throw from the boundary that ran out Wally Grout in the tied Test. In 44 Tests he averaged over 45 as an opener, and more recently he has been an enlightening force spreading the gospel of cricket in South African townships. Hines Johnson was thirty-seven when he made his amazing debut in the first Test of the series. A right arm fast bowler, he toured England in 1950, aged 40, having not played any first-class matches in the previous two seasons. Lester King's career was overshadowed by Hall and Griffith. A fast medium right arm bowler, he toured England in 1963 but did not play for the West Indies again until 1968, his only other Test. Clive Lloyd played 110 Tests, his 7515 explosive runs smashed at 46.68 per innings. Acknowledged as the mentor of the West Indian domination from 1976 until his retirement in 1985, after captaining the side to 36 victories in 74 matches. Deryck Murray made 24 dismissals in the 1963 series, a composed, reliable wicket-keeper who appeared in sixty-two Tests and later took up a post at the United Nations. Patrick Patterson formed a destructive presence in the company of a posse of lethal bowlers. In the mood, he blasted batsmen until injury slowed him, his 93 Test wickets struck at 52 balls a blow.

Lawrence Rowe's debut feat is without parallel, a graceful stroke player whose 2047 runs included a triple century against England. Eyesight problems and an allergy to grass disrupted his career, and after World Series Cricket he led West Indies rebel teams in South Africa. Collie Smith was a powerful right hander whose career was cut short by a fatal car accident in 1959 when he was playing in the Lancashire League. He scored two centuries against England in 1957, and in 26 Tests he picked up 48 wickets bowling off spin. Alf Valentine formed a match-winning partnership with Sonny Ramadhin—'those two little pals of mine, Ramadhin and Valentine' taking 59 wickets between them in the 1950 series. Bespectacled, he bowled left arm spin, capturing 139 Test wickets in a fourteen year span, including the famous 1960-61 tour.

The remaining categories include the 'instant' game, the one that pays the bills and guarantees audiences. Australia has played more one-day internationals than any other country, and for a time after their World Cup success in 1987 they set the standard. More recently the trend towards batting first and winning has reduced expectation, but the crowds still throng and, after all, they are the litmus test for a sport's commercial popularity.

The concluding combination of 'oncers' is a fleeting tribute to those players lucky enough to represent Australia on one occasion. A lot never have. You can spot the omissions: Allen, Angel, Davis, Eastwood, Guest, Joslin, Meuleman, Phillips, Sellers, Slater, Watkins. Matthew Hayden and Jo Angel may well play again, but at the time of writing they are still 'oncers'.

ONE-DAYISTS

	RUNS	S/R/100R	WKTS	S/R/100B
Allan Border _____ CAPTAIN _____	6524	71.15	73	36.45
Greg Chappell __ VICE-CAPTAIN __	2331	74.62	72	43.17
David Boon _____	5243	64.35		
Ian Healy _____	989	87.75	126/19 dismissals	
Dean Jones _____	6068	72.51		
Dennis Lillee _____			103	34.88
Craig McDermott _____			170	37.06
Geoff Marsh _____	4357	55.40		
Simon O'Donnell _____	1242	80.54	108	40.27
Shane Warne _____			44	27.00
Mark Waugh _____	2169	78.19	40	32.55
Steve Waugh _____	3401	73.20	152	44.94

ONCERS

Jeff Moss _____ CAPTAIN _____	22, 38★ v Pakistan 1979
John Rutherford __ VICE CAPTAIN __	30 v India 1956
Ian Callen _____	3/83, 3/188 v India 1977-78
Fred Freer _____	2/49, 0/25, 28★ v England 1946-47
Mervyn Harvey _____	12, 31 v England 1946-47
Matthew Hayden _____	15, 5 v South Africa 1993-94
Des Hoare _____	2/68, 0/88, 35, 0 v West Indies 1960-61
Len Johnson _____	3/66, 3/8, 25★ v India 1947-48
Mick Malone _____	5/63, 1/14, 46 v England 1975
George Thoms _____	16, 28 v West Indies 1951-52
John Wilson _____	1/25, 0/39 v India 1956
Ashley Woodcock _____	27 v New Zealand 1973-74

Draw straws for the wicket-keeper!